Esteban

Esteban

THE AFFICAN SLAVE
WHO EXPLORED AMERICA

Dennis Herrick

University of New Mexico Press ✦ Albuquerque

© 2018 by Dennis Herrick
All rights reserved. Published 2018
Printed in the United States of America

First paperback printing 2023 | ISBN 978-0-8263-6564-4

Library of Congress Cataloging-in-Publication Data
Names: Herrick, Dennis F., author.
Title: Esteban: the African slave who explored America / Dennis Herrick.
Description: Albuquerque: University of New Mexico Press, 2018. |
Includes bibliographical references and index.
Identifiers: LCCN 2017060736 (print) | LCCN 2018020657 (e-book) |
ISBN 9780826359827 (e-book) | ISBN 9780826359810 (hardback)
Subjects: LCSH: Esteban, -1539. | Explorers—America—Biography. |
Explorers—Spain—Biography. | Blacks—America—Biography. | Slaves—America—Biography. | Slavery—America—History—16th century. | Cibola, Seven Cities of. |
Southwestern States—Discovery and exploration—Spanish. | Southern States—Discovery and exploration—Spanish. | BISAC: SOCIAL SCIENCE / Slavery. |
HISTORY / United States / State & Local / Southwest (AZ, NM, OK, TX).
Classification: LCC E125.E8 (e-book) | LCC E125.E8 H47 2018 (print) |
DDC 910.92 [B]—dc23
LC record available at https://lccn.loc.gov/2017060736

Cover photograph: Bust created and photographed by sculptor John Sherrill Houser.
Designed by Felicia Cedillos
Composed in Minion Pro 12.25/14.25

*To all African Americans and other US minorities
whose accomplishments have been ignored, distorted, or diminished.*

On a May day in the year 1539, [Esteban] the Black unlocked for the world the gateway to the Southwest of the future United States.
—HISTORIAN JOHN UPTON TERRELL

The first white man our people saw was a black man.
—PUEBLOAN AUTHOR JOE S. SANDO

Contents

Preface ix

Acknowledgments xi

Noteworthy Dates xiii

Notes for the Modern Reader xvii

CHAPTER 1
A Man of Mysteries 1

CHAPTER 2
The Morocco Connection 13

CHAPTER 3
Terrorism in the Caribbean 21

CHAPTER 4
Esteban Arrives at Hispaniola 31

CHAPTER 5
Early Indian Resistance 37

CHAPTER 6
A Disastrous Beginning 41

CHAPTER 7
Invasion of Florida 53

CHAPTER 8
The Quest for Gold 59

CHAPTER 9
Arrows Penetrating "Good Armor" 73

CHAPTER 10
Fleeing in Rickety Boats 83

CHAPTER 11
Spaniards Forced into Slavery 93

CHAPTER 12
Faith Healing and Proselytizing 107

CHAPTER 13
Esteban's Rise and Fall 125

CHAPTER 14
Return to Slavery, but an Indispensable Man 143

CHAPTER 15
An African in Arizona and New Mexico 159

CHAPTER 16
A Mysterious Fate 175

CHAPTER 17
Death? Or Freedom? 181

CHAPTER 18
The Durability of Myth 191

CHAPTER 19
Inhumane Bondage and Historical Context 199

CHAPTER 20
What Isn't Known about Esteban 209

APPENDIX
An American Sculptor's Tribute 215

Notes 219

Bibliography 255

Index 273

Preface

This biography of Esteban is a true story, its principal origin being from the pen of a Spaniard named Álvar Núñez Cabeza de Vaca nearly five hundred years ago. The difference is that this biography switches the emphasis from Cabeza de Vaca to the African slave.

A note on the African's name: Esteban is spelled many other ways by writers, including Estéban, Estevan, Estebanico, Estevanico, Estebanillo, and so forth. When quoting from other works, the spelling used there is also used in this biography. Otherwise he will be referred to by his Spanish name of Esteban.

Because the world of the 1500s is so unfamiliar to most people, some explanations are in order to explain what would be alien concepts and situations today. If you're unfamiliar with the sixteenth century, before beginning chapter 1 you might want to read "Notes for the Modern Reader."

What little is known about Esteban comes from the writings of only a few Spaniards, beginning with Cabeza de Vaca's 1542 account known as *La relación*, which was titled "Álvar Núñez Cabeza de Vaca's account of what happened in the Indies during the expedition on which Pánfilo de Narváez went as governor." Cabeza de Vaca issued a revised edition in 1555. Its translated title is "The account and commentaries of Governor Álvar Núñez Cabeza de Vaca of what occurred on the two journeys that he made to the West Indies." That edition includes slight revisions of his earlier account of the 1528–1536 cross-continent ordeal with Esteban and adds his governorship in South

America. It is often referred to as *La relación y comentarios* or as *Naufragios*. As the titles of the 1542 and 1555 editions indicate, the emphasis was on Cabeza de Vaca, who always portrayed himself as the leader and overall hero on the expeditions.

Many people have never heard about the African expeditionary who went with him, and what they do know about him is more myth than fact. He is mentioned, usually very briefly, in other books about his time, but this biography will be one of the very few writings that does not portray Esteban negatively or insist that Zuni Indians killed him in 1539. Almost all other books that mention Esteban depict him that way. I confess that even one of my early books joined the overwhelming consensus about at least his death. In the 2013 first edition of my historical novel, *Winter of the Metal People*, I bought into the conventional wisdom that Zunis killed him. There it is, I'm embarrassed to admit, on page 10 and later. I hedged a bit by saying a Franciscan monk started the story that Zunis killed him.

I began to wonder. Why was all the evidence cited against Esteban based on assumptions and negative hearsay? And why were there so many different versions of his death? I no longer think it's necessarily true that Zunis killed him. To paraphrase President Harry Truman: There's nothing new in the world, except the history that someone doesn't want you to know. And there's also the observation by a noted British military writer, the late Richard Holmes. Skeptical of unverified and often fabricated elements in many popular so-called history books, Holmes said such writers "reinforce historical myth by delivering to the reader exactly what they expect to read."

My research of the last several years has refuted myths about Esteban, pointed out deliberate deceptions over the centuries, and raised reasonable doubt concerning his fate. This biography won't deliver what believers of conventional wisdom expect to read. Rather, this book comes much closer to the truth about one of the most remarkable figures of the sixteenth century.

Acknowledgments

Many people deserve credit for helping me tell the story of this unheralded African hero.

Special thanks to W. Clark Whitehorn, then executive editor of University of New Mexico Press, for his advice, guidance, and encouragement for this biography, and to Kathleen Meyer for her professional copyediting. Also to James Ayers for editorial, design, and production management, as well as to Felicia Cedillos for cover design. And to Elise McHugh, who early on recognized this book's poetential.

Thanks to Nancy Brown-Martinez, archivist for the Zimmerman Library's Center for Southwest Research at the University of New Mexico.

My wife Beatrice provided much support as well as detailed copyediting. I'm grateful to members of the Albuquerque Write Guild: Fred Bales, Jim Belshaw, the late Bob Gassaway, and Margaret Parks.

I depended upon Richard Flint and Shirley Cushing Flint, the best-known and widely published historians of sixteenth-century America and Mexico, for their research.

Any errors or omissions in this book are the fault of me and not them. Sources listed in the bibliography affirm John Bartlett's following quote: "I have gathered . . . other [people's] flowers and nothing but the thread that binds them is mine own."

Noteworthy Dates

1492 October 12	Christopher Columbus sails into the Caribbean Sea and sees its islands inhabited by the peaceful Taínos.
1496	Spaniards establish port of Santo Domingo on Hispaniola, later divided between Haiti and Dominican Republic.
1503	Estimated year Esteban is born in Azemmour, Morocco, or perhaps in sub-Sahara Africa.
1519	Alonso Álvarez de Pineda explores and maps the Gulf Coast from Florida to the Río Pánuco in Mexico.
1519–1521	Hernán Cortés with the help of smallpox and tens of thousands of Tlaxcalan Indian allies conquers the Aztecs. He turns the Aztec city of Tenochtitlan into Mexico City in its place.
1522	This year or soon after, Esteban is believed to have become a slave of Andrés Dorantes de Carranza in Spain.
1527 June 27	Esteban leaves Spain by ship on the Pánfilo de Narváez expedition, arriving two months later at the island of Hispaniola.

1527 October	Hurricane sinks two of Narváez's five ships on the south coast of Cuba.
1528 April 14	Esteban reaches Florida with the rest of expedition near today's St. Petersburg.
1528 June 25	Expedition occupies a small village in Apalachen.
1528 mid-July	Expedition abandons Apalachen village and retreats to the Gulf of Mexico coast at one or more settlements known as Aute. Continuing attacks by Apalachee warriors result in the surviving expeditionaries abandoning their campaign to conquer Florida.
1528 August 4	Expeditionaries begin building boats near Aute to escape from Florida.
1528 September 22	Esteban boards crude boat whose passengers include his owner Dorantes and Alonso del Castillo Maldonado to flee Apalachee Indians in Florida. His boat and four others built by expeditionaries float along the Gulf of Mexico coastline.
1528 October	The Mississippi River's current pushes the boats out into the Gulf of Mexico, forcing them to drift apart.
1528 November 5	Esteban's boat washes ashore on Malhado Island, near today's Galveston, Texas.
1528 November 6	Álvar Núñez Cabeza de Vaca's boat washes ashore about four miles south of Esteban.
1528 Early November	Two other expeditionary boats wreck along a hundred-mile stretch of the Texas coastline, all south of Esteban and Cabeza de Vaca's boats. After landing, the fifth boat is blown back out into the gulf with Narváez aboard and never seen again.
1528–1534	Esteban and three Spanish survivors—Cabeza de Vaca, Dorantes, and Castillo—spend nearly six years as slaves to Karankawa Indian tribes.

1534 September or October	The four survivors escape Indian captors and are welcomed by an Avavare tribe in Texas who treats them well without slavery.
1535 spring	Eseban and three Spaniards leave the friendly Avavares and head southward through Texas and then northward in Mexico and finally westward toward the Gulf of Califonia coast.
1536 March	Esteban and Cabeza de Vaca meet conquistador slave hunters in western Mexico.
1536 July 23	Esteban and the three surviving Spaniards arrive in an escort at Mexico City.
1539 March 7	After staying more than two years in Mexico City and additional months in west central Mexico, Esteban begins journey with Friar Marcos, traveling north from Culiacán, Mexico, to seek the Seven Cities.
1539 April 2	At Vacapa, Marcos sends Esteban on ahead. Marcos follows on April 17.
1539 early to mid-May	Esteban arrives at the Zuni village of Hawikku in western New Mexico near the Arizona border and disappears from the historical record.

Notes for the Modern Reader

A biography like this needs to make many compromises for the modern reader as it winds its way between Spanish and English spellings, and also in presenting concepts from the sixteenth century that do not exist today. For example, "Europe" was not a word then, let alone a continent-wide concept, and Spain was not the unified nation we know today. They are referred to as such for the modern reader, however. Another contrast is that in those days the word "Christian" was a synonym for Roman Catholic.

All mileage estimates based on Spanish leagues are approximate because guesses were by the Spanish travelers' memory, and the mile equivalents of leagues also varied at the time from 2.63 to 3 miles or more.

Centuries of Spanish warfare with North Africa Moors, along with unyielding Catholic Church dogma during the 1500s in favor of slavery and in condemnation of infidels, combined to create fanaticism by all Europeans, not just Spaniards, toward natives of the New World. Among the many reasons Europeans acted the way they did in the New World, other unfamiliar aspects of the sixteenth century include:

- Spain's practice of primogeniture, which resulted in disinheritance of second-born and later sons who were accustomed to wealth, resulting in them doing whatever they had to do to reclaim wealth and position in the New World.
- The impecunious peasantry that existed for nearly everyone else

in Europe, which motivated commoners to go to extremes in the New World as the one way to elevate themselves from poverty and become rich.
- Spain's need for great additional amounts of gold and silver to finance the Holy Roman Empire's relentless warfare across Europe during this period.

Foundational sources for this book are Fanny Bandelier's 1905 English translation of Álvar Nuñez Cabeza de Vaca's 1542 account of what happened in Florida and the cross-continent escape, known as *La relación*, and by the Frances M. López-Morillos translation of the *Relación* portion of his 1555 *La relación y comentarios*, edited by Enrique Pupo-Walker and republished as *Castaways* in 1993. Also key is Gerald Theisen's translation of the six chapters called the Joint Report in Gonzalo Fernández de Oviedo y Valdéz's *La historia general y natural de las Indias*. The Joint Report chapters were first published in 1547 and include the views about the cross-continent trek by Cabeza de Vaca's companion Spaniards: Andrés Dorantes de Carranza and Alonso del Castillo Maldonado. I used other translations and essays of interpretation when appropriate, as well as many resources featuring Esteban, from histories of that time to books and articles.[1] I also examined myths and exaggerations created by Spanish chronicles in the 1500s and US writers in the 1800s, 1900s, and even into the twenty-first century.

A major problem occurs in referring to sixteenth-century Castilian Spanish names, often in a compromise between making them historically accurate or in a form familiar to readers today. As one example, the spelling decided on for the Narváez expedition's treasurer is Álvar Núñez Cabeza de Vaca. Most English speakers are aware of how to read the diacritical marks of an accent and a tilde over certain letters, so they were retained in this book. However, the spelling of his Cabeza name was changed in this book from its original cedilla diacritical mark of ç to the more common z instead.

Spanish names are given in the Anglicized form most familiar to English speakers rather than the way they would have been used in Spain in the 1500s. For example, Americans know Francisco Vázquez de Coronado by the name Coronado, but he was not referred to that way in the sixteenth century. Instead, his full name was used, and contemporary Spaniards would have known him as Francisco Vázquez, not as Coronado. There are other exceptions to mesh with the times. The main one is that this book spells the conqueror of the Aztecs/Mexicas as Cortés with the accent mark and the original *s* instead of the *z* usually seen today. Also, Cíbola is spelled with the original accent mark rather than without, as the Anglicized version does today. When quoting from original sources, the spelling of a name used in that source is retained.

Into the 1800s, the Spanish spelling for the Zuni tribe was with a tilde—Zuñi. The more accepted modern spelling without a tilde is used in this book. Similarly, the word "Aztec" was not invented until the 1800s.[2] That tribe would have been known as the Mexica (meh-SHEE-kah) in the 1500s, but this book usually uses the term "Aztec" because that is how those Indians are known today.

A point of confusion is that people from all across what is today's Europe came to the Caribbean and Americas, not just Spaniards. Everyone in those days identified by where they came from, such as Castile, Aragón, Portugal, Germany, Italy, France, and so on. The collective noun at that time for all these nationalities was "Christian," because the continent was mostly made up of Christendom, or more specifically, Catholicism.

The usual Anglicized spelling of the Zuni village that Esteban visited is Hawikuh. Many Zunis prefer the spelling of Hawikku, so I used that in this book. The same is true for the spelling of "katsina," which many Puebloans prefer over the Anglicized "kachina."

By keeping these points in mind, the reader can more readily understand the differences between the sixteenth century and today.

CHAPTER 1

A Man of Mysteries

BOOKS ABOUT THE history of the American Southwest have ignored him or, even worse, attacked his character and belittled his importance. Spanish conquistadors said one reason they went to Arizona and New Mexico was to investigate what happened to him. The only public spaces honoring him are two small Arizona parks in Tucson and Phoenix, although he never visited the site of either city. He's known best by his condescending slave nickname. He is almost erased from America's historical record.

Nevertheless, the African slave Esteban was the first person from the *Old World* of Europe, Africa, and Asia to travel across the North American continent and also explore the American Southwest in the 1500s.

The remarkable story of Esteban is almost always told from the viewpoint of the Spaniard Álvar Núñez Cabeza de Vaca, with whom he traveled across the continent in 1528–1536 after a failed Spanish invasion of Florida.

In bringing Esteban out of the background and into the foreground, this biography remains true to facts that historians have come to agree upon, points out those still contested, and challenges numerous errors and myths about Esteban.

Nearly all writers maintain that Zuni warriors killed him in 1539 in the present state of New Mexico. If so, there is conjecture on why they killed him. Some speculate that his gourd rattle from another tribe or owl feathers he carried angered Zuni religious leaders. Others claim he demanded gifts and favors, or that his never-before-seen skin color startled the Zunis. None of these reasons to kill him seems serious enough for a tribe characterized as being inclined toward peace.[1]

The most persistent reason stated in book after book is that he was killed because he made advances toward Zuni women. However, Mexican Indians who accompanied Esteban reported that Zunis did not allow him to enter the village. Therefore, Esteban most likely never saw any Zuni women. The conquistador Francisco Vázquez de Coronado wrote the next year that Zunis kept women so protected that even he saw only two elderly ones.[2]

Zuni historian Edmund J. Ladd described Esteban as "a man either ignored or avoided by history, who is a very important Southwestern historical personality."[3] He wrote that the reason his ancestors would have killed Esteban was if they concluded he was a spy. They feared he would show the location of Zuni villages to slave-raiding Spaniards that trade-route Indians warned them about.[4]

But they allowed the Indians with him to escape with that same knowledge. So there's a possibility Zunis did not kill Esteban despite almost all accounts declaring they did, those accounts being rooted in comments by sixteenth-century Spaniards who never witnessed what happened.

What Really Did Happen?

This biography will present a series of counterarguments to the traditionalist views and analyze both possibilities of whether Zunis killed Esteban. It also will describe how slave-owning Spaniards in the 1500s created a negative attitude toward Esteban, which successive writers have built upon with fictionalized scenarios and exaggerations that have attacked Esteban's character despite lack of proof.

Esteban had earlier survived an escape from a Spanish expedition's invasion of Florida and traveled almost the width of the North American continent in 1528–1536 with three Spanish aristocrats on a journey that took almost eight years. Beginning with the invasion, that incredible feat is described starting in chapter 7.

Three years after Esteban's return, the Spanish viceroy in Mexico City chose Esteban to guide Spain's first expedition north of Mexico in 1539.[5] The slave was at last able to live as a free man, even if briefly.

This biography primarily will examine Esteban the man and the times he lived in so there can be a better understanding of what he accomplished and why he's been ignored.

His Spanish name, Esteban, is often spelled as Estevan because Spaniards pronounce the letters *b* and *v* nearly the same. The name translates into English as Stephen. In sixteenth-century Castilian Spanish, his name would be pronounced as es-STAY-bahn. In the United States, the usual Anglicized pronunciation is ESS-tuh-bahn.[6]

When reported on, he is almost always referred to as Estebanico or Estevanico, either of which translate to a nickname, "Little Stephen," or even "Stevie."[7] Spaniards of his day used that diminutive for a child—or, in Esteban's case, to convey condescension toward him because he spent most of at least his adult life as a slave.

The original disrespect of the nickname continues today in some history books, which still refer to him as Estebanico or Estevanico instead of his actual Spanish name. The reason for this is that is how he is referred to in most Spanish chronicles, the nickname being used at that time to demean and marginalize him. This book will use his actual Spanish name of Esteban.

Writers also refer to him to as an Arab Moor more often than as a black African because he was acquired as a slave in Morocco, and his possible Berber connection is almost invisible. The next chapter will examine this ethnic controversy.

Esteban remains an intriguing historical figure. His reputation remains under repeated disparagement despite his accomplishments, courage, and abilities.

Pueblo Tribes Remember

Ironically, the Zuni Indians who most writers accuse of killing Esteban are the ones who keep his memory alive in their oral history and through their ancient, traditional religion of kivas and katsinas.[8]

Esteban first entered the Pueblo world when he arrived at the hilltop Zuni village of Hawikku in today's western New Mexico in the spring of 1539. The encounter will be examined in chapters 16 and 17. But first, a reference to what might be Esteban from 1885.

Most researchers usually conclude that Smithsonian ethnologist Frank Hamilton Cushing must have been talking about Esteban when he regaled an audience at the Geographic Society of Boston in 1885 with what he called "the Zuni legend of the Black Mexican."[9] Cushing said Zuni elders told him a story from "eleven men's ages" ago about being attacked by black Mexicans and Indians from "the Land of Everlasting Summer."[10] Zuni historian Edmund Ladd, however, did not think the story was about Esteban and called it "poetic license" by Cushing.[11] Ladd said the so-called legend was not credible, citing reasons that include Cushing using English terms not in the Zuni vocabulary.[12] In addition, the legend involves "many" black Mexicans, not just one, and Cushing recalled the Zunis told him "one of the black Mexicans" was killed at the village of Kyaki:ma.[13] That village is at the base of Dowa Yalanne mesa, which is thirteen miles from Hawikku, the pueblo that most historians believe Esteban visited.[14] Was the legend based on Esteban, or did the term "black Mexican" refer to something other than an African?[15] And how long ago would eleven men's ages calculate to?[16] Also, what should one make of the event taking place at Kyaki:ma instead of at Hawikku? In addition, Cushing's tale has the Mexican Indians attacking the Zunis, in contrast to the usual version given about Esteban's arrival.

Regardless of whether Cushing's story is about Esteban or whether it tells of an actual event, or when, historians agree that Esteban walked up from Mexico accompanied by Mexican Indians, and most believe he arrived at the southwesternmost Zuni village named Hawikku, often Anglicized to Hawikuh.

A memory of Esteban continues in the pueblos' traditional religion featuring men wearing regalia and elaborate covers over their heads, often cylinder-shaped, to represent spirit-beings. Such figures are katsinas, often Anglicized to kachinas.[17]

A katsina can be the spirit of an ancestor, animal, bird, another tribe, or even a crop, depending on the ceremony.[18] Although sometimes referred to as Pueblo gods, they are not. They would be closer to the concept of Catholic saints, but even that is not an appropriate comparison.

"Borrowing the bodies of living men," writer Paul Coze explains, "[katsinas] visit the villages . . . to receive prayers to [the Creator]. He who wears the mask of a kachina believes he loses his personal identity and assumes that of the spirit."[19] This would be similar to religious leaders of any belief feeling a

Figure 1. The author carved, painted, and clothed this four-inch figure to illustrate an approximation of the Chákwaina katsina, named for Esteban, the African slave who was the first non-Indian to find Zuni. This figure is not authentic because it was created by a non-Puebloan. It's intended to give an idea of a katsina without a photograph of one, which some Puebloans would consider sacrilegious to their ancient religion. Wood carving and photo by Dennis Herrick.

sense of spiritual ennoblement when putting on their religion's clerical vestments.[20]

American culture routinely refers to the head coverings as masks. But many Puebloans, especially Hopis, consider that term offensive. They prefer to call the head cover a "friend" that unites the impersonator with the spirit of the katsina.[21]

Small carved representations of katsina figures, more properly *katsintithu* but commonly called "dolls," are still created in the Hopi pueblos as religion teaching aids, not toys, to instruct children in the ancient culture.[22]

Several anthropologists and historians believe the Hopi, Zuni, and some Rio Grande pueblos memorialized Esteban's arrival by creating a katsina spirit-being called Chákwaina (*Tsa'kwaina*, in Hopi).[23] It was always painted black and referred to as "the black katsina."[24]

Zunis tell often conflicting versions about Esteban's fate, depending on who is asked. For example, although early researchers were told that Esteban's arrival inspired creation of the Chákwaina katsina, several Zuni elders told one researcher a few years ago that Chákwaina existed as a demon katsina painted black long before they ever met their first black human in Esteban.[25]

Regardless, Chákwaina would emerge as a symbol of the ruinous Spanish conquest that Esteban's appearance at Hawikku foreshadowed.[26] As a portent of the event that so altered the life, religion, and culture of all Puebloans, they vilified Esteban as a monster katsina through Chákwaina with pointed teeth and dangling tongue.

Chákwaina is usually represented with a long, black goatee, a Puebloan kilt called a dance kirtle, and carrying a gourd rattle and a bow.[27] Over the past several decades, Chákwaina's head covering has often had a star painted on one side and a crescent moon on the other, signifying Esteban's Muslim heritage.[28] Chákwaina was introduced to Hopi First Mesa from Zuni and later adopted by some Rio Grande pueblos.[29]

Ceremonial dances have featured Chákwaina to commemorate Esteban's arrival in 1539.[30] The annual feast day dances at Jemez Pueblo often have had a performer wearing a darkened sheep pelt on his head to signify curly hair and with his face painted black to represent Esteban.[31] A painted face and wig were used because Catholic priests had banned katsina head covers.

A lesser-known katsina named Nepokwa'i has also been linked to Esteban.[32] Nepokwa'i is similar to the flute-player figure named Kokopelli, which is so prominent in Puebloan rock art. At the Tewa settlement of Hano on Hopi Second Mesa, Nepokwa'i's cylindrical head cover and body were painted black and the katsina was referred to as "a big black man." In Puebloan tales, Nepokwa'i appears with a buckskin on his back from which he makes moccasins for women.[33]

Today's feast day dances at the pueblos are reminiscent of the ancient katsina ceremonies, but only the western pueblos of Zuni and Hopi still feature katsinas in public. The essence of the religion remains hidden to outsiders at Puebloan villages along the Rio Grande, although katsinas still appear in ceremonies open to just pueblo members.[34] Because it's hidden, many non-Puebloans still don't realize that the ancient, traditional religion with its katsinas, ceremonial kivas, and sacred art has survived in secret despite centuries of suppression by zealous missionaries.[35] As a 1993 researcher observed: "The Pueblos have survived and flourished, retaining more of their old ways ... than any outsider can know."[36]

Spaniards would come to know the Zuni territory as Cíbola, a word of uncertain origin. Most think Cíbola was rooted in an Indian word for the American bison, also known as buffalo, on the Great Plains. Even today, Zuni Pueblo lands are partly in New Mexico's Cibola County, whose seal portrays a buffalo. Other theories about the word exist, including that it might be the name that a Mexican tribe used for the Zuni that was also applied to buffalo. Zuni historian Edmund J. Ladd said the Zuni word for buffalo/bison was *ciwolo*, and Spaniards in the late 1590s referred to the massive herds on the Great Plains as "cíbola cattle."[37]

Other Depictions

Esteban was almost memorialized on New Mexico's 1976 bicentennial medal. New Mexico bills itself as a land of three cultures—Indian, Hispanic, and American Anglo—but commission members discussed the possibility of including an image of Esteban or some other symbolic representation of the African race.

Doing so would have recognized that New Mexico has a fourth culture, African, because Esteban was the first non-Indian to enter the state, and US Army Buffalo Soldiers and other African Americans arrived afterward.

However, Myra Ellen Jenkins, the state historian, argued against Esteban's place in New Mexico history by claiming he was not a black African. Swayed by the controversial 1940 theory of amateur historian Cleve Hallenbeck, Jenkins asserted that Esteban "was actually an African Caucasian Moor or Arab."[38] Jenkins was paraphrasing Hallenbeck's personal theory about Esteban's race, which many books have since reprinted without question.

Charles Becknell, a commission member and then director of Afro-American Studies at the University of New Mexico, sensed racism in Jenkins's comment. "The man was from Africa and he was black," Becknell said.[39]

Nevertheless, Jenkins won the debate. Esteban and the African American contribution to New Mexico history were left off the medal.[40] Its reverse ended up depicting pueblo pottery, a conquistador helmet, and a miner's pickaxe.

Esteban's precise racial makeup can never be certain. However, the late Southwest historian David J. Weber wrote, "Most historians [are now convinced] that Esteban was a black man."[41]

In addition to inspiring creation of the Chákwaina and possibly the Nepokwa'i katsinas, although not honored on a medal, Esteban is remembered in a few old records. Though Africans were rarely mentioned and almost never identified by name in sixteenth-century Spanish chronicles, author Robert Goodwin noted in his 2008 book about Esteban:

"Esteban is one of the few examples of a sixteenth-century African slave whose achievements were so outstanding that it is possible to piece together his story from the contemporary Spanish documents."[42] Goodwin understates the case. Esteban is the *only* African slave named in Spanish documents whose exploits are told in detail.

However, there are no physical descriptions of him except he was tall and referred to as *el negro*, which translates from Spanish into English as "the black." For Spaniards to consider him tall he might have been six feet or so, a height few Europeans of his time attained.[43] He had a beard like many Caucasians and Africans of his day. Perhaps it was a goatee like on the Chákwaina katsina.

Several early historians and novelists perpetuated the falsehood that Esteban entered New Mexico and Arizona during his years-long journey across the continent. According to the latest estimates of their route, however, he and the three Spanish survivors of the disastrous Narváez expedition to Florida never entered those two states. Instead, they floated across the Gulf of Mexico and then walked across Texas and northern Mexico until they met up with Spanish slave hunters in 1536 and turned south toward Mexico City.

It was not until 1539 that Esteban entered Arizona and New Mexico. That year he guided the first Spanish incursion north of Mexico—led not by conquistadors, but by a Franciscan Catholic friar, Marcos de Niza.

Most references to Esteban's history focus on his meeting with the Zuni people. In those references, almost every American writer is critical of Esteban, promulgating errors and exaggerations not found anywhere in original Spanish chronicles, with the writers' negativity often morphing into hostility.

For example, a National Park Service booklet noted that Friar Marcos paused in his northward journey to wait for messengers, and then declared, "Esteban refused to wait." Actually, Marcos ordered Esteban to go on ahead. Then the writer speculates, "Away from the friar's restraints, [Esteban] ceased being a slave and became a king." The writer further assumes Esteban acted with connivance, greed, and lust although no eyewitness ever reported him acting that way.[44] This is typical of how most American writers have negatively dramatized Esteban's story. Additional writers who have passed off their personal opinions disguised as historical fact will be examined in chapter 18.

In contrast, Esteban comes across heroically in Cabeza de Vaca's account of the incredible trek across the continent that took eight years, despite being mentioned sparingly.

Historian John Upton Terrell conceded that Esteban had faults, like any human. But unlike most writers, Terrell expressed admiration for the African, writing in a 1968 book:

> [Esteban] spoke several Indian languages. He talked fluently in the language of the signs. He was a wilderness diplomat par excellence. ... He was trusted and respected by hundreds of Indians in numerous tribes between the Gulf of Mexico and the Gulf of California, between the mountains of Sonora and the Valley of Mexico, and he was revered by them.... He made the greatest journey into the unknown, into the unmapped wilderness darkness, in North American history—the first crossing of the continent from the Atlantic to the Pacific.... He was one of the most intrepid, brave, indomitable, and accomplished explorers of the New World.[45]

Traveling ahead of Friar Marcos on his final exploration in 1539, Esteban entered Arizona along the San Pedro River about fifteen miles southwest of present-day Bisbee. He then walked northeasterly, making his way along Indian trade paths. Coronado's expedition followed a route that Marcos said Esteban traveled the year before. The first researchers projected that route to be on the Arizona side of the state line, but archaeological research after 2010 reveals that Coronado and thus presumably Esteban traveled up the New Mexico side.[46]

In the often narrow-minded Eurocentric view of American history, some even consider Esteban as the *discoverer* of Arizona and New Mexico, although he found the Zuni tribe already living near New Mexico's western boundary.

History in Books

Distortions exist about Esteban because dominant societies write the history. It's also true that Esteban's life story has become, to paraphrase Voltaire, society's agreed-upon fable.[47] Both truisms pose obstacles in trying to understand Esteban's time, the people around him, and the man himself.

The essential aspect to remember about Esteban is that he was an African slave. All historical references to him are influenced by that singular fact, because Spanish slaveholder attitudes of the 1500s pervade the few contemporary records that mention Esteban.

Spanish chronicles during and immediately after the Middle Ages were xenophobic toward Africans, whether Arabs or Negroes. That's understandable after almost eight centuries of Christians fighting the darker-skinned Muslims of North Africa for control of the Iberian Peninsula, which would become the modern nations of Spain and Portugal. Warfare did not end until 1492 with the fall of the last Muslim stronghold in the Emirate of Granada in Spain.

Esteban first enters a written historical record thirty-seven years later. He is a shadow, shrouded by the fog of half a millennium of racial bias, assumptions, and inadequate historical documentation. Spaniards started mentioning him in 1529 with grudging acceptance because he became too important to ignore any longer.

A challenge in writing this biography of Esteban is that actual quotes and thoughts from Esteban exist only in novelists' imaginations. Conquistadors and a Franciscan friar who knew him and described his deeds never reported a direct quote, although what he said was sometimes paraphrased.

Nevertheless, novels attributing quotes by him include fanciful children's books such as Elizabeth Shepherd's *The Discoveries of Esteban the Black* (1970); Helen Rand Parish's *Estebanico* (1974); Carolyn Arrington's *Estevanico, Black Explorer in Spanish Texas* (1986); and the most imaginative of all in both content and title, I. Mac Perry's *Black Conquistador: The Story of the First Black Man in America* (1998).

The latest fictional novel, with fabricated quotes and imagined background, is *The Moor's Account: A Novel* by Laila Lalami, published in 2014.[48] Her novel presents a memoir she imagines a probably illiterate Esteban wrote in 1536–1538, just like Parish's novel.

This biography will examine the man and the myth, misinterpretations, and also deliberate deceptions fabricated over the years. Because of imagined events conjured up by novelists as well as many early supposed historians, who often mixed in their own prejudices and opinions with facts, this biography will often mention two or more reported versions of a particular event in Esteban's life. Such misleading accounts are included because distortions often evolve into today's conventional wisdom about Esteban, and their contradictions are indicative of their untruthfulness.

Despite these imagined events, no negative eyewitness accounts exist of Esteban's activities. Even if they did, they could not be accepted on face value. Eyewitness accounts tend to channel historical facts into folklore acceptable to the eyewitness's culture and with a concern for reputation. The eyewitness account often becomes a version of history that the eyewitness prefers to believe, rather than what actually happened.[49]

In a 2009 article, archaeologist Deni J. Seymour explains why eyewitness accounts cannot be trusted even if several agree with each other. They are subject to anthropologist Charles M. Hudson's principle about historical distortion that "a body of lore and shared experiences" can influence eyewitness accounts.[50] Seymour points out that this subconscious perspective was "reinforced as the Spaniards sat around the campfire and passed many tedious hours in the saddle. Those experiences most foreign to them may have been subjected to the greatest pressure of 'groupthink,' which holds unquestioned belief in the inherent morality and purpose of the group and a homogeneity of its members' social background and ideology."[51]

If everyone must therefore be somewhat skeptical of eyewitness accounts, which make up much of what little is known about Esteban, then where is truth to be found? Documentary evidence is scant, so writing about Esteban is often based on informed speculation—and influenced by writers' judgments for better or worse. Researchers often disagree over key points of Esteban's life and his fate. Much is uncertain when research stretches back almost five hundred years. The ambiguity and gaps in the vague historical record leave much room for scholars to reach differing conclusions.

One aspect of Esteban's early life that most historians agree upon is that he was a Muslim who converted to Catholicism. Some believe he might have been born into an African tribal religion. It's known he could speak Arabic and lived at least part of his life on Morocco's Atlantic coast in the city of Azemmour, also spelled as Azemour, Azemor, and Azemmur. It's southwest of the more famous city of Casablanca and was a Portuguese slave-trading center in the 1500s.

Besides speaking Arabic and Spanish, and perhaps also getting along in

Berber and Portuguese, Esteban's multilingual gift enabled him to learn several Indian languages and the Indians' sign language after he went to the Americas. He became the most important polyglot of the sixteenth century.

Nevertheless, even though Esteban was the first person from the Old World to appear in the American Southwest, most Americans, especially those outside the Southwest, know little or nothing about him. Most books based on biased Spanish chronicles barely mention him, ascribe bad motivations to him, reinforce fictions about his character, and divert credit to others for what he achieved.

Esteban was "one of a kind," NBA basketball star Kareem Abdul-Jabbar wrote in his book *Black Profiles in Courage*: "The only black in the first party to cross the North American continent. The first non-Indian to discover the [American] Southwest. The first to set foot in Arizona and New Mexico. His courage and ingenuity opened the Southwest. . . . But bring up this subject and people look at you funny. . . . The idea of black people involved in the discovery of this continent is still shocking news to most white people. I can understand that. It was shocking news to *me*."[52]

CHAPTER 2

The Morocco Connection

BECAUSE SPANISH ACCOUNTS report Esteban was found in Azemmour, Morocco, it's presumed he lived there from infancy and might have been born there.

Azemmour is a Berber city.[1] Esteban's origin in Azemmour indicates he was a Berber. Centuries ago the Berbers were described by Europeans as black, but after a thousand years of genetic mixing the skin colors today range from black to brown, and they can pale all the way to a Caucasian tone.[2] The Berbers have been known by other names throughout history, with Americans remembering the Berber homeland as the Barbary States. The distinction between a Berber and an Arab is relevant, because as recently as a few decades before Esteban's birth the Berbers fought against the Arabs in Morocco.[3]

Azemmour's residents consider Esteban to have been a Berber. American history books, on the other hand, almost always call him a Moor. He was a Moor in the European sense of the term, but the overbroad term of "Moor" has left the impression with many that Esteban was an Arab, not a black African, let alone a Berber or a sub-Saharan black. The Spanish term of *moro*, which translates in English to Moor, was common during Esteban's lifetime. Moors were the medieval Muslim inhabitants of much of North Africa, Sicily, and Malta. They conquered the Iberian Peninsula in the eighth century, controlling what is today Portugal, Spain, and southern France.[4]

Although some North Africans consider it a pejorative, Europeans use

"Moor" to refer to Muslims of North Africa in general—including Berbers and other peoples of the Maghreb, regardless of tribe. Thus, Esteban's Berber or sub-Saharan connections have been submerged in repeated references to him by the general term of "Moor." The Maghreb, a term little used in the rest of the world, refers to most of North Africa west of Egypt, including Algeria, Morocco, and Tunisia, but also often Mauritania and Libya. The Maghreb has been Islamic since Arab invasions in the seventh and eighth centuries.

Today, Arabic is the predominant language across North Africa. There also are Berber dialects along with European languages, the most common being French, Spanish, and English, in that order.

Hallenbeck's Deception

Álvar Núñez Cabeza de Vaca, who spent more than eight years with Esteban, concluded his account of their cross-continent journey together by describing Esteban as a "negro al árabe, natural de Açamor."[5] Writers in English have translated that phrase many ways, but the most accurate seems to be "Arabic-speaking Negro, native of Azemmour."[6] That translation combines both ethnicity and genetic heritage. Nineteenth- and twentieth-century US obsession with genetic heritage confused this distinction, although it was routinely recognized in late medieval Spain, which saw no contradiction in being both Spaniard and Negro.[7] However, T. Buckingham Smith's first English translation of Cabeza de Vaca's narrative in 1871 labeled Esteban as an "Arabian black," and ever since some Americans writing about Esteban have been lightening Esteban's skin.[8]

Ultimate responsibility for misidentifying Esteban's race falls to Cleve Hallenbeck. The head of the US Weather Bureau station in Roswell, New Mexico, Hallenbeck's hobby was writing books about the Spanish history of the Southwest.[9] He was aware that archaeologist Adolph Bandelier had questioned whether Esteban was a Negro or an Arab North African in 1905.[10] And historian Herbert E. Bolton referred to Esteban as a Moor and later as a black in 1921 in *The Spanish Borderlands*, although by 1929 Bolton settled on referring to Esteban as "a Negro."[11]

Hallenbeck went beyond such indecisiveness in his 1940 book. In it, he dropped the word "Negro" from the Castilian phrase "negro al árabe" in his translation of Cabeza de Vaca's account, coming up instead with "an Arab."[12] In an endnote to that translation, he insisted that Esteban was "not a Negro." Hallenbeck's description of Esteban as an Arab evolved into him later identifying Esteban as a Moor, because most but not all Moors are Arabic in European terminology. To add to his deception, everywhere that Cabeza de Vaca referred to Esteban as "el negro," Hallenbeck either changed the reference to "the Moor" or "the Arab," or he dropped the reference to Esteban altogether.[13]

Hallenbeck's distorted translation, changing Esteban's identity to an Arab or Moor, became the standard for American writers for the next several decades. That claim is still seen more often than not, and it's an example of how easy it is to start a myth and how difficult it is to kill one after it becomes popular.

Historian Cyclone Covey translated Cabeza de Vaca's description of Esteban as "Estevánico el negro," but despite that Covey added parenthetically in a 2004 book that he still thought Esteban was an Arab. José B. Fernández's 1975 book also identified Esteban as an Arab. As recently as 2013, a translator labeled Esteban "an Arab black man." And so it goes on.[14]

Historian Rayford W. Logan was quick to challenge Hallenbeck later in 1940, citing numerous documents that showed Esteban to be a Negro discoverer.[15] Nevertheless, Hallenbeck's distortion prevailed in books instead of Logan's rebuttal. In an examination of original Spanish documents referring to Esteban, Logan cited evidence that Esteban's origin was sub-Saharan black African. With the exception of Hallenbeck, Logan's analysis of numerous documents that mention Esteban found unanimity that Esteban was always referred to as "el negro"—the black.[16] Logan pointed out that the only other time in the *Relación* that Cabeza de Vaca referred to people by the Spanish word of "negro" was when he was on a Portuguese slave ship and describing the captive black Africans on board.[17]

Why did Hallenbeck categorize Esteban as an Arab instead of a black African? The answer might lie in the racism of the 1940s when attitudes could not grant heroic qualities to black men and especially not to a slave.[18] Some confusion over whether Esteban might have been an Arab stems from the Portuguese finding him in Morocco and because he could speak Arabic. Spaniards of the time considered Esteban to be a black African in race, although they thought of him as an Arab Muslim in culture because of where he'd been found.

Even if he was of a mixed racial background, the late ethnologist Carroll L. Riley wrote that Esteban was "sub-Saharan enough, phenotypically, for the Spaniards to feel comfortable in giving him a black ethnic classification." Historian Weber finalized Esteban's black African heritage: "The question of Esteban's race . . . is no longer a matter of contention among contemporary scholars."[19] It remains a point of confusion nevertheless for many people because of Hallenbeck's deliberate mistranslation.

The subtitle of Goodwin's *Crossing the Continent* labels Esteban an "African-American," although Esteban was not that. There was no such thing in the sixteenth century. Goodwin maintains that Esteban was a black African from south of the Sahara Desert, kidnapped by slavers. Or, Goodwin concedes, perhaps his parents were the ones captured, and Esteban was born in Morocco.[20]

In some uncertain year, possibly around 1522, Esteban was transported from Africa to Europe. This was at a time when Portuguese masters of Azemmour sold both Muslim Africans in the North African region called the Maghreb and black Africans from the rest of the continent as slaves on the Iberian Peninsula.[21]

Recent Moroccan Interest

Few researchers seem to have checked with today's Moroccan historians. But Moroccans' views are relevant because Azemmour claims Esteban as one of its own. *Lonely Planet*'s Morocco guide for travelers states, "The town's most famous inhabitant was Estevanico the Black."[22]

Researcher and author Hamza Ben Driss Ottmani notes that "Recently Moroccan historians have revived the memory of our man" amid a growing awareness of their nation's sixteenth-century connection to the United States and Mexico.[23]

In 2006 Ottmani wrote the first history of Esteban's story for a North Africa audience. His *Le fils du soleil: L'odyssée d'Estevanico de Azemor* (The Son of the Sun) was published in French and named Morocco Book of the Year. Ottmani reports that Moroccans' research had not yet found documentary evidence of

Esteban's sixteenth-century birth or name. But he mentions that Moroccans have settled on "that beautiful family name that his Moroccan admirers affectionately gave him, namely: Mustapha El Azemmouri."[24] Now, although they often revert to the Spanish name when discussing Esteban, Moroccan writers start by giving him the name of Mustapha or some variant such as Mustafa.[25] For example, in Morocco native and novelist Laila Lalami's Pulitzer Prize finalist for fiction in 2015, *The Moor's Account: A Novel*, she mentions that Esteban's name was Mustafa.[26] The name and its variants for Muhammad are very common in Arabic. It's a generic reference in this case, because the name translates into English as "Mustapha from Azemmour." Today's websites for Azemmour and the surrounding Doukkala-Abda rural area report the tradition that Esteban was born in 1503 as "Mustapha al-Azemmour" in that Moroccan city.

The Arab, Spanish, and English names of Mustafa/Mostapha/Mustapha, Esteban, and Stephen have similar pronunciations in different languages. Arab scholar Chouaib Halifi points out how close the name of Esteban/Stephen is to the Arabic variations.[27] When spelled in Arabic, the name is pronounced as Istfan. When the name is transliterated in Arabic from another language, it is pronounced Steefaan.[28] So by choosing any variation of Mustapha, Moroccan writers picked the closest name in Arabic phonics to Esteban's eventual name in Spanish.

Another reason to consider Moroccan sources involves Esteban's presumed origin in the city of Azemmour, its name coming from the Berber word for "wild olive tree."[29] Although the tourism website reports Esteban was born in Azemmour, some Moroccan scholars and authors assert he was captured as a child from elsewhere in Africa.[30] In other words, he was captured from below the Sahara Desert either by "marauders" or by African tribes selling fellow Africans into slavery.

Usually, a slave's origin is described as the place where a European slave merchant purchased the person, not the place of birth. "So, as Esteban was described as a . . . native of Azemmour, we can assume that he was sold into captivity there," author Goodwin concludes. "But the history of Azemmour makes it likely that he was from farther south, beyond the desert, from the Land of the Blacks."[31]

No one can know his birthplace for sure. As for his future, Ottmani's book notes that "Estevanico of Azemor has gone almost unnoticed in the history of the New World." Esteban's achievements have been hidden behind a "veil made thick of oblivion, myth, and sometimes lies, to the point that the man, although the first of the Old World to discover the Southwest of the United States, remained obscured for centuries."[32]

Moroccan scholar Lhoussain Simour made the same point. He wrote in the *European Review of History* in 2013 that Esteban, whom he referred to as Mostafa al-Zemmouri, "turns into a real hero" despite Cabeza de Vaca's attempt to keep him in the background. "Yet why is it that [Esteban's] name and achievements have remained almost in obscurity for so long?" Simour asks. "He is still one of the most important adventurers and explorers of America's Southwest, who transformed the cultural and historical landscape of the New World."[33]

Azemmour's citizens honor the memory of Esteban as a hometown hero. The theme of the 2013 Remp'Arts d'Azemmour festival in Morocco was "Estebanico: A Journey of Discovery and Encounter." Several Moroccan and French scholars presented a symposium about Azemmour's famous citizen. At least one mural depicting Esteban was painted on Azemmour's medina wall.[34] The small square is now named Place Estévanico. That festival in Morocco emphasizes how there is little public recognition of Esteban in the United States, although at least two US festivals have honored the memory of Esteban, both in Pensacola, Florida: the Estevanico Arts and Gospel Festival in 2011 and the Estevanico International Festival, which celebrated the diversity of cultures along the state's Gulf Coast that Esteban visited.[35]

If he were born in about 1503, whether to Moroccans, Berbers, or sub-Saharan Africans living in Azemmour, he would have been about twenty-four years old in 1527 at the start of the ill-fated Pánfilo de Narváez expedition to Florida. That date would agree with a common belief that he was in his mid- to late twenties by 1529, when he is first mentioned in a Spanish account.

Historians assume he must have been about that age, because by then he was strong, able to endure the harshest hardships, resourceful, and a leader despite Spaniards' disdain for his race and his enslavement. And the same could be said ten years later when he set out northward with Friar Marcos.

If Esteban was already a slave while living in Azemmour, a Moroccan master might have sold him to the Iberian slave markets.[36] But he might also have been a free man in Morocco who had volunteered himself for sale into slavery in a desperate bid to survive drought-related famine.

An exceptional dry period struck the agricultural area around Azemmour in the early 1500s.[37] In 1522, Portuguese merchants arrived at Azemmour to pick up their annual loads of fish, and a chronicler tells how crowds of starving people gathered around the ships, beseeching the merchants to take them to the Iberian Peninsula as slaves. They had been suffering through years of famine and plague. In their despair, they saw slavery as their last chance for food and survival.

Alert for a profit, the merchants agreed. They set sail with their unexpected human cargo to the Portuguese and Spanish slave markets. Esteban is believed to have boarded one of those ships in 1522 or soon afterward.[38]

Iberian Slavery

Slavery on the Iberian Peninsula was not seen as such a hopeless option to Azemmour refugees. Slaves suffered abusive treatment in many countries, and they were then being cruelly treated in the Americas, where slaves on the Caribbean island of Hispaniola suffered the hardest labor and meanest discipline. Portuguese and Spanish laws, however, required masters there to clothe, feed, and shelter their slaves.[39]

African slaves on the Iberian Peninsula lost their freedom and could never resign like a salaried servant could. Even so, that would have been preferable to starving to death in Morocco. Slaves in Spain served as nursemaids, cooks, stable keepers, personal attendants, bodyguards, valets, porters, and waiters. The Catholic Church at that time sanctioned slavery of non-Christians, so Spanish families of means often owned two or more household slaves in the sixteenth century.[40]

The possibility that Esteban sold himself into slavery might explain the loyalty he demonstrated toward his Spanish owner. Many have wondered why he didn't desert his owner and other Spanish companions after Narváez's disastrous expedition to Florida, when Esteban and other expeditionaries fled from Florida and began traveling the continent's width. Esteban had several opportunities before reaching western Mexico in 1536 when he could have abandoned the Spaniards because the Indians accepted him as a friend. If he had deserted, the three Spaniards might have wandered lost and perished.

The fact that he stayed with them all the way back to Spanish control makes more sense if it's true that he sold himself into slavery. Historian Richard Flint also points out that Esteban might have become acculturated as Spanish, and so he might have been reluctant to abandon what had become familiar to him for the unknown life of Indian tribes. The native peoples of south Texas especially, and perhaps of northern Mexico as well, might have seemed as uncouth to him as they did to most Europeans of the day.[41] Esteban proved able to accommodate himself well enough to the Catholicism of his Spanish masters that he won their trust and at least tolerance.

Even if he remained in his heart a Muslim, Esteban was baptized in adulthood as a Catholic after becoming a slave. Until about the time Esteban left for the New World, Spain did not knowingly allow non-Catholics to go to the Caribbean and the Americas.[42] By 1527, however, the monarchs had come to believe that converted Africans, *ladinos*, were too independent, and that instead African captives not converted or assimilated, *bozales*, should go. Thus, Esteban's owner, Andrés Dorantes de Carranza, probably had to receive special permission to take the Catholic convert Esteban on the Narváez expedition to Florida.[43] Dorantes, from Extremadura near the Portuguese border in western Spain, must have developed full confidence in Esteban to take the African with him to the other side of the Atlantic as his personal slave, and he bestowed on his new slave the Spanish name of Esteban de Dorantes.

CHAPTER 3

Terrorism in the Caribbean

TO KNOW ESTEBAN, it's necessary to have an understanding of the times he lived in amid the ruthless conquest mentality of sixteenth-century Europeans and many Muslim people, including Ottomans under Suleiman, who were at that time repeatedly attempting to conquer eastern Europe.

Growing up in Morocco, and later as an adult slave in Spain, Esteban would have known about a "New World" that Columbus had found across the Atlantic Ocean.[1] He would have heard stories about the riches of the islands there, and although he might have heard about the warfare or cruelties against the native people, he probably couldn't have appreciated the extent of what was genocide then in the Caribbean.[2] Gold and exotic foods and materials traveled from the Caribbean to Spain on Spanish treasure ships in unbelievable quantities throughout the early 1500s, dazzling Spain's royalty and populace enough for them to ignore how the riches were acquired.[3]

Columbus Arrives

Christopher Columbus underestimated the planet's size so much that he assumed the Caribbean Islands were near India. He called the natives *indios*, a misnomer that has persisted in the English term of "Indians."

Columbus anchored next to the first island he saw, Guanahaní, which he renamed San Salvador, in the Bahamas northeast of Cuba. Columbus reported he made landfall on a beach in front of a Taíno village. The words "Arawak" and "Taíno" as terms for the Caribbean people, language, and culture date from the mid-nineteenth century. Nevertheless, Taíno will be used here because it is the term most people use today.[4]

The remains of such a village reported by Columbus were found on San Salvador at Long Bay Beach, and no similar village has been located in the Bahamian Archipelago. Mixed in with European potsherds at the site were a Spanish coin minted between 1471 and 1474 as well as glass trade beads and two belt buckles.[5]

Columbus reported that the natives walked onto the beach with food and water to welcome his ships. Columbus wrote to the Spanish royalty to say, "Your highnesses may believe that there is no better nor gentler people in the world."[6] Then he made a chilling observation in the *Santa Maria* ship's log.[7] He wrote, "These people are very simple as regards the use of arms." In an omen of events to come, he boasted in the same sentence that "with fifty men they could all be subjugated and made to do what is required of them."[8] He soon seized six Taínos to train as interpreters and be shown to the royal court. "They should be good servants," he wrote in his journal, using the frequent euphemism of the time for slaves.

A few days later Columbus wrote, "With the force I have under me, which is not large, [I] could march over all these islands without opposition.... They have no arms, and are without warlike instincts. They all go naked, and are so timid that a thousand would not stand before three of our men. So they are good to be ordered about, to work and sow, and do what may be necessary."[9] Most Taínos did not have even bows and arrows, although island Caribs and the Taínos of Puerto Rico and northeast Hispaniola did, so most Taínos were almost defenseless.[10] Scientist Jared Diamond seems to have been right when he wrote, "Some societies seem hopelessly conservative, inward looking, and hostile to change."[11] The Taínos' pleasant island existence up to that point had not required weaponry beyond clubs and hand-propelled atlatl darts.[12] A Spaniard described Taíno wars as "little more than games with sticks, such as children play in our countries."[13]

The new arrivals from across Europe massacred and enslaved them at will.[14]

All the islands were given Spanish names. Columbus christened the island

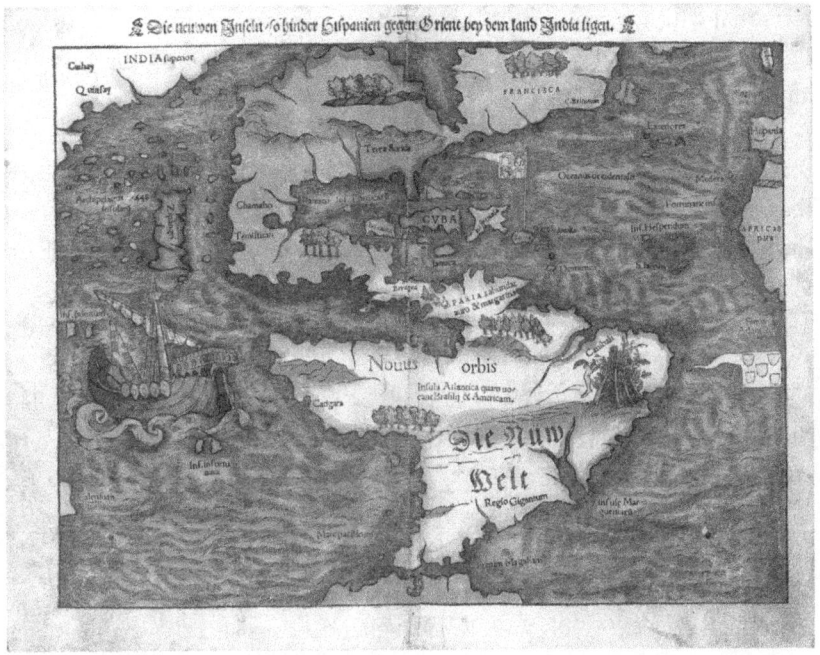

Figure 2. This map, published in 1550, fourteen years after Esteban's arrival in Mexico City, is the first to show the Americas as a connected continent not attached to any other landmass. The Great Lakes are shown descending almost to the Atlantic Ocean. Note the depiction of the Spanish flag of the time just east of Hispaniola, and the Portuguese flag at map's far right edge, because in 1493 Pope Alexander VI divided the New World between the two countries. Portugal was given Brazil, while Spain received everything else. The map's title in German refers to the discovered "new islands . . . against the Orient on the land of India." In both Latin, "Nouus Orbis," and in German, "Die Neue Welt," the Americas are identified as *The New World*. Sebastian Münster's edition of *Geographei*; map from Library of Congress.

where the city of Santo Domingo would be established as La Isla Española, meaning "The Spanish Island." The name morphed to Hispaniola, which is the term most familiar for the early history of the island, which is divided today between the Dominican Republic and Haiti.[15]

In Columbus's first voyage, the Spaniards were amazed to see that Taínos raised dogs that did not bark—*perros mudos*, mute dogs.[16] The Spaniards would find these or similar barkless dogs throughout the Caribbean islands, Mexico, and the southern United States. They decided the animals were so tasty that within a century the barkless Taíno dogs were eaten to extinction. Barkless dogs were described in the 1540s as small, long-bodied, short-legged, and plump.[17]

In his second voyage, Columbus shipped back hundreds of Taíno captives that he intended to sell into slavery in Spain. Queen Isabella made him return the Taínos to their islands, insisting he had no right to sell her subjects into slavery, so Columbus began enslaving Taínos to mine for gold and work on the islands without the queen's knowledge to make his voyages profitable.

Slavery was acceptable to that period's way of thinking because Spaniards, Portuguese, and other Europeans considered inhabitants of this so-called New World to be non-Catholic infidels—"idolaters," as Columbus called them—and as subhumans. The Catholic Church at that time approved of enslaving or executing infidels.

It would be more than forty years before Pope Paul III tried to change that attitude in 1537, declaring that Indians were humans with souls and should be treated humanely and not enslaved. In *Sublimis Deus*, the pope declared that "the Indians are truly men," and further decreed: "People who may later be discovered by Christians are by no means to be deprived of their liberty or the possession of their property, even though they be outside the faith of Jesus Christ; and that they may and should, freely and legitimately, enjoy their liberty and the possession of their property; nor should they be in any way enslaved."[18] Such a declaration of the Indians' humanity was still a decade in the future when Esteban arrived at Hispaniola. When it was issued, the pope changed few minds among Europeans in the Americas. By then it was too late anyway. Whole islands in the Caribbean were already depopulated of natives by warfare, slavery, and disease. After the pope's declaration, colonists continued to consider the inhabitants of the Americas as inferior beings in defiance of the pope.

Protector of the Indians

Friar Bartolomé de las Casas was among the priests, mostly Dominicans, who continued to preach in vain amid the gold fever, slavery, and almost risk-free wars against Caribbean Indians as well as the indifference of colonists toward providing religious instruction or caring for the Indians.[19] He was on Hispaniola when Esteban arrived, as were friars of the Hieronymite and Capuchin orders.

Another order of friars, the Franciscans, also were active during the Conquest, engaging in little more than converting any survivors of warfare to Catholicism. Put another way by one historian, "[The Franciscan] attitude seemed to be . . . that the destruction of the Indians was some sort of divine retribution for idolatry."[20]

Las Casas and other Dominicans repeatedly censured their rival order of Franciscans for a general willingness to be accomplices to the conquest's cruelties and slaughters. Las Casas campaigned for the rest of his life against conquest brutalities, making him both admired and reviled with the title of "Protector of the Indians."[21] Colonists and most non-Dominican clergy opposed him. Las Casas preached that Christians who worshiped Jesus Christ should also follow Christ's teachings, which condemned greed. "Christ did not come into the world to die for gold," Las Casas declared in vain from the pulpit against colonial greed.[22]

But even Las Casas exploited Indian labor at first on an *encomienda* he'd been granted, although he rationalized it by saying he treated his Indians better than other encomienda owners. Las Casas gave up his encomienda once he decided it was a form of slavery and that slavery was immoral and against God's wishes.[23] His lifelong quest to win freedom and kind treatment of the Indians was inspired by hearing one of the first cries for justice in the Americas in a sermon by Dominican Friar Antonio de Montesinos in 1511.[24]

The encomienda was a hallmark of the conquest and usually used agricultural labor. To understand it, one must realize that sixteenth-century "legislators, governors, judges, and colonists alike and even the clergy, shared the general notion that the Indians (all of them, everywhere) had, by some mysterious dispensation of Providence, been placed there for the particular glory and profit of the Spaniards."[25] Therefore, the Indians owed tribute to Spaniards and other Europeans. But because they did not have money, they paid their tribute in the form of labor. In return, the *encomendero* was supposed to provide for the Indians' welfare and religious instruction, although all these reciprocal conditions were so universally flouted that a historian described the early encomienda as "a thin disguise for slavery," in other words, slavery in every sense except legal definition.[26]

However, a Spanish encomienda in the 1500s was not by definition chattel slavery because the encomendero did not own the people unless they were war captives or purchased from other Indians. Instead, they worked with levies of commoners to perform forced labor. One reason Indians adapted to Spanish encomienda labor and even enslavement in the conquest was that they were accustomed to having other tribes or even their own tribe impose forced labor one way or the other.[27] So when Cortés distributed Indians to encomiendas after conquering the Aztecs, the Aztec commoners often accepted the encomienda assignment with relief. Their former Aztec masters had regularly sacrificed them to their gods if there weren't enough prisoners. Their slavery had been so dangerous, historian Lesley Byrd Simpson wrote, that "it was only necessary to threaten to return them to their native masters in order to make them serve the Spaniards very willingly."[28]

Indians enslaving other Indians is not often considered in histories about the conquest, but it reveals the age-old reality of humans treating other humans cruelly regardless of race, ethnicity, religion, or cultural background. This is described in more detail in chapter 19.

Las Casas developed great influence with Spanish King Ferdinand II and Queen Isabella I, and later King Carlos I, in his opposition to forced labor on Spanish encomiendas.[29] He charged encomienda owners with using Indian labor but rarely making any attempt to Christianize their workers. "That encomienda interfered with conversion was therefore a most serious charge," according to Christopher Schmidt-Nowara.[30] Early on, Las Casas had urged that Africans replace Indians as slaves because the Indian population had been decimated. But he later repented, declaring, "It is as unjust to enslave Negroes as it is to enslave Indians, and for the same reasons."[31]

Another priest with a dramatic change of mind was Dominican Friar Domingo de Betanzos, who'd gone to Hispaniola in 1516. In a deathbed declaration, he confessed he'd made statements that "the Indians were beasts, that they had sinned, that God has condemned them, and that they would all perish." He worried on his deathbed that his statements encouraged Spaniards to kill Indians and commit brutalities against them, so he declared, "I swear and beseech the Royal Council of the Indies . . . and all others . . . not to give credence to anything I have spoken or written against the Indians. . . . I believe that I erred. . . . It grieves me I cannot retract my statements in person."[32]

Centuries later in 1974, there was a gesture of reconciliation by Robert F. Sanchez, archbishop of the Diocese of Santa Fe in New Mexico and the first

Hispanic archbishop in the United States. He issued a formal apology to Puebloans of the American Southwest for how his Spanish ancestors and the Catholic Church had mistreated them for centuries.[33]

Two popes also have apologized on behalf of the Roman Catholic Church. In 2000 Pope John Paul II begged God's forgiveness for sins committed or condoned by Catholics over the past two thousand years, including complicity in the African and Indian slave trade, sexism, racism, persecution of Jews and Protestants, and violence in defense of the Catholic faith. In a 2015 South America trip to Bolivia, Pope Francis asked forgiveness for the "grave sins" committed by the Catholic Church against native peoples in the conquest and colonization of the Americas.[34] Pope Francis doubled down on his condemnation during a 2016 trip to Chiapas in Mexico.[35] The two popes' apologies vindicated Las Casas and his relentless campaign against such evils, although his church has never granted sainthood to the sixteenth-century friar despite efforts by his many advocates.[36]

As other denominations came into existence, many of them also condoned slavery, especially of blacks like Esteban, or participated in discrimination. The Southern Baptist convention in Atlanta issued an apology to African Americans in 1995 for its history of supporting slavery and opposing civil rights for blacks, saying, "We genuinely repent of racism of which we have been guilty."[37] Official apologies to blacks for racism also were issued in 2000 by the United Methodist Church and in 2006 by the Episcopal Church. In 2013 the Church of Jesus Christ of Latter-day Saints disavowed its past racist policies.

Esteban could not understand how Christians who practiced a more lenient form of slaveholding in Portugal and Spain could be so merciless in the way they exploited Indian and African labor in the New World. A few slaves such as Esteban were fortunate enough to escape the sunrise-to-sunset brutality of the mines and encomiendas, opening to them an opportunity to demonstrate that they were men or women of exceptional talents and strong character.

Narváez Eyes Florida

If Esteban did not know about Pánfilo de Narváez's cruelties toward Indians before he left Spain, he was bound to hear of Las Casas's opposition to the expedition's leader once he arrived in the islands because Las Casas was on Hispaniola when Esteban arrived. The friar's rage at Narváez had festered for years. Las Casas would write in *A Brief Account of the Destruction of the Indies* that conquistador Narváez allowed his men to slaughter thousands of peaceful Indians at a Cuban village called Caona in 1512–1513.[38]

Narváez had sat on his horse, watching his men killing Indians for no reason other than they felt like doing so. Among piles of bloody corpses, Narváez looked toward Las Casas, who'd tried to stop the murders. Narváez asked the priest, "How does Your Honor like what these our Spaniards have done?" Las Casas replied in a fury, "I commend you and them to the Devil."[39]

Priests opposed to mistreatment of Indians did not sway European colonists in the Americas. In one recorded instance, a priest asked for time to convert the Indians, which was one of the king's stated reasons for the conquest. The conquistador replied: "I have not come for any such reasons. I have come to take away from them their gold."[40] Cortés described the attitude of many colonists when he refused a grant of land in 1504, saying, "I came to get gold, not to till the soil like a peasant."[41]

It's unclear if Cortés was a hidalgo, as were many of the conquistador leaders. The Caribbean Islands, and later Mexico, swarmed with jobless young hidalgos disinherited under Spain's primogeniture law in which all of a deceased father's estate went to the firstborn son. Accustomed to a wealthy home, these later-born sons went to the Americas to seek their fortune either through wars against Indians or by finding a rich widow. Spoiled young nobles, they refused manual or commercial labor, which influenced other young men.[42] Colonial civic leaders as late as 1540 declared their city would be better off if such men left on expeditions because they were bachelors and "most of them were youthful and licentious *caballeros* without [anything] to do. . . . except for eating and being idle."[43]

Narváez, who was a hidalgo, was not the first conquistador to see possibilities in exploiting Florida for wealth similar to what was being wrested from Indians in the Caribbean and Mexico. He'd learned of its potential from Juan Ponce de León, who'd gone to Florida on two journeys. Like Narváez, Ponce was another conquistador seeking fame and fortune over the bodies of his own men and any Indians who got in his way. Or, as historian John Upton Terrell put it, Ponce "had won a great reputation by slaughtering helpless natives."[44] As for Narváez, Terrell wrote, "He was acclaimed as one of the most proficient butchers of natives among the many *conquistadores* who possessed outstanding talent" in killing, torture, and enslavement.[45]

Ponce earned additional notoriety by owning a vicious war dog called a boar-hound that was named Becerillo. Las Casas wrote how Spaniards "trained the boar-hounds to tear an Indian to pieces . . . these hounds made great havoc and slaughter."[46] Becerillo killed many Caribbean Indians before Carib warriors riddled the dog with arrows in 1514 as it was swimming across a river to attack them.[47]

Ponce took ship-borne expeditions to Florida in 1513, when he was surprised to be met by a Spanish-speaking Indian, and on his final trip in 1521 when he met his match.[48] Calusa warriors in canoes with powerful longbows surrounded Ponce's ships and launched a devastating attack in what is now Florida's Charlotte Harbor along the southwest coast.[49] The conquistador retreated to Cuba and died, reportedly from a thigh wound from an arrow poisoned by sap from the manchineel tree. Ponce's probable age was forty-seven.[50]

With Ponce's governorship of Florida buried with him, Narváez stepped forward to claim the potential riches of such a title for himself. He thought the Indians of Florida would be the same as the vulnerable Taínos. The Indians on the mainland, he and other Spaniards would learn, were far more formidable than island natives. One could wonder how the conquest would have gone if the Europeans had first encountered the strength of the warlike Iroquois Confederacy of New York instead of the weakly armed Taínos in the Caribbean. In his 1909 book, Francis Augustus MacNutt refers to the differences between mainland Indians and the Taínos: "The fiercer and stronger types of American Indians receded before the Anglo-Saxon invasion of their territories, leaving a trail of blood behind them, while the weaker nations of the islands . . . went down before the Spaniards with hardly more than a plaintive cry for mercy."[51]

What might have happened if Aztecs had recognized the Spaniards as invaders instead of as gods, or if the Spaniards had encountered Incas before their great civil war weakened them? What if Aztecs and later the Incas had not been decimated by diseases brought with the European presence? Would victory have been possible over the Aztecs and Incas if millions had not died from smallpox and other diseases while fighting the Spaniards?[52]

Cortés needed tens of thousands of Tlaxcalan Indian allies to defeat the

Aztecs in disease-ravaged Mexico. And it took the Spaniards with many thousands of Indian allies forty years of warfare to conquer the divided and smallpox-ridden Inca empire in Peru.

One fact is certain: conquest of Mesoamerica would not have been possible except for conquistadors recruiting large armies of Indian allies.[53] In a sense, the Spaniards did not conquer the Americas. Indians fighting alongside the Spaniards and killing other Indians made the conquest possible.

Like Hernando de Soto's disaster a decade later, Narváez made the mistake of attempting an all-European conquest of Florida Indians. Narváez's doomed expedition against Florida tribes was one of the few Spanish expeditions without Indian warriors and will be described in later chapters.

CHAPTER 4

Esteban Arrives at Hispaniola

WHEN ESTEBAN'S SHIP sailed into Santo Domingo's harbor in 1527, occupation by Spaniards and other Europeans had transformed a quiet tropical paradise into a hell for the natives and African slaves. Hispaniola was the second largest island after Cuba in the Caribbean. In front of Esteban's ship spread Santo Domingo's late-medieval style of streetscape with its teeming chaos as the Caribbean's largest shipping port.

Esteban would have looked out upon an island with few Indians left alive. The Taínos had been pushed toward extinction, resulting in the importation of African slaves starting about twenty years earlier. Many male Africans had been warriors, so adding them to the mix of Hispaniola's slaves led to violent slave revolts.[1] What is considered the first major African slave insurrection on Hispaniola erupted in December 1522, just five years before Esteban's arrival.[2]

In an early 1500s drawing of Santo Domingo, a stone wall fortifies the west and north sides, while the castle-like fortress and its tower control the entrance to the Ozama River and docks, all built with forced Indian and African labor. The east side was toward the river, and the south side faced the Caribbean. Tilled farm fields had already eradicated the original tropical forest of palms and other trees closest to the city, as had ranches and sugar plantations farther out.

What did Esteban think when he first saw Hispaniola's fields of crops and the ranches, businesses, and colonists' households, all worked by slaves? He

Figure 3. Old Santo Domingo in Esteban's time of the early 1500s. From Samuel Hazard, *Santo Domingo: Past and Present*, 1873.

saw the city's great stone church buildings, government buildings, and Spanish houses, all built with slave labor. Esteban could not realize how the work was carried out in the cruelest hard-labor conditions. He'd lived under enforced laws giving at least some protection to slaves on the Iberian Peninsula, contrasted to conditions on Hispaniola. Nothing in his experience would have prepared him for the cruelties there against Indians and Africans. Esteban would never venture into Santo Domingo without staying by his owner Dorantes's side. On any trips into the city, Esteban would have noticed young people of mixed European, Taíno, and African descent.

The docks were bustling places year-round, with sailing ships unloading cargo from other islands and from today's South America, Mexico, and from across the Atlantic. The best description of the scene comes from Terrell's *Journey into Darkness* about Santo Domingo: "Vessels of every size and description crowded the harbor: small, square-rigged caravels, light frigates, two-masted brigantines, bulky galleons, men-of-war. Merchantmen arrived with luxury cargoes of wines, silks, silver and glassware, carved furniture and fine linens, as well as an array of ordinary foodstuffs. They departed with gold and silver bullion, rare woods, fruits, parrots, spices, maize [early corn], copper, tin, iron, diamonds, emeralds, pearls, opals and turquoise, hides, cotton, cacao, peppers, and amber."[3]

And slaves, both arriving and departing. Esteban could not have avoided seeing lines of starving sub-Saharan black Africans as well as Berbers and Moors from North Africa being marched into the city crazed with despair coming off the ships. Their fate would be wretched lives as slaves, often measured in months. Indians from other islands, Mexico, and South America also were unloaded, terrorized by hardships and beatings. They would be sold to owners of encomiendas or transferred onto other ships for sale on other islands. "Indian slavery [was] a necessary introduction to the general topic of the labor supply," notes Lesley Byrd Simpson, the late historian and author of *The Encomienda in New Spain*. "Enslavement of the natives was the most ancient and obvious solution for the chronic labor shortage."[4]

Slaves were defined in the earliest years as prisoners taken in wars against the Spanish, known as *indios de guerra*, or natives purchased who were already enslaved by other Indians, known as *indios de rescate*. Very quickly, the Indians working for encomiendas became slaves in effect as well, even though they were not bought and sold like the others.

Esteban had to feel grateful to already be a personal slave from Spain claimed by Dorantes. He wouldn't need to endure Santo Domingo's merciless slave market. From the decks of the squalid ship on which he'd crossed the Atlantic, he'd have been able to see the city's streets stretching out before him in rectangular blocks, dominated by the multistory stone cathedral, which priests had forced slaves to build at the points of guns and swords in the central section.

Not far from the Cathedral Plaza stood the imposing stone buildings of the palace occupied by the governor. The slave-built stone government buildings controlled everything on all the islands at that time. Cortés controlled Mexico from the newly emerging Mexico City.

Around the grandeur of fine stone buildings, however, were the unsanitary conditions of a typical European colonial city of the 1500s. Crosses were painted on building walls to designate public latrines. Garbage pails and chamber pots were emptied onto dirt streets already mired in mud and animal excrement. Abandoned and starving half-breed children lived in the alleys and gutters with stray dogs and pigs. At the same time amid the squalor, historian Terrell describes a contrast of elegance. European gentlemen and ladies walked about, dressed in fine clothes with lace and jewels, trailed by a line of black slaves in bright clothes with flowers between their bare toes. Terrell notes that Esteban would have heard "the sweet music of players brought from Spain. And he heard the screams of the tortured in rat-infested dungeons."[5]

Spaniards did not bathe much in that time because of polluted wells, rivers, and lakes on the European continent. Queen Isabella (1451–1504) reported she bathed only twice in her life: when she was born and when she was married.[6] Europeans always considered the Taínos' custom of washing their bodies and hair as odd and even dangerous. Amid the unsanitary conditions, waves of epidemics struck down European, Taíno, and African alike. In such a crowded urban setting, Esteban would have difficulty envisioning why Christopher Columbus once marveled at the islands' natural beauty.

The Lure of Gold

The New World's natives were doomed because gold was so easy to find.

The invaders knew from the first day about Hispaniola gold because the near-naked Taínos wore gold jewelry. The first placer mining operation for gold was established in 1496. Soon Taíno males fourteen years old and over were forced into labor panning gold from the streams, where it was said 90 percent died within three months or less.[7] They were replaced with new Indian captives forced to work in conditions comparable to the worst World War II concentration camps.

A decade after Columbus's arrival, a Taíno girl working at a Hispaniola gold mining site found a disk-shaped nugget weighing thirty-five pounds.[8] In 2016, that one nugget would be worth about $640,000 for its gold alone. Its size would enhance its value several times. For example, a 6.07-pound nugget, about one-sixth the size of the Hispaniola nugget, was sold in 2014 to a collector for an estimated $400,000.[9] An equivalent 2016 value for the Hispaniola nugget would be at least $2.5 million for its gold and size. The largest gold nugget ever found weighed fifty-four pounds, discovered in

California in 1859. Loaded aboard a ship to be delivered to Spain's king, the Hispaniola nugget was lost with five hundred Europeans when a hurricane sank a treasure fleet returning to Spain in 1502.[10]

Besides the mining, Europeans used forced labor to grow and process sugarcane.[11] They also ran cattle ranches and other slave-labor enterprises based on crops and animal husbandry.

Infectious diseases, wars, slavery, exhaustive overwork, executions, starvation, and even thousands of Indian mass suicides struck down Hispaniola's Taíno population.[12] Many Taínos starved as their food supply became diminished because of the invaders' demands for food. There also was a decline in native food production, caused by Taínos being taken out of their fields and hunts and used for labor instead. Foreign animals such as pigs, sheep, goats, and cattle multiplied and overran the island, further destroying the native food supply.[13] Starvation stalked Taínos everywhere. Both free and enslaved Indians became sickly, weak, and emaciated.

Another factor in the declining Taínos population was the crashing birth rate because sexes were separated. Most men not killed outright were sent to work in gold mines in the beginning, while the women went to work in crop fields. Malnutrition was so acute that the mothers' milk dried up and countless babies died.[14] Once numbering at least in the hundreds of thousands on Hispaniola alone, a census in 1514 counted only about fourteen thousand Taínos still alive on the island, twenty-two years after Columbus arrived.[15] African slaves were being imported because so many natives had perished.[16]

By 1518, a judge on Hispaniola lamented that the island's Taíno population had plunged from his exaggerated estimate of more than a million to about eleven thousand.[17] "Judging from what has happened, there will be none of them left in three or four years," he wrote.[18]

A smallpox epidemic hit the Taínos that year.[19] The introduction of smallpox, which killed millions in the New World, is usually described as unintentional. However, conquistador Bernal Díaz reported that the disease spread rapidly after Narváez took an African slave covered with smallpox pustules from Cuba to Hispaniola and then to Mexico.[20] If so, Narváez might have deliberately introduced smallpox to Mexico in 1520. Of course, the whole Spanish nation should not be blamed for one unprincipled conquistador's action. And for perspective, someone not appearing infected with the disease would have inadvertently introduced smallpox at some point.

Las Casas estimated fewer than a thousand Taínos survived the smallpox epidemic on Hispaniola. It becomes clear why by 1527 Esteban would have seen few pureblood Taínos, if any. Most still alive retreated to the mountains and forests. The loss of Taíno life was appalling. Full-blooded Taínos apparently went extinct, although Taíno DNA can still be found in Caribbean residents.[21]

Although Las Casas became more critical of the Spanish monarchy over the years, he recognized the disinterest that King Carlos I displayed toward treatment of natives in the Americas by writing an age-old complaint: "You see how easy it is to deceive kings, how destructive to the kingdom to listen to poor advice, and how oppression rules when truth is silent."[22]

Meanwhile, despite Las Casas's efforts, the conquest continued as a means to acquire wealth with mines and encomiendas through forced labor by Indians and Africans. For at least the first few decades, arrivals to the Caribbean were greeted with encouragement that they were in a land of riches. "There is much gold," a chronicler quoted people on Hispaniola's Santo Domingo docks shouting to passengers as they arrived on ships in 1502. "And there is a war with the Indians, so there will be plenty of slaves."[23]

Gonzalo Fernández de Oviedo y Valdéz, the Spanish historian who lived in Santo Domingo for a time, admonished a group of young male hopefuls upon their arrival. "Don't say that you come to the Indies to serve the king ... since you know that the truth is just the contrary," he told them. "You come with the desire to get more wealth than your father or your neighbors."[24] Friar Las Casas wrote: "All, small and great, go there [Hispaniola] to pilfer, some more, some less, some publicly and openly, others secretly and under disguise; and with the pretext that they are serving the king, they dishonor God, and rob and destroy the King."[25]

CHAPTER 5

Early Indian Resistance

ESTEBAN AND THE others who accompanied Pánfilo de Narváez would learn the lesson in Florida, but Columbus was the first to discover, on his fourth voyage in 1502, the warlike prowess of mainland natives when he arrived along the Caribbean coast of what is now Central America. Expecting little resistance because of his ease in conquering the poorly armed Taínos, he soon learned that mainland Indians were courageous and aggressive in war.[1]

At a Panama province called Veraguas, it was the Indians who attacked first, rushing Columbus's men with their weapons amid a din of shouts, drums, and conch-shell trumpets.[2] Diego Méndez, one of the men with Columbus, described the battle years later in his will: "I stayed on shore with about twenty men ... when suddenly more than four hundred natives [probably a typical Spanish exaggeration] came down upon me.... They began to shoot their arrows and hurl their darts ... thick as hail, and some of the Indians separated themselves from the rest for the purpose of attacking us with clubs.... With our swords we cut off their arms and legs and killed them."[3] Méndez's description belies the romanticized notion about sword fighting often depicted in movies. In paintings of the period showing Europeans in battle, the battlefield is littered with the arms, legs, heads, and disemboweled torsos of Indians. Méndez said seven of his men were killed along with "nine or ten of those who advanced most boldly against us."

More Spaniards arrived in the final two small boats from Columbus's ships out at sea. Their captain, Diego Tristán, decided to take twelve men up a river. "I advised and warned him not to go," Méndez reported, but Tristán went anyway. The natives killed Tristán and all his men, "except one who escaped by swimming and from whom we heard the news." The Indians also destroyed Tristán's boats, which caused Méndez "great vexation." Columbus could not send reinforcements, and Méndez was trapped on shore.

For the next four days, Méndez reported, "the Indians came continually to assail us, every instance playing [conch shells] and kettle-drums, and uttering loud cries."[4] The dozen or so Spaniards managed to keep from being overrun with two small brass cannons and "plenty of powder and ball" for their matchlock, muzzle-loading arquebus muskets.[5] The fighting continued until the Spaniards found two Indian canoes and tied them together. Ferrying men and supplies, the surviving dozen escaped to Columbus's ships anchored in deep water off shore.

Méndez had encountered warriors from the Guaymi tribe. The Guaymi were such formidable fighters that the conquistadors avoided fighting them in later years.

The most famous Guaymi chief, who defeated Spaniards in several battles throughout the 1520s, was called Urraca, which is the Spanish word for the magpie bird. Spaniards tricked Urraca once into meeting with them for peace talks. Instead of negotiations, they bound him in chains and imprisoned him on a ship to take to Spain. Urraca managed to escape in such dramatic fashion that Esteban might have heard about it. Embarrassed by Urraca's feat, Spanish chronicles never explained how a man in iron shackles could escape from a ship. Urraca fought the Spaniards for several more years until dying of natural causes in 1531, still a free man. His successors carried on the Guaymi resistance.[6] Columbus reported that another Guaymi chieftain he called Quibian escaped custody in 1502 and, like Urraca, Quibian's sons also managed to escape from Columbus's ship.[7]

Even the Taínos managed to become formidable foes toward the end in an Indian war that's little known outside the Caribbean. While on the ship for the forty-five days it was in port, Esteban would have heard worried Spaniards talking about the success of Indians rebelling on Hispaniola. Enrique's Rebellion by then was in its eighth year. Enrique was a hereditary Taíno chieftain, which Taínos and later also Spaniards called a *cacique*. As they did in referring to Esteban as Estebanico, the Spaniards showed their

Early Indian Resistance

sense of superiority by referring to Enrique by the diminutive of his name: Enriquillo.

The Taíno leader started his revolt in 1519. He was about twenty years old and might have been in his teens. By the time Esteban arrived, runaway African slaves had joined Enrique's Taíno forces. Many of the runaways had been warriors in Africa before their enslavement and had earlier established safe havens in Hispaniola's mountains and forested interior. The runaway African slaves combined with free and formerly enslaved Taínos to make a formidable combat force.[8]

With a few hundred warriors, Enrique established a base in what is now the Dominican Republic's Bahoruco Province in the island's mountainous southwest and fought the Spaniards for fourteen years. Esteban must have felt a pride he dared not admit to his Spanish masters when he learned that escaped African slaves made up large numbers of Enrique's rebels.

The Spaniards had crushed all previous Taíno resistance. So why was Enrique's rebellion so successful? The answer is that Enrique was raised in a far different way than his ancestors. Enrique was orphaned as an infant in 1502 when Spaniards gathered his parents, relatives, and eighty regional Taíno leaders into a large wood house, its roof thatched with grass and palm leaves, under the pretense of calling a peace conference. They then set the building afire and burned the Taínos alive inside it.[9] Friars rescued the child and raised him in a Franciscan monastery. The boy's Taíno name was Guarocuya. The friars renamed him Enrique, a Spanish name that translates to "Henry" in English.

Enrique learned the Spanish mindset and gained an understanding of Spanish military tactics. In a mistake the Spaniards would not repeat with future Indians, Enrique also learned how to ride horses and how to use Spanish weapons. Most of all, he possessed the rare natural ability of military genius.

As his rebellion continued, Enrique acquired more horses and weapons. His standing order was to strip all weapons and armor from Spaniards who surrendered. He then released them, making it more likely they would surrender again in battle rather than risk death.[10] A Spaniard complained that Enrique's Taínos "know our forces and customs and further use armor and have swords and lances."[11] Taínos and Africans raced in on horseback to raid plantations—killing owners, destroying crops, and rescuing more Taíno and African slaves, who joined Enrique's uprising.[12]

Every year the Spaniards sent forces against Enrique and his mountain holdouts, but he always either evaded them or defeated them in pitched battles. Two Spanish leaders wrote in 1528, shortly after Esteban arrived on the island, "the rebels know the land, and so they mock the Spaniards."[13] With Spanish weapons and horses, and an instinct for guerrilla warfare, Enrique became invincible. The rebellion would not end until King Carlos I authorized Spain's first treaty with warring Indians in 1533–1534, granting freedom to Enrique and his rebels.[14] Enrique could not enjoy his triumph for long. About a year after the treaty, he died from a European disease. His followers also became sick and soon died.[15] Lake Enriquillo in the Dominican Republic is named in his honor, and he is a Dominican Republic national hero.

Even while Enrique's rebellion flared, Hispaniola's gold was becoming depleted, which motivated conquistadors in the 1520s to start looking for gold elsewhere. The success of Hernán Cortés in wresting vast amounts of gold from the Aztecs turned conquistador eyes to the surrounding mainland. With Cortés claiming the Mexican gold, Narváez looked toward Florida, and he began preparing for what he believed would be another profitable war against Indians. He purchased supplies and horses for a journey to unclaimed Florida, where he could enjoy full authority to commit whatever atrocity he deemed necessary for conquering. His expedition would cost Narváez his life at the age of fifty-eight. And it would set the historical stage for the African slave Esteban who went with him.

CHAPTER 6

A Disastrous Beginning

ESTEBAN IS INVISIBLE in Spanish chronicles during the first year of Pánfilo de Narváez's expedition. He would not be mentioned until a future crisis became so severe that Spaniards considered his abilities essential, and the African slave would become a key but understated figure in the continent's most amazing survival epic.

Narváez, who'd lost an eye fighting Hernán Cortés's men in Mexico a few years earlier and wore a patch over the empty socket like a pirate, led his force into the swampy wilderness of Florida. Spaniards gave the peninsula that name because of its profusion of flowers, based on the Spanish word *flores*. Because the king refused to commit men and money to expeditions in the Americas, his granting Narváez permission to launch an expedition to conquer Florida and become its governor was the conquistador's first step.

When the king agreed to appoint Narváez governor of Florida, he wasn't just thinking of the present state's peninsula. The Spanish concept of *florida* at that time extended from the River of Palms in Mexico on the west coast of the Gulf of Mexico and encompassed all of today's US southern states from Texas eastward. At his own expense, Narváez outfitted five ships and recruited about six hundred men-at-arms and sailors from Spain, Portugal, Greece, Italy, and other parts of Europe.

Esteban lived in Spain during the Holy Roman Empire's continuing wars throughout Europe in the early and mid-1500s. His relief must have been keen when his master, Andrés Dorantes de Carranza, declined to become involved. If Dorantes had gone to war, Esteban also probably would have had to go as Dorantes's personal slave. However, Narváez's temptation of gold and glory was too much for Dorantes to resist. He signed on as captain of infantry and took Esteban with him.

Because Spanish kings required conquistadors to raise their own funds and rely on volunteers, Europeans on every expedition to the New World were armed militia. For the most part, conquistador leaders and their men-in-arms had no military training. The vast majority never served in the military of any nation. The men-in-arms paid for the opportunity to go on expeditions, mortgaging what they owned to pay the amounts required and provided their own weapons and supplies. They considered expeditions as investments toward the goal of becoming rich. When not on expeditions, conquistadors were colonists.

Despite that, history books continue to refer to conquistadors in the Americas as "soldiers" who made up "armies," implying that conquistadors were trained and equipped by Spain, overlooking the fact that the New World's conquistadors were undisciplined adventurers who signed up to get rich. "Far from being interested in establishing new farms or businesses," one historian wrote of the earliest Europeans who went to the New World, "these individuals included penniless noblemen, convicts, criminals, ex-soldiers, adventurers, and assorted castoffs from society."[1] By 1500, even Columbus complained, "I vow that numbers of men have gone to the Indies who did not deserve water from God or man."[2]

Gold-seekers like Juan Ponce de León, Cortés, Narváez, and other conquistadors gambled that the up-front personal cost of an expedition would make them richer. As more African slave revolts flared and gold production fell, Hispaniola was starting to look like too much trouble with diminishing chances for fortune. Florida was not far away and seemed to offer new promise.

After winning the king's permission to invade Florida, Narváez set sail with his flotilla of five caravel ships from southern Spain in the summer of 1527. Because he didn't want to risk horses on the eight-week Atlantic voyage, he planned to purchase the animals on Hispaniola.

Esteban arrived in the New World on one of those ships after the perilous voyage over the Atlantic Ocean and the Caribbean Sea, which were already graveyards for scores of Spanish and Portuguese ships and thousands of crew members and captive Africans.

No one realized how dangerous the expedition would be.

Out of more than three hundred expeditionaries who landed in Florida the following year after two ships and many horses and men had been lost to hurricanes, Esteban was among only six who survived: the four cross-continent travelers and two others kept by Indians.[3] A survivor with Esteban in the escape from Florida was the expedition's royal treasurer, Cabeza de Vaca, who was also given the rank of provost marshal, which made him second in command to Narváez.[4] What is known of the expedition to Florida and the journey across the continent comes primarily from Cabeza de Vaca, whose *Relación* was published a few years afterward. The opinion of Esteban the slave never was recorded, if indeed anyone ever asked for it.

Cabeza de Vaca started the *Relación* at the expedition's point of embarkation, writing: "On the 27th day of the month of June 1527, the governor Pánfilo de Narváez departed from the port of San Lucar de Barrameda [in southern Spain], with authority and letters from Your Majesty to conquer and govern the provinces [of Florida]."[5]

John Upton Terrell writes about what it must have been like for Esteban and sixteenth-century Europeans crossing the Atlantic Ocean. What would seem unimaginable hardships today were endured for a chance at the New World's riches by six hundred men and ten wives, with more than 120 packed into each ship with war dogs, goats, sheep, and cattle: "The two-months' trip across the Atlantic was nothing less than a constant nightmare. . . . The stubby, clumsy caravels pitched and rolled tremendously. . . . [The sea-going vermin] throve with increasing immunity to all assaults. Bilge rats stood at bay like wild boars. . . . Cooking was done, weather permitting, in a brick galley where, sailors maintained, cockroaches achieved the size of ocean wild fowl."[6] Each passenger was given a quart of wine every day to wash down a diet of biscuits, bacon, and salted meats and fish. Terrell notes, "This diet, unsubstantial as it was, was not always maintained. Narváez's table, however, was weighted daily with such luxuries as pork roast, breast of fowl, green vegetables, suitable condiments, pastries, fine cheeses, fruits, and vintage wines."[7]

A sixteenth-century priest recalled his ordeal across the ocean: "A ship is a very narrow and stout prison from which no one can flee. . . . Closely compressed into its narrow confines, heat and suffocation are unbearable. The deck floor is usually one's bed. . . . One remains eternally seated, for there is no place to walk.... An infinite number of lice eat one alive.... And bad odors pervade everywhere, especially below deck.... The thirst one endures is unbelievable and is increased by the hardtack and salt beef constituting our fare."[8] Esteban bore the hardships with everyone else. As a slave, he experienced an even more difficult time.

Knowing what the passengers endured, it's no wonder the expedition's first setback occurred right after Narváez pulled his leaky, stinking ships into the Santo Domingo harbor. Once there, 140 men deserted.[9] They apparently had just wanted a ride to the New World. Or perhaps they'd heard stories of the fate suffered by Juan Ponce de León and many of his men when they had gone to Florida in 1521. They also might have heard about more than a thousand European expeditionaries, most of them Spaniards, who were killed in Cortés's battles with Aztecs and other Indians in Mexico. Adding to the bad news were 150 or so survivors in Santo Domingo from the 600 Spaniards who'd tried to establish a colony a few months earlier in what is now South Carolina.

Early Mainland Attempt

Esteban and the others soon learned about them. Drunk or sober, those survivors went around Santo Domingo telling tales about powerful Indian tribes that attacked them relentlessly to avenge an earlier slave-raiding expedition.

They had sailed with Lucas Vázquez de Ayllón, a sugarcane encomendero and Spanish official on Hispaniola, who'd secured the king's permission to establish a colony on the coast north of Florida. Ayllón heard about the coastal area after he'd purchased one of the Indians that a slave ship captain kidnapped along the South Carolina coast in 1521. That Indian was a remarkable man whose native name is unknown. Spaniards renamed him as Francisco de Chicora.

Francisco learned Spanish and was baptized as a Catholic. He accompanied Ayllón to Spain to testify about his people and his land to Pietro Martire d'Anghiera of the royal court. His testimony included several fanciful tales that Indians liked to tell to gullible Europeans.[10] Francisco pretended to accept his position as a Spanish slave, but he never gave up hope of returning to his own people. He encouraged Ayllón with assurances he could guide the

Spaniards once he was back in his homeland, which he called Chicora, which might have been a Spanish mispronunciation and simplification for the Cofitachequi chiefdom. Upon Hernando de Soto's arrival thirteen years later, the natives there showed him European arms and armor that the expeditionaries believed came from Ayllón's colonization attempt.[11]

Like the stories of a wonderful, imaginary land of Cíbola that Esteban would later tell to lure Friar Marcos forward into Arizona and New Mexico, Francisco tempted his Spanish owner with tales of an extraordinary land where he once lived. Finally, he convinced Ayllón to go there.[12] The Spaniard's obsession for glory, fame, and riches won out over common sense. Francisco must have barely believed his good luck as he boarded the ship. The ships with colonists, livestock, and African slaves landed first at Winyah Bay, near present-day Georgetown, South Carolina.[13] Not long after the Spaniards first went ashore, Francisco fled and rejoined his people. The Spaniards never heard from him again.[14]

Ayllón's colonists traveled over land and by ship more than a hundred miles to look for a site on which to settle. But historians are not certain in what direction, so the location of his eventual settlement, named San Miguel de Gualdape, is in dispute from Georgia to Virginia.[15] That colonization effort was the first European community established, although only briefly, in what is now the United States. At some point in late 1526, the Africans who'd been brought along rose up in the first slave rebellion in what were to become the United States, escaping into the forests.[16]

It took three months for disease, Indian attacks, and physical hardships to cost Ayllón three-fourths of his colonists. When he died of fever, the 150 survivors sailed away in 1527, towing his body in a boat behind their ships.

Ayllón's survivors returned to Hispaniola a few months before Esteban arrived. The news they brought of such strong Indian opposition on the mainland might have caused the Narváez deserters to realize Indian wars outside the Caribbean could be more dangerous than they thought. In any case, they went ashore and never returned to Narváez's ships, disappearing into Santo Domingo's businesses, taverns, and brothels. They were the lucky ones. The deserters would not die violently in the next year, unlike almost everyone who would go ashore in Florida.

Undeterred by the desertions, Narváez recruited men to replace them and also bought a sixth ship. He quickly learned it was a seller's market in Santo

Domingo, so he bought the immediate supplies he needed plus some horses. In October 1527 he ordered his ships to weigh anchor and sail west for Santiago in Cuba. He hoped to find lower prices there for armaments, horses, and other supplies he still needed for Florida. He left during the hurricane season. Everyone watched the sky, felt for the wind, and watched the height of the waves.

Spanish Chronicles

Because he wrote the primary account of the doomed expedition, Cabeza de Vaca takes over the narrative about what Esteban and the rest experienced from that point on. Events were mostly seen through his eyes, clouded as they were by his misunderstandings and biases. Cabeza de Vaca became the de facto chronicler of the expedition and the incredible cross-continental escape that followed with Esteban. However, it still would be another year before Cabeza de Vaca's *Relación* would move from considering Esteban to be a slave not worth mentioning to being a man taking on a larger role in the account and finally to seeing him as indispensable.

A major secondary source to the *Relación* is an account known as the Joint Report, which includes additional and sometimes different details provided primarily by Dorantes and to some extent by Alonso del Castillo Maldonado, who were Esteban and Cabeza de Vaca's cross-continent companions. This Joint Report was based on the three Spanish survivors' testimony to Viceroy Antonio de Mendoza in 1536. No copies of the testimony survive, but it became the foundation document for both Cabeza de Vaca's *Relación* and a six-chapter section in Gonzalo Fernández de Oviedo y Valdéz's *La historia general y natural de las Indias*. Oviedo was King Carlos's court chronicler for the Indies.

The *Historia*'s section was titled "Cabeza de Vaca, Álvar Núñez, Alonso del Castillo, and Andrés Dorantes de Carranza, Joint Report." Esteban's slavery barred him from being included in the title with the Spaniards. It's doubtful his testimony was even given upon returning to Mexico, although he and Viceroy Mendoza must have had many informal conversations. The *Historia* section is now known just as the Joint Report, and it seems to primarily reflect Dorantes's testimony.

Perhaps due to Dorantes's influence, the Joint Report mentions his slave on the first page, referring to a black man he called Estéban.[17] The Joint Report refers to the African by name one more time when he refers to "the black man who was a Christian called Estéban," affirming that Esteban had been baptized as a Catholic while in Spain.[18] Esteban is referred to as *el negro* in the rest of the Joint Report.

The Joint Report chapters referring to Esteban appear in Oviedo's *Historia*, published in 1547.[19] The account is colored by many of Oviedo's interpretations, conclusions, sermonizing, and assumptions.[20] Cabeza de Vaca's *Relación* was published first, in 1542, and he doesn't mention Esteban until about halfway through his account. If Oviedo's rendition of the Joint Report, written in the third person, can be considered a Dorantes version of what happened, the *Relación* of 1542 in the first person consists of Cabeza de Vaca's viewpoint, even when the voice turns to the third person in his 1555 second edition.

Friar Bartolomé de Las Casas denounced Oviedo's pro-colonization and pro-conquest perspectives in historical writings such as the *Historia*. Las Casas called Oviedo "one of the greatest tyrants, thieves, and destroyers of the Indies, whose *Historia* contains almost as many lies as pages."[21] Las Casas was referring to Oviedo's exaggerated tales of Spanish daring and Indian submissiveness while at the same time glossing over massacres and mistreatment of natives.

Oviedo was vulnerable to such criticism because he had written a chivalric romance novel in 1519. It's considered the New World's first novel because Oviedo said he wrote it while he was in Santo Domingo.[22] Las Casas was the first to compare Oviedo's romance novel to his later *Historia*. Oviedo's account of what happened in the Indies immortalized many events that he distorted or fabricated. Nevertheless, his glamorized versions of events are still commonly accepted as the *history* of the Caribbean.

Entrenched fables of history like Oviedo's pose a challenge in deciphering Esteban's story. Sixteenth-century Spanish chronicles were notorious for exaggerations, omissions of inconvenient facts, and lies put into the record to justify or rationalize behavior by conquistadors and colonists from throughout Europe. The invaders also often misunderstood what they were seeing, while xenophobia and jingoism influenced them so much that mistaken perspectives and conclusions were inevitable.

Despite Oviedo's faults, the Joint Report chapters in the *Historia* seem exceptional because historians believe they are based on the lost testimonies given to Mendoza and are generally parallel to what Cabeza de Vaca wrote in his *Relación*.

Pánfilo de Narváez

Although only glimpses are seen of Esteban, all of them through Spanish perceptions colored by condescension toward him as a slave, Narváez was so rich and well known that several Spaniards described him for posterity. Las Casas, who knew him personally, wrote, "This Pánfilo de Narváez was a man of authoritative personality, tall of body, somewhat blond, inclined to redness."[23] The Mexico conquistador Bernal Díaz, also a personal acquaintance, wrote: "Narváez was . . . tall of body and of rigorous limbs, and he had a long face and a blond beard."[24] In addition to his bearded, often flushed face and his height, Narváez had a loud, deep, and arrogant voice. Diaz observed that Narváez's voice boomed as if it were coming out of a cave. The historian Oviedo said Narváez was headstrong and stubborn. He compared Narváez to a donkey that must be hit a third time because it forgot the first two blows.[25]

This last attribute would be Narváez's fatal flaw. Cabeza de Vaca reported how he and anyone else who tried to give him advice were ignored if their ideas did not conform to what the conquistador had already decided.

First Hurricane

In the *Relación*'s account of what happened over the next eight years, Cabeza de Vaca steps into the spotlight from the beginning. Esteban is ignored at the start, as are the expedition's other slaves and servants.

After Narváez bought more horses and supplies at Santiago, Cuba, he decided to buy additional supplies at a small Spanish colony farther up the coast. The weather turned bad on his way, so Narváez pulled his ships into the Gulf of Guacanayabo, on Cuba's southern shores, near today's city of Manzanillo. Then, despite the weather that he was not willing to venture into, Narváez sent Cabeza de Vaca with two caravels onward to pick up his promised supplies at the port of Villa de la Satísima Trinidad, founded in 1514 to the west and halfway along the southern Cuban coast. It's not known if Dorantes, and therefore also Esteban, accompanied the two ships to Trinidad. They might have gone, or they might have stayed behind in the safer anchorage with Narváez.

Cabeza de Vaca's two ships arrived at Trinidad, where he wrote, "The next morning the weather looked ominous."[26] Spaniards had not yet adopted the Taíno word for "hurricane," but everyone on the ship feared the possibility of a *tormenta terrible*—a terrible storm. Cabeza de Vaca went ashore with thirty men. But he assures his readers that he first instructed the caravel captains to run the ships aground if the storm hit so the horses and supplies aboard might be saved. This sets the tone for the rest of his book, in which other events would have turned out okay if everyone had just followed Cabeza de Vaca's advice.

Regardless of whether Esteban went on Cabeza de Vaca's ships or stayed behind, he survived an incredible ordeal. Esteban had seen many ocean storms while he lived along Morocco's Atlantic coast, but he never saw a storm as violent as the one that hit Cuba in the fall of 1527.

Although Spaniards were well aware and had often been victimized by hurricanes, Cabeza de Vaca's book contains the first detailed account of one. He told about the frightening experience at Cuba:

> The rain and storm increased in violence at the village, as well as on the sea, and all the houses and the churches fell down, and we had to go about, seven or eight men locking arms at a time, to prevent the wind from carrying us off. And under the trees it was not less dangerous than among the houses, for as they also were blown down we were in danger of being killed beneath them. In this tempest and peril we wandered about all night. . . .
>
> On Monday morning we went down to the harbor, but did not find the vessels. . . . So we followed the shore, looking for wreckage, and not finding any turned into the forest. Walking through it we saw, a fourth of a league from water [more than half a mile], the little boat of one of the vessels on the top of trees, and ten leagues [almost twenty-seven miles] farther, on the coast, were two men of my crew and certain covers of boxes.[27] The bodies

were so disfigured by striking against the rocks as to be unrecognizable. . . . Sixty people and twenty horses perished on the ships.[28]

Dread of the wrath of a God that Spaniards believed was usually pleased with them struck a mortal fear of hurricanes into the surviving ships' crews.

Narváez was in a hurry to get to Florida, but he faced a mutiny. With the weather continuing to look threatening, the terrified crews refused to venture farther. The best Narváez could do was persuade them to move the four surviving ships a few miles west to a protected harbor, where the city of Cienfuegos is now located on the south coast of Cuba. Esteban spent the next four months aboard a ship there with the rest of the expedition. Everyone went ashore at times, with Dorantes always wanting Esteban by his side as a bodyguard.

Narváez spent a pleasant winter on his plantations at Cuba, where slave labor made him one of the richest conquistadors in the Indies. At some point, he traveled overland north to Havana. There he bought another caravel, hired a captain named Álvaro de la Cerda, and recruited forty infantrymen and twelve cavalrymen from among the colonists.[29] However, events would develop that would prevent any of these reinforcements from joining Narváez in Florida.

He also bought a shallow-draft brigantine and hired a new pilot named Diego Miruelo, who claimed to be familiar with the mainland coast all the way from Florida to the River of Palms in Mexico.[30] Miruelo claimed his knowledge happened to cover the exact extent of the governorship the king promised to Narváez. It would turn out, however, Miruelo was exaggerating his sailing experience and knowledge of the Florida and mainland coastlines. He'd heard where Narváez wanted to go and lied about his knowledge so he could be hired.

Narváez rejoined his ships at the end of February, sailing to Cienfuegos on Miruelo's brigantine while Cerda remained in anchorage with Narváez's newly acquired caravel at Havana. Crews on the ships with Esteban had regained their courage after warm, calm months and were ready to continue. The prospect of riches stiffened their backbones.

Narváez must have been overwrought with eagerness to be underway again toward Florida and the wealth and power he assumed waited for him there. His small fleet of four caravels plus Miruelo's brigantine pulled away

Figure 4. The approximate route Esteban traveled on one of Pánfilo de Narváez's ships from Santo Domingo in Hispaniola to different points in Cuba and while fighting storms until landing near today's Tampa Bay in Florida. The storm-tossed voyage to Florida is speculative. Map by Dennis Herrick.

from Cuba on February 21, 1528, with about six hundred men, ten wives, eighty horses, and some man-killing war dogs aboard.[31]

Then the disastrous Caribbean storms resumed, earlier in the season than usual. Miruelo's bad piloting hung the ships upon shoals near the Isle of Pines, now known as Isle of Youth. They remained trapped for two weeks with the ships' wooden hulls wedged atop sandbars. The next storm turned out to be their savior, because the wind drove so much water over the shoals that the ships were lifted and able to sail off.

After rounding the western tip of Cuba, the *Relación* reports, "another tempest came up in which we nearly perished." Hugging the Cuban coast, they ran into a third storm that battered them for three days near Havana. Wind drove them out to sea in late March 1528, forcing them to leave behind Cerda's ship and reinforcements at Havana.

Narváez's caravels and one brigantine meandered northward alone, battling even more storms. A short sailing between Havana and Florida ended up being a storm-tossed and confusing weeks-long voyage across today's Gulf of Mexico.

History is silent on why Cerda did not leave for Florida until Miruelo returned to Cuba, docking his brigantine in Havana after failing to find the entrance to Tampa Bay. When Miruelo returned to Narváez's disembarkation site, Cerda sailed his caravel along with him. They reached Florida in early to mid-1528, linking up with at least two of Narváez's ships.[32] With the reinforcements and supplies that Cerda and probably also Miruelo carried to Florida, the Spaniards searched for a year for Narváez and his men.[33]

They never found them, and they returned to Cuba after exhausting their supplies.

CHAPTER 7

Invasion of Florida

IT'S NOT CERTAIN where Pánfilo de Narváez intended to land. A major unclear portion of the story is that some historians think Narváez intended to go to the River of Palms in Mexico, but storms drove him instead to the Florida peninsula on the opposite side of the Gulf of Mexico.[1] If Narváez had intended to go to the Florida peninsula, a caravel could have traveled the three hundred or so miles almost due north to Tampa Bay in about four days.[2] The River of Palms in Mexico was about a thousand miles west of Havana. After storms pushed them around the Gulf of Mexico for weeks, they didn't know where they were and their original goal became irrelevant.

Regardless of their initial goal, Narváez's crew was glad to see any land when they spotted the northern Florida coastline on April 12, 1528, as reported in both the *Relación* and the Joint Report. The ships then sailed south along Florida's western coast for two days until dropping anchor near a spit of land near present-day Tampa Bay on the peninsula now known as Pinellas County. The ships arrived on April 14, 1528, at what is now called the Jungle Prada site in St. Petersburg, Florida.

Though he was an early arrival, Esteban was not the first African in Florida.[3] Juan Garrido, known as "The Black Conquistador," had accompanied Juan Ponce de León on his expeditions there in 1513 and 1521. A free African, Garrido arrived on Hispaniola in 1502 or 1503 and became the most famous of Spain's many, but little-mentioned, armed African auxiliaries in the conquest. He fought Indians on Cuba and Puerto Rico. He then went with

Figure 5. Map shows the ships' storm-tossed route (conjectural), their landing point, the projected route that Esteban and the rest of the expedition traveled up through Florida, the retreat to Aute, and the launching of the boats into Apalachee Bay—which the survivors called the Bay of Horses—for their long and perilous voyage across the Gulf of Mexico. Map by Dennis Herrick.

Hernán Cortés to help conquer the Aztecs.[4] If Garrido ever disembarked the ships in Florida, it would have been for brief visits.[5] As a result, Esteban ended up spending the most time by far of any African on the mainland in the 1520s or earlier—except for the dispersal of Lucas Vázquez de Ayllón's escaped slaves. Esteban was not the sole African accompanying Narváez to Florida. It's known that at least two Spaniards each took four black slaves with them, and with so many noblemen on the expedition there were also numerous unrecorded Africans as well as Caribbean Indian slaves.

After landing in Florida, Narváez remembered how Florida Indians fatally wounded Ponce de León seven years earlier, so he proceeded cautiously. As soon as the ships anchored, he sent ashore the king's controller, Alonso Enriquez, and some sailors. They must have felt like sacrificial lambs to Narváez's caution, rowing a small boat to the beach. From there they walked to a village that could be seen a little way inland. Staying behind on the ships in the harbor were all four of the eventual cross-continent companions: Esteban, Álvar Núñez Cabeza de Vaca, Andrés Dorantes de Carranza, and Alonso del Castillo Maldonado.

The natives, whose tribe would become known as the Tocobaga, weren't too surprised to see Spanish ships bobbing in the water. They'd seen ships before and had come to think of the Europeans as looters and slave hunters. The wonder is that they didn't flee immediately, but they came out of their wood and thatch houses to greet Enriquez's group. Enriquez tried to convey the usual first impression to newly encountered Indians. Through hand signals and perhaps drawings in the sand, he told them the Spaniards wanted to be their friends. The Tocobagas didn't believe a word of it, but they gave him some fish and meat anyway. Enriquez and the sailors went back to the ships, congratulating themselves on having fooled the Indians into thinking there would be peace. After dark, however, all the village's Tocobagas fled in their canoes.

Because Enriquez and the sailors hadn't been attacked and the village was now abandoned, Narváez went ashore the next day, April 15, and took a contingent of men armed with arquebus muskets, lances, crossbows, and swords. It's likely Esteban also went ashore because Dorantes would have accompanied Narváez as the expedition's infantry captain. The Spaniards searched the abandoned village. Cabeza de Vaca reported that one house was so big it could accommodate three hundred people. He might have exaggerated to convince his readers how Spaniards were so courageous and powerful that a vast number of Indians would flee at first sight of them.

Excitement came when an expeditionary plucked out of a fishing net a small gold item, referred to in different translations as a rattle, bell, or jingle.[6] Even that small object was all the encouragement Narváez and his men needed to rejoice. Gold could be found in Florida! There was much celebration on the ships that night. The songs, music, and excited chatter on the ships floated across the water to the land, sweeping over the swamps and filtering through moss-draped trees.

Narváez returned ashore the next day with Esteban, Dorantes, and as many armed men as he could cram into the ships' small boats. Before Narváez could begin any military action in Florida, certain duties had to be performed by his force. Spaniards valued the rigid protocols of legalism and documentation. Such obsessiveness has benefited researchers, who have rooms and shelves of records and chronicles to study centuries later. Historian John Upton Terrell wrote that the records are riddled with political deceit, ecclesiastical humbugs, self-serving machinations, Eurocentric rationalizations, and fables.[7] But at least the information exists to evaluate.

Esteban stood on that jungle-lined beach in exotic Florida to watch the commissions of his master and other officers presented, accepted, and signed. There were documents and Narváez's royal credentials to be read, witnessed, and notarized. Expeditionaries needed to swear to pledges, affirming Narváez as Florida's new governor and consenting to be bound by royal authority to obey him. Everything would be gathered and sent to the Spanish bureaucracy's eternity of the ages inside depositories, libraries, and warehouses. Cabeza de Vaca gave the order of business on that momentous day of April 16, 1528, writing as if he were addressing the king: "[Narváez] hoisted flags in behalf of Your Majesty and took possession of the country in Your Royal Name, exhibited his credentials, and was acknowledged as governor according to Your Majesty's commands. We likewise presented our titles to him. . . . He then ordered the remainder of the men to disembark, also the forty-two horses left [almost half had perished at sea]. . . . and these few [horses] were so thin and weak [having been aboard ship almost eight weeks], that they could be of little use for the time."[8] Many men had also died. After assigning minimal crews to operate the ships, Narváez was reduced to about three hundred men-at-arms on land.

Esteban would have seen flags raised and the Franciscan and Capuchin friars erect a cross that was taller than the men. Thus, Florida was claimed for Spain and also for Christianity—or more precisely, for Catholicism. That was an important religious distinction, because religious hatreds had resulted in people's deaths for centuries, and after 1480 the Inquisition had imprisoned, tortured, and executed non-Catholics as well as those Catholics suspected of not adhering to the church's teachings. The Inquisition's zealous extremism intensified when Martin Luther launched the Protestant Reformation with his Ninety-Five Theses in 1517.

Even after Esteban saw the flags and cross raised and all of Florida and its people claimed for Spain, one more duty remained for Narváez. Esteban watched as Narváez read *El Requerimiento*, which is best translated into English as "The Ultimatum."[9] Spain mandated all conquistadors to read the theological and political manifesto to Indians and their villages before any hostilities could be commenced. It was an absurd bit of bureaucratese written years before that postulated a worldview of Christianity and European history incomprehensible to Indians. Nevertheless, any resistance was a legal pretext to attack. The document was filled with threats of what would happen if natives did not agree to everything, regardless of whether they understood it. Las Casas once wrote he didn't know whether to laugh or to weep about the requerimiento's wording.[10] Its absurdity was heightened by the fact that conquistadors read the document in Spanish and often far away from any village. And that's what Narváez proceeded to do. There were no Indians around to hear Narváez, so he read the requerimiento to the trees, swamps, beach, and sky.

In the chauvinistic thinking of sixteenth-century Spain, that fulfilled the letter of the law. No matter how or where, the act of reading the document gave the Indians fair warning that Spaniards felt a legal right to rule natives and do whatever they wanted with them. The requerimiento declared that Indians must accept that their land now belonged to the Spanish monarchy, agree to be ruled by the king of Spain who was also the Holy Roman Emperor, obey the pope in Rome as their spiritual leader, and convert to Catholicism. Refusal to accept the requerimiento would result in warfare, death, and enslavement.

The requerimiento ended with a threat. Narváez must have relished reading its directive to the wilderness:

> But, if you do not do this, and maliciously make delay in it, I certify to you that, with the help of God, we shall powerfully enter into your country, and shall make war against you in all ways and manners that we can, and shall subject you to the yoke and obedience of the Church and of their Highnesses; we shall take you and your wives and your children, and shall make slaves of them, and as such shall sell and dispose of them as their Highnesses may command; and we shall take away your goods, and shall do you all the mischief and damage that we can, as to

vassals who do not obey, and refuse to receive their lord, and resist and contradict him; and we protest that the deaths and losses which shall accrue from this are your fault, and not that of their Highnesses, or ours, nor of these gentlemen who come with us."[11]

No Indians heard the requerimiento that day. But the next day a group of Tocobagas came to the village the Spaniards had taken over. They didn't realize Narváez had already claimed all their land by fiat and declared them to be subjects of Spanish sovereigns and the pope. Cabeza de Vaca seemed surprised by the Indian mood when he wrote, "They made many gestures and threats, and it seemed as if they beckoned us to leave the country."[12]

During his conquest of Cuba, Narváez would have slain Indians with swords or burned them alive for what he considered insolence if any questioned his authority. But for some reason he didn't do that with the Tocobagas. Perhaps he even considered the directives from King Carlos I to avoid unnecessary war or unjustifiable force and to treat natives well. With annoyed gestures and grimaces, the Tocobagas left.

Narváez didn't know what tribe his visitors were from, because the Tocobaga name would not be identified in Spanish chronicles for thirty-nine more years. A tribal name didn't matter, because to Narváez all Indians were pagan savages. In a few days he would prove that Christians were now in charge with his order to slice off the nose of a Tocobaga chief named Hirrihigua. For added terror, the murderous Narváez forced Hirrihigua to watch vicious Spanish war dogs kill the chief's mother and tear her body to pieces as they fed on her corpse.[13]

Esteban surely was present and must have been stunned to see such conquistador brutality. All nations' armies had used war dogs in Europe for many centuries, but Esteban had never served in the military, so he never would have witnessed such violence. Narváez would soon learn that, unlike the Caribbean's docile and mostly helpless Taino natives, Florida's Indians were well-armed and formidable warriors.[14] Over the next three and a half centuries, Europeans and later Americans would discover to their horror that natives of what is now the United States were as brave as and could be as vicious and cruel as any enemy.

CHAPTER 8

The Quest for Gold

THE TWO WEEKS after landing were spent letting most of the men and horses recuperate from the ordeal of the ship's journey. Thirty-eight horses had died on the ship and been dropped overboard, leaving the forty-two that reached Florida.

Narváez took possession of the gold item found in the fishing net. It wasn't much, but the promise of it heralding many more thrilled the conquistador. He no doubt often examined the object in his hands, rubbing it with his fingers in his excitement until it shined with a luster that captured his reflection. He either dismissed the idea or it didn't occur to him that such a solitary artifact might have been lost from a Spanish ship and snagged by an Indian net.

The Tocobaga tribe faded from the area, which reinforced Narváez's conviction that his force could handle any Indians if they tried to resist him. He only knew the ease with which conquistadors subdued natives of the Caribbean islands. His biggest problems so far were heat and humidity.

Friar Juan Suárez conducted a Mass for the expeditionaries after landing on April 17. In his homily, Suárez prayed for God to help them conquer Florida.[1] Esteban and several other slaves were present, while other expeditionaries included Cabeza de Vaca as treasurer and provost marshal as well as Alonso de Solís, the inspector. Both were to protect the king's financial interest if they were to find gold or other riches. The monarch was due the "king's fifth," the *quinto real* in Spanish, a tax of 20 percent of all riches realized.

Friar Suárez went along as the expedition's religious leader and also as the expedition's commissary.

After Mass, a day after claiming Florida for Spain, Narváez organized a force to explore this new land where he planned to be governor. Most men were too weary from the voyage, but Narváez selected the sixty hardiest men-at-arms for an exploration on foot. Six more men hoisted their lances and saddled a half dozen of the least debilitated horses. The animals were in such bad shape that Cabeza de Vaca thought they would be of little use. Esteban, his presence still ignored in Spanish chronicles, must have been included on this first reconnaissance. Because Dorantes was captain of the infantry, he would have gone along with his personal slave at his side.

On this first foray was Friar Suárez's constant companion, an Aztec prince named Tetlahuehuetzquititzin. Despairing of pronouncing such a name, the Spaniards just called him Don Pedro. A traitor to his people, he'd fought on the side of Cortés in the conquest of the Aztecs, then known as the Mexica (meh-SHEE-kah).

The force of about seventy or more men, including slaves and servants, slogged through the Florida swamps and forest, moving through a sopping, vegetation-choked, watery jungle inches above sea level. Garlands of Spanish moss hung from tree branches. All around them were birdsongs, the buzz of insects, and splashes and movements of unseen animals. They stepped past snakes larger than any they'd seen before. They eyed black-scaled alligators that slave hunters had warned them about. The jungle must have seemed primordial.

Esteban and the Spaniards would have been awed by the tangled, flooded wilderness that filled their view. Europeans knew of tropical forests in the Caribbean, but nothing that resembled Florida's everglade wilderness. Expeditionaries would find the jungles impenetrable in places, forcing them to slosh through swamps filled with snakes and alligators. And they would soon discover the most dangerous predators of all: Indian warriors as relentless and skilled in war as the conquistadors.

That evening they reached what the *Relación* described as "a very large bay, which seemed to sweep far inland."[2] Because of the water's salty taste, they knew it was a bay from the sea that would become known as the Gulf of Mexico. They camped that night and the next day on the shore of what would become known as Old Tampa Bay.

Figure 6. Esteban and other expeditionaries entered a swampy wilderness in Florida. 1872 print from John Bakeless, *America as Seen by Its First Explorers.*

Upon returning to the original encampment, Narváez felt disoriented because he wasn't sure how far he was up the coast of Florida. The pilot Diego Miruelo said he knew of a large bay that would protect the ships from hurricanes. He'd seen it, he said, on previous trips along the coast. He was thinking of today's Tampa Bay, but he didn't realize they were on an inlet about fifteen miles north of the bay's entrance.

Perhaps the heat, humidity, mosquitoes, and confusion of not knowing where they were addled their brains. In hindsight, it would seem Narváez should have thought, *We saw a huge body of water when we walked north. Maybe it's coming up from the south.* Instead, he agreed with Miruelo that the entrance to that bay must be even farther north and they'd sailed past it without noticing it. Miruelo's mistakes and Narváez's trust in him would combine to become the expedition's fatal error.

Narváez ordered Miruelo to sail the brigantine north and find the bay. If unsuccessful, they agreed, Miruelo's brigantine was to return to Cuba and pick up more supplies and return with Álvaro de la Cerda's caravel with its supplies and reinforcements of men on foot as well as cavalrymen and more horses. Narváez needed the supplies and reinforcements. Taking so long fighting the storms around Cuba and even on the way to Florida had left the expedition short of food. And at some point he'd lost another caravel when it sank or wrecked as the fleet sailed south along the coast. The loss of the ship is mentioned with just one nine-word phrase in Cabeza de Vaca's account, when he reported "one having been lost previously on the wild coast."[3] Were more horses and men lost in that incident? Narváez purchased used ships, so perhaps the caravel was leaking so badly from saltwater woodworms that Narváez abandoned it and transferred everything to the other ships, which would explain Cabeza de Vaca and Dorantes's lack of concern about its loss.

The brigantine departed, leaving the expedition's three surviving caravels anchored offshore. The expeditionaries would never see Miruelo or the brigantine again.

Inexhaustible, unlike many of his men, Narváez ordered another exploration inland. He reinforced the ones who'd gone earlier, and everyone proceeded about ten miles beyond the earlier encampment on the bay's western shore. Dorantes kept Esteban close by, not knowing what they might encounter in the Florida jungle. Some might have wondered about the formed mounds seen along the way. The mounds were Tocobaga ceremonial and communal places built as much as five hundred years earlier.

They found and seized four Tocobagas, probably after tempting them to come close with beads and other trade items. Showing the prisoners some kernels of maize, they asked through a language of signs if the natives knew where more could be found. "They told us that they would take us to a place where there was maize and they led us to their village, at the end of the bay nearby, and there they showed us some that was not yet [ripe]," Cabeza de Vaca reported in his *Relación*. That Tocobaga village is believed to have been in what is today's Philippe Park in Safety Harbor, on the west shore of Old Tampa Bay.

The Indian maize of the 1500s had small blue, yellow, white, black, and red kernels in slender ears and was eaten after drying and grinding. Maize had small ears compared to modern yellow corn.[4] Maize was a principal food for Indians all through the Americas in the sixteenth century and a predecessor of today's corn. Although Europeans often mentioned Indian maize, it would be forty years later that a Frenchman would write a description of what maize looked like, at least as grown in the Florida climate. He wrote that maize was planted twice a year in large fields, grew up to seven feet tall with foot-long ears, and took about three months from planting to harvest.[5]

In the unnamed village of unripe maize the expeditionaries were surprised to find several merchandise crates from Europe. "In every one of them was a corpse covered with painted deer hides," according to the *Relación*. "[Friar Suárez] thought this to be some idolatrous practice, so he burnt the boxes with the corpses. We also found pieces of linen and cloth, and feather head dresses that seemed to be from New Spain [Mexico]."[6] Historians are convinced the bodies were of drowned Europeans who'd washed ashore from shipwrecks. If Suárez had understood that, he would have had the bodies buried instead of burned.

Most importantly, the *Relación* reported Narváez and his men found "samples of gold." That gold probably also washed ashore from Spanish wrecks along the coast, like the gold rattle found in the fishing net, but Narváez's grasping nature assumed the gold originated with the Indians. Using impromptu sign language, Narváez questioned the village's Tocobagas where he could find more gold like the samples.

The burning boxes and commotion caused by the Spaniards must have brought the village's chief, Hirrihigua, down from the mound that he dwelled on. The Spaniards' frantic questioning about gold focused on the chief. Gold items had been found in the village. Where could more be found? Where is the gold? Narváez became ever more aggressive in questioning Hirrihigua. The chief must have continued to show disdain toward the conquistador and refused to cooperate. Cabeza de Vaca chose not to describe what happened next. He was more concerned with describing the Spaniards' tribulations than reporting the common barbarities that Europeans committed in those days.

A chronicler of the Hernando de Soto expedition, which journeyed through the same area eleven years later, revealed what Tocobagas later told Soto and his men. Garcilaso de la Vega, who was half Spanish and half Inca, wrote in his history about Narváez ordering Hirrihigua's nose cut off and his mother killed by war dogs. Garcilaso's information came from interviewing some Soto survivors and reading reports they'd written afterward.

Bloodied but still defiant, Hirrihigua employed a tactic that Indians often used to rid themselves of European invaders. He said that gold would be theirs if they left and went to the territory of a different tribe—which, although this tactic was unspoken, was always a powerful enemy tribe. In the words of Cabeza de Vaca, the Tocobagas "gave us to understand that, very far from there, was a province called Apalachen in which there was much gold."[7] Seeing Narváez's one remaining eye light up with excitement, Hirrihigua continued to add to the wonders the Spaniards could expect if they would leave his territory and go find the Apalachee tribe. "They also signified to us that in that province we would find everything we held in esteem," Cabeza de Vaca wrote. "They said that in Apalachen there was plenty."

So far, the Tocobagas gave Narváez no more concern than the Taínos had after they'd been ravaged by slavery and disease starting in the 1490s. He knew nothing about Apalachee Indians, other than Hirrihigua's claim that they possessed gold. The conquistador objective for decades was to find Indians with gold and take it from them. Narváez's vision of golden riches in Florida seemed within reach.

Narváez led the expeditionaries farther until they found a village with some maize ready for harvest. They stayed there for two days. Then they returned to the ships with exciting news that there was plenty of gold to the north with a tribe called the Apalachee.[8]

Left behind with his mutilated face and memory of his mother's cruel death, Hirrihigua vowed vengeance. It would take him a year.[9]

Fateful Decision

Narváez made up his mind about what he would do even before he got back to the ships. The day after his return, on May 1, 1528, he called together his four royal officials to announce his decision. A notary was included to record his decision, a necessary requirement in the legalistic Spanish system. Cabeza de Vaca as treasurer, Alonso Enriquez as comptroller, Friar Suárez as commissary, and Solís as inspector listened with mounting apprehension as Narváez announced his plan. He intended to plunge with all of his men and horses into the interior while the sailors would take the ships and search for a good harbor.

Historians have debated ever since why Narváez would do such a foolish thing, separating his men from ships that were the best hope for supplies and escape if necessary. He might have been influenced by the success of his hated nemesis, Cortés. Sent to arrest Cortés in Mexico, Narváez was defeated in battle, lost an eye, and spent two years humiliated as Cortés's prisoner. He learned how Cortés scuttled his ships upon arrival in Mexico, leaving his men no choice but to fight armies of Mexican Indians on his way to eventually capture tons of gold and a kingdom. Was Narváez thinking of the same strategy in his otherwise inexplicable decision to send his ships away? Once the ships were gone, Narváez's men would be forced to follow him to his gold and his governorship.

Cabeza de Vaca claimed he was the most vocal in arguing against Narváez's plan. He might have been, because he was second-in-command. His *Relación* is told from his point of view, so it can't be certain if he or someone else was the main opposition leader. Regardless, Cabeza de Vaca took on the wise counselor's role in his account. "I replied that it seemed to me in no manner advisable to forsake the ships until they were in a safe port, held and occupied by us," he wrote. "I told him to consider that the pilots were at a loss, disagreeing among themselves, undecided as to what course to pursue."[10] But that wasn't all. Although it now sounds like 20/20 hindsight, Cabeza de Vaca reported he told Narváez, "Neither did we know what to expect from the land we were entering, having no knowledge of what it was, what it might contain, and by what kind of people it was inhabited, nor in what part of it we were."

The royal officials weakened their case by disagreeing among themselves. Cabeza de Vaca thought everyone should get back on the ships and look for a harbor that would protect the ships from hurricanes. Friar Suárez, however, thought they should walk along the coastline while keeping the ships in sight until a harbor was found. To have everyone get back on the ships, the friar said, was to tempt God because of storms that had already killed so many men and horses and destroyed ships. Jeronimo de Albaniz, the notary, had another proposal.[11] Let the ships find a harbor, he said, and stay there until the expedition could join them and then move inland.

Narváez rejected all their ideas. He'd send the ships off, he said, and they would lose no time by leaving immediately to find Apalachen's gold. They could link up with the ships later. How, he didn't say, but Narváez was a man of supreme confidence in his ability to accomplish anything. He'd become rich by being aggressive, confident, insistent, and ruthless.

Narváez thought his royal advisers were too timid as they looked around at the green wall of Florida's trees and swamps in every direction. He even accused Cabeza de Vaca of cowardice and said he should leave on the ships, but Cabeza de Vaca refused. Narváez had put up with frightened expeditionaries before, sitting out an entire winter in Cuba because of their fear of storms. Now it seemed all of his royal officers were afraid to do what he considered necessary to find Florida's riches. Dropping all pretense of asking for advice, Narváez issued his decision. His mind was made up. The Indies had turned into a gold rush, and he was determined to get his share in Florida. He'd lead them into Florida to the riches he felt certain were ahead for the taking.

One of the ten wives on the ships predicted that Narváez and his men would never survive and urged the others to find new husbands. Narváez chastised the woman, declaring, "He and all who went with him expected to fight and conquer many and very strange people and countries so that, while many would need to die in the conquest, he was sure from the accounts he had of the richness of the country that the survivors would be fortunate and become very wealthy."[12]

Narváez told the expeditionaries to ready themselves and issued two pounds of ship biscuit and half a pound of bacon to each man. He ordered the expedition inland as the ships sailed away. Cabeza de Vaca remembered the fateful day, writing afterward: "Thus we set out upon our journey inland. The number of people we took along was three hundred, among them . . . Father Juan [S]uarez, another friar called Father Juan de Palos and three [diocesan] priests, the officers, and forty horsemen."[13] Cabeza de Vaca's total of three hundred men on the march is a suspiciously round figure. His writing is ambiguous and translations differ.[14] Bandelier's translation of the *Relación* assumes the forty horsemen should be counted among the three hundred. But the original Spanish states, "trescientos hombres y quarenta hombres de á caballo" (three hundred men and forty men of horse), which implies the horsemen should be counted separately.[15]

Regardless of whether the cavalry is counted among the three hundred, it's certain that many more than three hundred ventured forth because an unknown number of servants and slaves, including Esteban, also were taken along, none of whom were counted. One estimate is that up to four hundred stepped into the Florida wilderness.[16]

Most wealthy members of Spanish expeditions considered it unthinkable to travel without their slaves and servants, but such aides are never included in rosters. For example, Francisco Vázquez de Coronado took seven of his slaves on his expedition of 1540, including three women. None are listed in the official roster. Records show that on the Narváez expedition several expeditionaries took their slaves besides Dorantes, but none are mentioned by name except, eventually, Esteban.[17]

Esteban and the rest of the expeditionaries set out and walked into the Florida wilderness for fifteen days. They crossed a land full of game, but the wildlife fled at the noisy advance of hundreds of men and horses tromping through the wilderness amid shouting orders, clanging weapons, talking, and grumbling.

They were not hunters, and soon they were starving. The sharp edges of tall grasses cut their exposed flesh, and brush and tree branches snagged the men's clothes. Their armor of metal, thick leather, and quilted cotton tunics stiffened by soaking in brine made the heat and humidity terrible. They clambered over trunks of trees fallen in storms, many of them shattered by lightning. They waded through swamps that rotted their shoes. Florida has several species of mosquitoes, which, along with other biting insects, tormented them day and night.

Although it's speculation, Spain and Africa were rife with malaria, so it's possible some men arrived with malaria dormant in their bodies. If it became active again, mosquitoes that bit them could infect others, in effect introducing malaria to Florida.[18] Men began suffering unidentified fevers and chills, malnutrition, dysentery, other illnesses, and injuries. "We were not used to such exposures, we felt greatly exhausted, and were much weakened by hunger," Cabeza de Vaca lamented. "In all this time we did not meet a soul, nor did we see a house or village."[19]

But they were being watched. Tocobaga warriors behind trees must have laughed at the sight of the struggling, bearded strangers as conditions worsened every day. After crossing a river on rafts, horsemen were able to run down and capture five or six Indians. Narváez persuaded the captives—most likely with torture or threats—to guide them to a village with fields of maize. The village's inhabitants fled, and the maize saved the ravenous expeditionaries. They rested there for several days. All except Narváez recognized their desperate situation.

Cabeza de Vaca obtained permission to take forty men north to look for Miruelo's purported bay. He'd learned from Indians that the Gulf of Mexico was not far away. The biggest problem, however, was that Tampa Bay was to their south, not north. When Cabeza de Vaca gave up and returned, Narváez sent a captain named Valenzuela on a second exploration with forty men on foot and six on horse. The second patrol experienced no better luck. Valenzuela traveled more than eleven miles to a river and shallow swamps near today's Yankeetown, Florida. Because of the number of infantry, it can be assumed that Dorantes and therefore Esteban went on both explorations.

Meeting the Timucuans

On May 21, 1528, Narváez started the expedition farther north, this time driving his men on for twenty-eight days. The total distance from Hirrihigua's village to Apalachen was about two hundred miles. Confusion and detours forced by natural barriers caused them to walk much farther, and after twenty-eight days they still had not reached Apalachen. They followed a route probably west of today's Florida State Highway 55 and US Highway

129, both of which are west of Interstate 75. The denseness of Florida wilderness can still be seen along these highways. They fared as best as they could by scavenging maize and other food found in villages.

The expeditionaries suffered all the misery short of death they could endure. Historian Terrell wrote a vivid description of their suffering: "Both the heat and the insects were unmerciful. There was no relief, no escape night or day, from either. The earth steamed ... and a man felt as if he were rotting before he had died. The necks and shoulders of the horses were sheaths of blood. ... The faces of the men were swollen ... by the bites of mosquitoes, which came in such swarms that a man could not avoid breathing them."[20] They persevered. Whatever else is said about conquistadors, no one could doubt their courage, determination, and fortitude. Tales of Apalachee gold motivated Narváez's expeditionaries to put up with any misery and keep trudging onward.

Indians were not encountered until June 17, when a Timucua chief named Dulchanchellin approached them with raucous fanfare.[21] The *Relación* reported that the chief was carried into the Spanish camp on the back of another Indian. He wore a painted deerskin and was preceded by several young male pipers playing a cacophony shrill and alien to the Europeans. The music came from tubes with a hole at each end.[22] More than thirty years later, the French artist Jacques le Moyne de Morgues described a similar approach by another Timucua chief. "Twenty pipers," he wrote, "who produced a wild noise, without musical harmony or regularity, but only blowing away with all their might, each trying to be the loudest."[23] Like all the rest, Esteban had to be astonished by the Timucua chief's approach. Even conquistadors with years of experience in the Americas had never seen Indians put on such a spectacle.

The Timucuans, like the Apalachees later, were several inches taller than the Europeans. Cabeza de Vaca described them as giants. The Indians of today's Florida, Georgia, and Alabama were elaborately tattooed. A later observer described the tattoos: "Commonly the sun, moon, and [stars] occupy the breast; zones or belts or beautiful fanciful scrolls wind around the trunk of the body; thighs, arms, and legs, dividing the body into many fields or tablets, which are ornamented or filled up with innumerable figures, as representations of animals or battle with their enemy, or some creature of the chase, and a thousand other fancies."[24] Le Moyne said the Timucuans grew long hair that was wrapped into a bun on top of their heads, secured with "a lace" and festooned with feathers and other items. The Apalachee encountered later would appear much the same.

The expeditionaries were near the border dividing the territories of the Apalachee and Timucua tribes. Dulchanchellin was rewarded for his friendliness with beads, copper bells, and other European trade trinkets. Somehow he managed to convey that the Apalachee were his enemy. He said his Timucua warriors would guide the Spaniards in an invasion of Apalachen.

That night they encountered a major physical obstacle, which the *Relación* described as "a broad and deep river, the current of which was very strong."[25] It undoubtedly was the Suwannee River. Terrell pinpoints the site as being a few miles south of Branford, Florida, downstream from where the Suwannee is gorged from its confluence with the Santa Fe River. The expeditionaries had taken about three weeks to travel what would have been sixty miles in a straight line, which reveals the difficulty of their passage.

Fearful of the river's power, the expeditionaries used a canoe on which to pull a raft and spent all day ferrying everyone and the horses and equipment across. One cavalryman, Juan Velázquez, grew impatient with what he considered an overly cautious crossing. Fired with Spanish machismo, he spurred his horse into the river to show his companions how a real man crossed a river. But the strong current swept him out of his saddle. Weighed down by clothes, weapons, and armor, Velázquez hung onto his horse's reins, and they both drowned. Dulchanchellin's Indians recovered the horse's body and said the rash conquistador's body had washed farther downstream. The *Relación* reported, "His death caused us much grief."

The dead horse provided many expeditionaries with their first meal of meat in many days, although Esteban and other slaves probably never tasted a morsel. Without the benefit of hunting, food remained so high a priority that Narváez put aside his quest for gold to go to Dulchanchellin's village with its stored food.

At some point the new alliance between Narváez and Dulchanchellin came apart over some disagreement, perhaps because some expeditionaries abused tribal members, most likely women. Hostility occurred the first night. A warrior shot an arrow, narrowly missing a Spaniard who'd gone to a river for water. Timucua and Apalachee warriors were skilled archers with their powerful longbows, so the man who shot the arrow might have intended a warning shot. In any case, the arrow was an effective announcement that Dulchanchellin had changed his mind and no longer welcomed the expeditionaries. That same night, all of Dulchanchellin's people disappeared into the jungle, leaving the expeditionaries to fend for themselves.

Onward to Apalachen

Dulchanchellin had indicated that Apalachen was off to the northwest. So Narváez led his men in that direction. It wasn't long before aggressive-acting warriors materialized in front of the expedition. At least one historian believes they were Timucua warriors from Dulchanchellin's village.[26] When the Spaniards called out to them and prepared to fight, the warriors withdrew into the dense jungle. Arquebus shots were probably fired.

The Indians reappeared at the rear and began following the expeditionaries. Men grew nervous as they looked over their shoulders, spotting armed warriors behind them. Narváez left some horsemen behind in ambush, the horses gagged with grass stuffed around the bridle bits in their mouths to keep them from whinnying. As the pursuing Timucua warriors entered an open area, the lancers charged out of the brush and trees. Trained to aim their lances at the heads and necks, they killed several Timucuans. The harassment stopped.

The horsemen managed to capture "three or four Indians, whom we kept as guides thereafter."[27] Torture and beatings persuaded the captives to guide the expedition toward an Apalachee town. These new guides were guarded closely. A decade later Soto is known to have carried chains and neck irons to control captured Indians, and it's likely Narváez did as well.[28] Narváez thought he'd coerced them to guide him to Apalachen, but he hadn't counted on shackled Indians continuing to defy him as best as they could. Instead of the guides taking him directly to Apalachen, the *Relación* reported, "These led us into a country difficult to traverse and strange to look at, for it had very great forests, the trees being wonderfully tall and so many of them fallen that they obstructed our way so that we had to make long detours and with great trouble. Of the trees standing many were rent from top to bottom by thunderbolts."[29]

The Apalachee Village

Instead of a couple of days, it took a week before they reached sight of an Apalachee village on June 25, 1528. It was located in a prairie on the edge of a large, shallow body of water known today as Lake Miccosukee, which often separates into large pools during dry summers. The village consisted of forty "small and low" Indian houses in an area surrounded by "dense timber, tall trees, and numerous water pools" and built in an area somewhat sheltered from Florida's severe storms.[30]

Narváez thought he'd arrived in the heart of Apalachee territory. However, the Timucuans had conspired to lead him instead to a small village. The countryside around Apalachen was a bit hilly, although elevation is a relative term in Florida, where much of the state is at sea level or only a bit higher. The area was covered with immense trees, and there were lakes, ponds, and marshes larger and more numerous than any the expeditionaries had seen.

It had taken the expedition fifty-six days to travel a distance of 220 straight-line miles since leaving the ships, an average of less than four miles a day and an indication of how much farther they traveled because of detours and difficult terrain. They made crawling progress compared to the speed that conquistadors usually covered distances.

The *Relación* reported the men "gave many thanks to God" for having delivered them to Apalachen. They forgot their terrible hardships, Cabeza de Vaca wrote, because "we had been assured so much food and gold" could be found there. Instead, they found a war more dangerous than anything Spaniards had ever experienced in the New World.

CHAPTER 9

Arrows Penetrating "Good Armor"

NARVÁEZ STARTED THE hostilities. Someone read the *requerimiento* on the village's edge, too far away to be heard and in Castilian Spanish. Then Cabeza de Vaca led nine horsemen and fifty men on foot to storm the town. Dorantes as captain of infantry and his slave Esteban must have been members of this attack. Castillo was the only one of the four eventual cross-continent companions who might have stayed behind with the main force. No men were in the village, but the conquistadors rounded up several women and children and forced them to start grinding maize for food while the main force of hundreds of expeditionaries also entered the town.

As historian Paul Schneider observes, "Reports from other expeditions of the period suggest it was not a fortunate thing to be a young woman in a village where a Spanish army encamped."[1] The *Relación* only described the women's hard labor, but rape was always a threat and might have occurred, as it often had in occupied villages of the Americas. Unknown to the expeditionaries, at least one villager escaped to alert the village's tattooed warriors elsewhere, probably on a hunt. "Soon, while we were walking about, [warriors] came and began to fight, shooting arrows at us," Cabeza de Vaca wrote.[2] An arrow killed Solís's horse. That must have shocked the expeditionaries, who were used to Caribbean bows so weak that usually they could only wound a horse. It was an omen of intense warfare to come.

After fighting off the attack with crossbows and frightening blasts of arquebus muskets, the expeditionaries began looting the village of deer hides and stored food. It's not known if Esteban had a weapon during this attack. If he didn't, Dorantes probably turned him into an armed bodyguard soon afterward. Two hours after the battle, the town's few warriors returned, but this time to beg the expeditionaries to give them back their women and children. Did they worry about their women and children with these strangers, as well they should, or was their request a ruse to take civilians out of harm's way for future attacks? Regardless of the reason, the women and children were released, perhaps because Narváez didn't want more mouths to feed.

Narváez demanded the Indians give over their leader as a hostage, and an old, crippled man stepped forward so shackles could be put on him. Narváez thought keeping an Indian leader as a hostage would avert any future attacks, copying Cortés's example of taking Moctezuma captive in Mexico.[3] But Narváez didn't yet understand the warlike nature of Florida Indians. He also thought his volunteer Apalachee hostage was a major leader, but the man was from a small village, and he might not have even been a chief.

The villagers left with their women and children. Then they went for reinforcements from other towns. Many more Apalachees from at least one other town attacked the very next day. "They did it so swiftly and with so much audacity as to set fire to the lodges we occupied [with fire arrows]," Cabeza de Vaca wrote.[4] Spanish casualties went unmentioned as usual, but he admitted the Spaniards were able to kill only one Apalachee.[5] Another attack was launched the next day, with one more warrior slain. Cabeza de Vaca rarely reported expedition casualties, although some had to have been killed or at least wounded in both attacks.

The Apalachees demonstrated a form of warfare unfamiliar to Europeans—the stealthy approach, the swift attack, the strategic withdrawal. The Apalachees decided against any more frontal attacks against the town because of the expedition's arquebuses, crossbows, and horses. They would find ambushes and guerrilla warfare much more effective. The resistance of Florida Indians was still evident a decade later in the way a Timucua chieftain named Acuera replied to a Soto request for a meeting to discuss peace. A Spaniard quoted him as responding: "[He] already had much information from other Castilians [Narváez's expedition] who had come to that country years before . . . robbing, pillaging, and murdering those who had not offended them in any way. He by no means desired friendship or peace with such people, but rather mortal and perpetual warfare . . . [and]

Figure 7. Print by Jacque Le Moyne, engraved by Theodorus de Bry, showing Florida warriors attacking a village with flaming arrows as occurred during the Narváez expedition. From Jacques Le Moyne de Morgues's *Brevis narratio eorum quae in Florida Americai provincia Gallis acciderunt*, 1591.

he promised to wage war . . . by waylaying and ambushes, taking them off guard."[6]

Narváez stayed in the village for more than three weeks.[7] All during that time, the Apalachees maintained constant war, killing and wounding expeditionaries and horses when they ventured outside the village. The Apalachees had the village under a siege. The expeditionaries had been impressed at first by the amount of wild game around the village. They'd spotted three kinds of deer, rabbits, bears, Florida panthers, geese, ducks, egrets, herons, partridges, and many other animals and birds. Their starving days could have been over, but they didn't dare hunt very far from the village. Three horse-mounted scouting expeditions ventured out, discovering land less populated and poorer than the village they were in. They were less than twenty miles northeast of the largest Apalachee town, Anhaica, at present-day Tallahassee, Florida, but the patrols never found it.

As the days went by, the village's food reserves and the wild game, all so plentiful when they arrived, diminished. When Apalachees killed the expedition's Aztec prince Don Pedro, Narváez decided it was time to leave. They'd found no gold. Several expeditionaries had been killed and wounded by then, and many more were sick. They were forced to admit that the Tocobaga and Timucua Indians had sent them on a chimerical quest leading to Florida's most aggressive tribe. No gold, and worst of all not enough food to feed hundreds of hungry Europeans.

Now the shackled Apalachee leader told Narváez that just a few days walk to the south near today's Gulf of Mexico was an Apalachee village called Aute.[8] The so-called chief and hostage assured Narváez that the Indians at Aute had maize, squashes, beans, and fish. It was again that trick Indians often used, telling Spaniards that what they sought could be found someplace else. But this time, the captive knew Apalachee warriors would be attacking the bearded strangers all the way to Aute. And he knew Aute's people would be warned.

The crafty old Apalachee man's promise of food at Aute now replaced the alluring rumors of gold. The Spaniards' hope was to leave Apalachen, the source of so many dashed dreams and hopes. Retreat to Aute.[9] Aute was about thirty miles southwest, near present-day St. Marks, Florida.[10] But that was thirty miles through a water-soaked Florida jungle where it was impossible to walk in a straight line. The expeditionaries walked many more miles than that through a gauntlet of relentless hit-and-run Apalachee attacks that cost more men and horses.

Narváez was depressed with disappointment. He now realized he would be lucky if he and his men escaped alive. He was on a fruitless quest for gold that didn't exist in Florida, and as historian Terrell notes, "He was governor of a worthless kingdom, a miserable land in which even an effort to survive taxed a man almost to an unendurable limit."[11]

After slaughtering Indians at will on the Caribbean islands, Narváez never could have imagined the ferocity and fighting ability of Florida natives with their powerful bows. Cabeza de Vaca was moved to grudging admiration for Apalachee warriors: "Those people are wonderfully built, very gaunt and of great strength and agility. Their bows are as thick as an arm, from eleven to twelve spans long [seven to eight feet or more], shooting an arrow at 200 paces with unerring aim."[12] In the Soto expedition a few years later, the strongest Spaniards could not draw the deerskin bowstring to their face, but the Indians could draw it to behind an ear with ease.[13] Spanish accounts then and later reported that Apalachee bows were so powerful they could send an arrow through a horse and embed arrows six inches into a tree.

In killing expeditionaries or wounding them, the Apalachees' cane arrows even pierced the "good armor" of the time.[14] When Cabeza de Vaca referred to armor, he wasn't talking about steel plate armor. Not even an arquebus ball or crossbow bolt could penetrate that. He was referring to the armor used successfully against Caribbean Indians, consisting of chain mail, cotton-padded quilt tunics like the Aztecs wore, and jackets covered in thin metal plates or made of several layers of stiff elk leather. Only the richest expeditionary members, the officers, wore the steel breastplates thought of as armor today.

No inventory exists of the arms and armor taken in the Narváez expedition. In a similar Spanish expedition twelve years later, however, an inventory recorded two percent of the expeditionaries wore European-style armor. Just a half dozen or so of them owned anything approaching a full suit of armor, and others were limited to chain mail or a stray piece of armor such as a helmet. The overwhelming majority wore quilted tunics or leather armor, chain mail, and cloth hats.[15]

When shooting at men wearing chain mail, the Apalachees removed their arrowheads so their powerful bows would split the arrow shaft upon impact and drive long splinters through the body. Thus, the chain mail so valued against the weak bows in the Caribbean proved dangerous and ineffective against Apalachee arrows. Likewise, the power of Apalachee bows could drive arrows through the cotton quilt tunics and leather armor that used to provide adequate protection to Spaniards.

Narváez's men found themselves at another disadvantage. In the time it took them to fire a matchlock arquebus or a crossbow and then reload, an Indian could launch several arrows at them. Matchlock arquebuses were so heavy that a barrel needed to be propped on a forked pole. Being smoothbore muskets, they were inaccurate at much distance, and it took half a minute or more to reload the muzzleloaders for another shot. Crossbows were more accurate for fighting at a distance, but that was offset by them taking so much time and effort to reload.

There also remained the tangled, flooded Florida landscape to frustrate the expeditionaries.

Retreat

Esteban and the Spaniards headed south toward Aute. On the second day, while expeditionaries were wading in a jungle swamp with water up to their chests and encumbered by standing and fallen trees in every direction, the Apalachees struck. Cabeza de Vaca described a nightmarish ambush:

> Once in the middle [of the swamp], a number of Indians assailed us from behind trees that concealed them from our sight, while others were on fallen trees, and they began to shower arrows upon us, so that many men and horses were wounded, and before we could get out of the lagoon our guide [the old man who had told them to go that way] was captured by them. After we had got out, they pressed us very hard, intending to cut us off, and it was useless to turn upon them, for they would hide in the lake and from there wound both men and horses.[16]

A hailstorm of arrows ripped through the ranks. Men and horses bloodied the swamp water, the men screaming in pain and terror.

If they'd managed to keep their powder dry, arquebusiers would have been able to fire one shot. But it would have been awkward at best to reload in chest-deep water. Similarly, crossbow men also would have been able to shoot only once. To reload a crossbow, a man held the weapon on solid ground with a foot and levered or cranked the bowstring back to firing position. Submerged and in a battle, this would have been difficult.

The horses were useless in the watery tangle of fallen trees, so Narváez ordered the lancers to dismount and join the infantry in a counterattack. More were killed or wounded as they struggled forward, but the expeditionaries managed to advance well enough that the Apalachees melted away into the surrounding jungle. It was as if the Indians had never been there—except for the dead, dying, and wounded Europeans and horses left in the aftermath.

Esteban would have slogged through the swamp's trees and plants with the rest, staying close to Dorantes. Under such dangerous conditions, it's likely Esteban was allowed weapons at least by this time. As a large, strong, twenty-something man, Esteban would have been an ideal bodyguard for Dorantes. One never knows when an armed slave might be needed during such harrowing times. Esteban would have carried a sword. If he had carried an arquebus or crossbow as well, he would have saved his first shot in case he needed it to protect Dorantes.

The Europeans braced themselves for another attack more than two miles farther, at another body of water they described as a debris-choked lake. Like the first one, this was a large, shallow swamp surrounded by jungle. The expeditionaries concluded the reason they weren't attacked was because the Apalachees used up their arrows in the first ambush.

With a fresh supply of arrows the next day, however, the Apalachees attacked again at another swamp. "They pursued us still," Cabeza de Vaca recalled. "We attacked them twice, killing two, while they wounded me and two or three other Christians."[17] Being wounded by the powerfully driven arrows was often tantamount to death. But Cabeza de Vaca survived what must have been a minor wound, although he implied it was serious. He never revealed in his writing how many wounded men from these battles died afterward.

The warriors were moving targets, running between trees and ducking behind cover. It was difficult for an arquebusier to hit them because of the split second between pulling the trigger and making the gun fire. The expeditionaries had never seen Indians with such agility, strength, courage, and fighting ability. A Spaniard with Soto eleven years later praised the Apalachees as "the bravest of men . . . they repeatedly killed many Christians . . . they were never willing to make peace. . . . If their hands and noses were cut off they made no more account of it. . . . Not one of them, [even facing] death, denied that he belonged to the Apalachee."[18]

A description of Apalachee Indian warfare about thirty years later by Pedro Menéndez de Avilés gave another insight into their formidability as fighters. Menéndez described the tactics that Narváez's men also must have dealt with:

> Small groups lay in ambush to shower arrows on any stray Spaniard looking for palmetto shoots or shellfish. . . . They could dart in and out among the Spanish force without endangering themselves; for in truth, these Florida natives were more swift and lithe than any Spaniard. They are so sure of not being caught that they venture very close to the Christians before discharging their arrows. These arrows are loosed

with such force that they pierce any clothing as well as coats of mail. So quick are the Indians in releasing the arrows that they can wait for a harquebus to be discharged at them ... and then release four or five arrows in the interval during which the soldier reloads his piece. As soon as the Spaniard pours in the powder to prime his piece, the Indian hides among the grass and woods, for the terrain is very luxuriant and covered with forests and underbrush. By the time the powder is ignited in the harquebus the native has crouched and is crawling through the grass and undergrowth. When the soldier has fired, the Indian rises at a place different from the spot aimed at, as if he had been swimming underwater. So adept and clever at this maneuver are they, that one can only be astonished.

They fight by skirmishing, and jump over the brush like deer. Any Christian would be worn out pursuing them.... When the Spaniards retreat, the Indians return in pursuit and, emerging from amidst the thickets, again loose their arrows upon the Christians. They lose no opportunity for making use of this maneuver, so that to wage war upon them is a bad risk.[19]

For five days, the Apalachees stayed invisible, but the Spaniards knew that fierce, naked giants were stalking them. The retreat continued with the surviving horses carrying those too sick or wounded to walk. So many horses had been killed, and so many men were sick and wounded, that the horses' effectiveness for carrying lancers into battle was compromised, if not eliminated, while on the move. Many men were lashed to the saddles to keep them from collapsing off the animals. Esteban and other slaves and servants also carried sick and wounded men on litters, while other ill expeditionaries staggered forward on foot, dazed and suffering. Sickness raged through the ranks with feverish diseases, many spread by mosquitoes and an environment unhealthy to Europeans. Tick-caused diseases, infections, injuries, and physical debilitation also took a toll.[20]

A little more than two miles from the expedition's destination of Aute, the Apalachees struck from the rear. A nobleman named Avellaneda, wearing his helmet as well as full back and breastplate armor, charged forward to rescue his servant boy. He was shot off his horse by an Apalachee arrow through his neck. His companions carried him dead the rest of the way to Aute.

Aute and the Coast

They found food but no shelter at Aute because Apalachees had burned all the lodges to the ground. They were trapped, not daring to go elsewhere. They sprawled in the open, exposed to wind and rain, tormented by mosquitoes, enduring hot and chilly weather alike, and always sapped by the humidity. They knew they were close to the Gulf of Mexico but did not know how close. Cabeza de Vaca's dates are confused, but it was probably late July or early August 1528 when they reached Aute.

The original plan had been to use the ships for supplies and reinforcements. But now everyone faced the consequences of Narváez's decision to abandon the ships to seek his gold, leaving expeditionaries stranded without hope for easy escape. More than a hundred men were so sick or wounded that they were, in Cabeza de Vaca's words, "out of condition to be of any use whatever." Because Africans acquired immunity to many fever diseases, Esteban might have avoided sickness throughout the expedition, although his health was never mentioned. Expedition officers recognized their hopeless situation and needed to figure out how to save the men who were left.

After two days of increasing desperation, Cabeza de Vaca reported that Narváez entreated him to try to find the coast. The proud Narváez must have been very sick or demoralized to be reduced to begging Cabeza de Vaca for help. The next day, Cabeza de Vaca led a reconnaissance in force along a river near Aute that flowed to the south. With him went seven horsemen and fifty men on foot. Esteban accompanied them, although he still is not mentioned. The *Relación* did report that Dorantes went along, however, and he would have taken Esteban with him. The scouting party struggled through the overgrown landscape, listening and watching for Apalachee ambushes the entire way. At sunset, they found an inlet of the Gulf of Mexico that was about three miles from Aute. They rested and feasted on oysters. Twenty men were sent out the next day to explore farther. It's probable Esteban and Dorantes also went again. This patrol returned before finding the coast, but Cabeza de Vaca thought they'd come close enough to the gulf that the entire expedition should go there together. Upon their return to Aute, they learned that while they'd been gone the Apalachees attacked the encampment, putting the men "at great stress, owing to their enfeebled condition." The Indians also killed another horse. Again, there's no mention whether expeditionaries were killed or wounded.

Everyone set out the next day to reach the coast. There were so few horses left that two or more sick expeditionaries rode on each horse while the sick Narváez rode his own horse. Many men were barely able to function. With death as the single prospect for failure, the ragged expedition managed to make it to near the gulf's waves on the Florida coast. "One-third of our people were dangerously ill, getting worse hourly, and we felt sure of meeting the same fate," Cabeza de Vaca recalled.[21] At one point he made an odd statement about summertime Florida being very cold, indicating he might have been suffering some of the same chills that were taking down so many men.

Cabeza de Vaca reports he learned at this time that the remaining cavalrymen were conspiring to take horses and desert as a group so they could try their luck on their own.[22] Most, perhaps all, were talked into staying to ensure safety in numbers and to share whatever fate awaited the rest. Cabeza de Vaca took credit for convincing the horsemen to stay, but he would have needed a lot of help from other officers. There was no chance for a man on foot to escape, and everyone knew they were doomed if the cavalry abandoned them because Indians feared horses more than men. Cabeza de Vaca said the cavalrymen agreed to stay as a point of honor. If any did leave in secret, they couldn't have gotten very far before Apalachees killed them. That mutinous near-desertion proved how Narváez, sick at heart and of body, had lost control of the expedition. His officers were in charge now.

Ambushes remained a constant danger. Men remained forever vigilant, but sometimes that was not enough. Apalachees attacked a group of men sent out to collect fish and oysters from the inlet and coves. Unable to go to their aid in time, those in camp saw ten men killed before their eyes. "We found them shot through and through with arrows," Cabeza de Vaca wrote. "Although several wore good armor, it was not sufficient to protect them, since, as I said before, [the Apalachees] shot their arrows with such force and precision."

Stranded on the beach, with men sick and dying, Apalachee warriors lurking in the jungle around them, and the ships gone forever, the ailing Narváez called a meeting. The officers decided their one chance for survival was to build boats and launch them into the Gulf of Mexico. But how? "It seemed impossible, as none of us knew how to construct ships," Cabeza de Vaca wrote. "We had no tools, no iron, no smithery, no oakum, no pitch, no tackling. . . . Above all, there was [not enough food] to eat."[23]

CHAPTER 10

Fleeing in Rickety Boats

SO ENDED NARVÁEZ's plan to conquer Florida. It conquered him instead.

Spaniards would attempt to colonize Florida many times over the next three decades in efforts costing the lives of hundreds of men. The first attempted Spanish settlement in Florida was in today's Pensacola in 1559–1561, fewer than two hundred miles west of Narváez's first Apalachee town.[1] A hurricane ruined that effort. Archaeologists discovered the site by accident 450 years later.

It would not be until 1565 when Captain Pedro Menéndez de Avilés founded St. Augustine, the first successful Spanish settlement in Florida. Two years later he established a small fort on the Pinellas County peninsula near where Narváez landed. Tocobaga Indians, with long memories of Narváez and Soto outrages, destroyed the fort, killing all Europeans in it. Almost two centuries would pass before Europeans returned to Tampa Bay.

The king's contract granting Narváez governorship of Florida and the entire Gulf Coast across to Mexico and beyond had ordered him to establish two towns with a hundred persons each.[2] However, Narváez had long ago given up any hope of colonizing. He just wanted to survive. Narváez was as sick as so many others when they reached Aute, suffering with fever and chills. He seems to have turned over more and more of his daily decisions to his officers.

The officers decided on August 4 to begin building five boats, a task that would take them almost seven weeks. The expedition's two biggest heroes of that time stepped up, their presence proving the expedition's international makeup. The first man, Alonso Fernandez of Portugal, let it be known that he was a trained carpenter. A crude anvil was fashioned atop a tree stump, and Fernandez cobbled together wooden flues and a bellows made of deerskin to melt metal items such as chain mail and stirrups into new uses. Later a Greek, Doroteo Teodoro, discovered that a workable pitch for sealing boat seams could be made from the resin of certain pine trees.[3] Construction of boats could begin.

The hardest labor would have been assigned to Esteban and other slaves still alive, by then reduced in number to at least two other Africans and one Cuban Indian.[4] They and all other able-bodied men set to work with tasks needed to build five boats. Work groups were appointed by the cadre of officers with or without input from an ill Narváez. The most able men and their horses were sent four times to raid Aute's fields. Despite opposition from Apalachee defenders, the horses proved such an advantage that they were able to bring back beans, squashes, and maize. Others were sent on the dangerous job of looking for seafood in the coves.

Fewer than twenty of their forty-two horses were left. At some point, expeditionaries started butchering a horse every third day to feed men working on the boats and the sick. In Spain, horses were so valued that to eat one was considered "a sin against the Holy Ghost."[5] Cabeza de Vaca, always taking the superior moral stand in his account, wrote that he refused to eat horsemeat. The other starving survivors put aside their scruples and feasted.

At the forge, expeditionaries melted all the metal they felt they could spare to make nails, saws, chisels, and axes. They gathered piles of palmettos, using the fiber and husks for oakum combined with the Greek's pitch for sealing their boats' wood. They made ropes and tackles out of the horses' manes and tails. They sewed clothing of the living that could be spared and all the clothing of the dead together to make sails. Tree limbs were split and formed to make oars, the floor, and the sides. Skins from legs of slain horses were put to use as water containers.[6]

By September 20, almost two months after arriving at the coast, they had eaten all the horses except one. That one was saved for a celebratory feast before pushing off. A little more than a decade later, members of Hernando de Soto's expedition would find horse skulls scattered across that beach.[7]

They had completed five wood boats, each one about thirty-three feet long. Cabeza de Vaca never reveals a width, but because he refers to them as boats rather than rafts, they were rectangular with their sides built up and with a mast, oars, and a tiller. The boats were flat-bottomed or with a shallow draught, so they resembled a smaller, crude version of Miruelo's brigantine. In the time it took to construct the boats, about forty men had died in their makeshift shipyard on the beach. It's unclear, but the deaths might or might not have included those who'd been killed outright by Indians or had died of their wounds later as well as those who had died of diseases.

The expeditionaries decided they'd walked more than seven hundred miles since separating from the ships. That was a major miscalculation. A straight-line distance of their route was more like about 250 miles, although they must have traveled many miles farther by meandering around obstacles and looking for food. They had no idea how far it would be if they floated along the Florida coast by boat to their starting point. The second major mistake was believing Miruelo. The clueless ship's pilot often boasted of sailing the northern coast of the Gulf of Mexico from Florida to the River of Palms in Mexico. That river was supposed to mark the western border for Narváez's phantom governorship. Miruelo left the impression with officers that the River of Palms in Mexico was about twenty-six to forty miles along the coast of Florida, and that some distance farther would be a river opening to a Spanish-controlled settlement. Cortés had founded that town on Río Pánuco in 1522 and named it Santisteban del Puerto.[8] It now is called Pánuco, as it often was then.

It's possible no one knew about a chart made nine years earlier by Alonso Álvarez de Pineda showing that the River of Palms and Spanish settlement of Pánuco were hundreds of miles away from the Florida peninsula. If they'd known, they would have fled back the way they came in hopes of their ships returning for them near Tampa Bay. Cortés also had drawn a rough map of coastal America in 1522, but Narváez might not have known about that map either.

There was no navigator with them. They were confused, lost, disoriented, and frightened. Many of their fellow expeditionaries were dead, and many more were so sick as to be near death. Everyone knew that Apalachee warriors were all around them with their powerful bows, stalking and killing them. All of that stress combined for poor judgment.

If they'd followed the coastline east and then south, they would have ended up at their original landing site after sailing a bit more than two hundred miles. Perhaps the ships would have returned there, expecting them to show up. However, they feared the ships would not find them, stranding them in what they now considered murderous Florida. On the other hand, if they went west they'd be heading toward Mexico, and they thought Mexico would be a sure haven. They wanted to travel as far away as possible from Florida's warlike tribes. The egregious errors in estimating the distances sealed their fate.

Because Miruelo had told them the distance to Pánuco was close to the west, which they might have misunderstood, they decided to go that way across the Gulf of Mexico. They could not have known that by going in boats west to the mouth of Río Pánuco, now the site of Tampico, Mexico, they would need to float about 1,300 miles hugging the coast as much as possible. As it turned out, they never made it that far.

Traveling west in five makeshift, frail boats was the worst decision. Yet, that's what the expeditionaries did, not realizing the extent of their ignorance of Gulf Coast geography. Cabeza de Vaca never identified the leading opinion-maker on that decision. But with Narváez sick, it probably was Cabeza de Vaca as second-in-command. Knowing how badly that decision turned out, it's no wonder he avoided admitting in the *Relación* to being among those who made the decision.

As sick as he was, Narváez still used his authority to assign himself to the first boat with the strongest and healthiest expeditionaries. There were about fifty men in each boat. The second boat contained the purser, Alonso Enríquez, and the commissary, Friar Juan Suárez. Esteban, his owner Andrés Dorantes, and Alonso del Castillo Maldonado, departed in the third boat. Thus, three of the four expeditionaries who would survive the cross-continent trip were in the same boat. Captains Téllez and Peñalosa commanded the fourth boat. Cabeza de Vaca brought up the rear in the fifth boat. With him was the inspector, Alonso de Solís. Like Esteban traveling with his owner, any remaining slaves and servants were distributed among the other boats with their masters.

Cabeza de Vaca reported that scores of men were sick. The totals he gave for men who climbed into the boats varied, depending on whether officers were included in his count, between 242 and 251. With the deaths known or implied by this point, it becomes clear that many more than 300 expeditionaries had started into Florida's interior five months earlier. Servants and slaves were not counted, although they faced the same or worse risks as the men-at-arms. By the time the expedition reached Aute, it was obvious that many men had perished unnamed by then and at least twenty-two horses had vanished along the way. Of the survivors who fled in the boats, only about half of them would live long enough to reach beaches in Texas, starving and weak.

Into the Gulf

The expeditionaries climbed aboard their boats and pushed the flimsy watercraft into the inlets leading to the Gulf of Mexico, using sails and oars to begin their escape by water on September 22, 1528. They were so crowded that the men could not stir once they found a place to sit.[9] Their weight brought the water level to within six inches of the top of the sides. Only desperate men would have ever thought they'd have a chance across the unpredictable and stormy Gulf of Mexico, even if sticking to shallow waters along the coast.

Behind them they left the area where so many men had died, and where they'd killed their horses in an attempt to save themselves. As they looked back, they named it Bahía de Caballos, the Bay of Horses. Today it is Apalachee Bay.

Sometimes with sails, sometimes with oars, the motley fleet bobbed and floated along shallow waters of the coast in boats that resembled elongated tubs. At the first island where they thought they would be safe from Apalachees, they worked on the boats to build the sides higher. Then they resumed their voyage.

Blistered by the sun, starving, desperate for every sip of fresh water, the men rolled dead companions over the boats' sides as they went along. For a miserable month and a half they would make their way across the gulf with their crude sails and oars, keeping the boats together, taking turns leading the way.[10] Sometimes the wind would fill their ragged sails and push them along. Other times they used oars to move forward day and night.

They kept the coastline in sight, but whenever they saw spires of smoke from Indian villages they dared not go within arrow range. Five men died from drinking the gulf's saltwater, and three others were killed in an Indian attack in which several were wounded. Many died of their illnesses in the boats. In another incident, the Greek Doroteo Teodoro and his African slave went ashore in a canoe with Indians who said they would provide fresh water. Teodoro and his slave never returned.¹¹

Soto's expeditionaries learned years later that the Narváez group had entered Mobile Bay, Alabama. "Here we got news of the manner in which the boats of Narvaez had arrived in want of water," a Soto chronicler reported, "and of a Christian, named don Teodoro, who had stopped among these Indians with a Negro, and we were shown a dagger that he had worn."¹² It's believed Choctaw Indians killed them at a town called Piachi on the lower course of the Alabama River.¹³

Teodoro's African slave is one of the fleeting glimpses Cabeza de Vaca gives of just five of the expedition's numerous slaves and servants. Esteban is the only one he ended up naming. Cabeza de Vaca referred to Teodoro's slave in this incident several months before he ever identified Esteban. Earlier he'd mentioned Avellaneda's servant boy, and later he would refer to a Cuban Indian slave, who would perish on the Mexico coast, and after that another African slave who was found alive from one of the other boats but then disappeared from the record. The expedition's other slaves and servants died without mention.

Incredibly, none of the storms the expeditionaries encountered sank their boats. They managed to keep together until they reached the mouth of the Mississippi River, hundreds of miles from the Bay of Horses. The river was then known as Río del Espíritu Santo. The river's strong current emptying into the gulf pushed all of the boats farther into the gulf, scattering them out of sight of one another. And out of sight of land. Three of the boats managed to regroup temporarily before being separated again, but Esteban's boat was fated to travel the rest of the way across the gulf alone. Esteban and the other strongest men took turns steering the craft with the tiller while others lay inside the boat, "so near dying that few remained conscious."¹⁴

Landfall

On November 5, 1528, the leaking, battered boat with Esteban, Dorantes, and Castillo was cast ashore by large waves onto what is believed to be today's Velasco Peninsula, near Galveston, Texas.

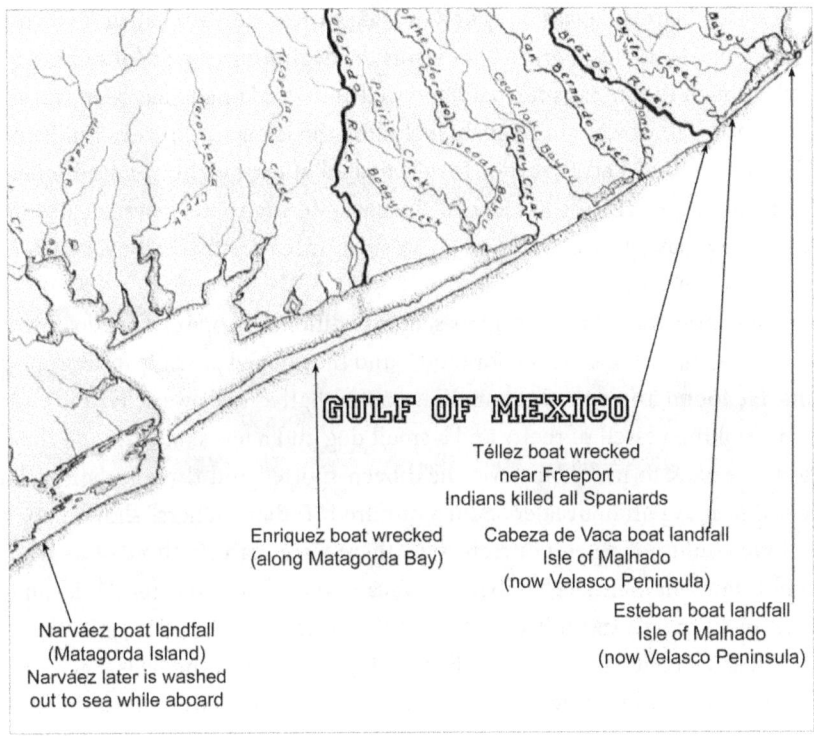

Figure 8. All five Narváez boats were swept ashore or wrecked along this Texas coastline on the west side of the Gulf of Mexico, south of Galveston. All the boats sank or were unsalvageable except the boat Narváez was on, which was blown or washed out to sea with him aboard. He was never heard from again. Based on US Coast Guard Chart 1117.

The next day, waves threw Cabeza de Vaca's boat "a horse's length" onto the shore about four miles farther south. It would be a few days before the two boatloads of men learned they'd landed close to each other. As waves hurled each of the boats in turn onto Texas beaches, Cabeza de Vaca recalled how "the people who lay in [his] boat like dead came to themselves, and, seeing we were close to land, began to crawl out on all fours."[15] Esteban had to wonder where the other boats had landed after they were separated in the gulf, or even if they'd made landfall. He'd eventually learn that Cabeza de Vaca's boat had been swept ashore about four miles to the south the day after his boat.

Velasco Peninsula was an island in 1528. Cabeza de Vaca called it Isla de Malhado, Island of Ill Fortune, for it was the beginning of years of suffering, even though the Indians treated them well at first. Malhado has been translated many other ways in English, including the Island of Ill Fate, Evil Fate, Misfortune, and Bad Fortune. They'd floated at least eight hundred miles from the Bay of Horses because of their wandering route, staying close to shore. Few have ever traveled so far in such unseaworthy craft over such a large body of water.

Cabeza de Vaca's boat survivors sent expeditionary Lope de Oviedo down a trail into the woods to look for food—and they hoped possibly for Europeans. He found an empty Indian village about half a mile away. "He took an olla [cooking vessel] of theirs and a small dog and a few skate fish and thus he came back to us."[16] However, he'd been spotted and three Indians followed him. A half hour later about a hundred "Indian archers" showed up.

"We could not defend ourselves, as there were scarcely three of us who could stand on their feet," Cabeza de Vaca wrote. "The inspector [Solis] and I stepped forward and called to them. They came and we tried to quiet them as best as we could and save ourselves, giving them beads and bells. Each one of them gave me an arrow in token of friendship."[17] The Indians returned the next day with fish and roots that tasted like nuts for the famished survivors. That evening they returned with more food and also brought their women and children to see the Europeans.

The Indians who found the two boats about four miles apart on Malhado Island were from the Han and/or Capoque tribes, eastern branches of the Karankawa tribe.[18] The Texas Indians might have realized there were white and black people in the world because Spanish ships had sailed along the Gulf Coast. But they probably had seen some only from an indistinct distance, so the sight of these strangers who came out of the gulf awed them.

After the shipwrecked men had regained some strength under the Indians' care, they decided to try to resume their voyage to Pánuco, farther down the coast. Taking off their clothes, they wrestled their dilapidated boat out of the sand and managed to get it back into the gulf. They only made it "two crossbow shots" from shore when waves swamped the boat and sank it.[19] Three men drowned and the rest struggled back to the beach without their clothes or supplies.

Cabeza de Vaca recalled bitter cold weather on those November days.

Figure 9. An old print depicts one of the Narváez boats capsizing along the Texas coast.

"Naked as the day we were born ... we [were] in such a state that every bone could be counted, and we looked like death itself."[20] Two men died that night.

The coastal Indians would have eventually reunited occupants of the islands' two boats, but that was expedited after someone on Esteban's boat gave an Indian a Spanish item, most likely out of gratitude for food. Cabeza de Vaca later saw the Indian with the item and learned of the other boat. The two crews joined up, each having heard of the other from Indians. Esteban's boatload of men still had their clothes and meager supplies, according to the *Relación*, but nothing else. Dorantes reported that the men from his boat shared what clothes they could spare with Cabeza de Vaca's men, probably stripping Esteban and any other slaves first.

The crews joined forces and tried to repair the boat that Esteban and the others came on, but "when they put to sea, these Spaniards were not able to keep themselves afloat, because of the woodworms and other problems." That boat's sinking would turn out to be their final chance to continue by water down the coast to Pánuco.

The Indians had canoes, and it's baffling that the expeditionaries never reported trying to appropriate any and continue on their way to the River of Palms and their ultimate goal of Pánuco. Neither the *Relación* nor the Joint Report explained that odd lack of action. Perhaps the Indians wouldn't allow them to use canoes, or the castaways considered them too undependable for the gulf's waters, although they'd crossed the gulf themselves on lesser craft and the Indians were willing to venture out. Whatever the reason, it cannot be known.

None of the other boats were seen again except as wreckage surrounded by corpses. The Téllez-Peñasco boat wrecked near today's Freeport, Texas, about twenty miles southwest, and all on that boat were too weak to defend themselves against the Camone Indians who found them. The Camones might have considered killing the men an act of mercy because the expeditionaries were so emaciated and feeble. Enriquez's boat with the friars wrecked near Matagorda Bay, seventy miles southwest of Malhado Island. None from that boat survived the year in an ordeal that Cabeza de Vaca reported included starvation, murder, and cannibalism. Cabeza de Vaca later learned that Narváez made landfall on Matagorda Island. The conquistador was still in the boat with two others when wind and waves sent it back out into the gulf. As the Joint Report says, "The sea swallowed them up."[21]

After Esteban's boat sank, the survivors decided their last chance was to have some men walk to Pánuco and bring back help. Realizing rivers would need to be crossed and bays walked around in the coastal waterlands, everyone agreed that the five best swimmers should go, who included the Portuguese carpenter who helped build the boats, three Spaniards, and a Cuban Indian slave. Still desperate to believe Miruelo's statement that Pánuco could not be far away, the survivors didn't realize they were stranded about 550 miles from that Spanish town. After they left, a "cold and tempestuous" storm swept from the gulf across the land with rain, wind, and freezing temperatures, dooming four of the five. Indians killed the fifth man.

The record is silent, but it's possible Esteban was one of only two slaves still alive from the unknown number who'd been taken to Florida. He was not chosen to make that escape attempt because he could not swim. That inability saved his life.

CHAPTER 11

Spaniards Forced into Slavery

ESTEBAN SAW SCORES of expeditionaries die that first harsh winter. Danger heightened after the storm along the coast that doomed the five who'd left for the south, because Malhado Island Indians began falling sick from a stomach ailment. About half of the Indians died, and so did about 80 percent of the expeditionaries.[1] A group of Indians blamed the strangers and were on their way to kill them when one Indian leader talked them out of it, reasoning that if the strangers were to blame for the disease they would not have suffered an even greater death rate than the Indians. Some writers have theorized expeditionaries might have transmitted the disease, but a 2008 study concluded that the disease was caused by a pathogen already existing in Texas.[2]

Cabeza de Vaca was taken into an Indian village on the mainland because he was so sick that everyone was convinced he was about to die. Lope de Oviedo and the notary Albaniz remained debilitated on the island and unable to travel.[3] Esteban and most of the surviving expeditionaries crossed over to the mainland in search of food. Dorantes recalled in the Joint Report that they went to swamps and lagoons on the mainland to eat oysters like the Indians did for three or four months every year. They stayed there until the end of March 1529.[4] Even with oysters to eat, Esteban and the others suffered from exposure. Like the Indians, Dorantes reported they experienced great hunger and found unbearable the swarms of mosquitoes day and night.[5] It was a harsh reminder of what they'd experienced in Florida.

The most dramatic incident that winter took place with five men in a shore-side hut on the island who stayed there because they either feared going to the native village or were posted to watch for Spanish ships. Starving, they ate each other until the last one died with nobody left to eat him. That incident turned the Indians away from friendship. It was an ironic twist in history. For decades the Spaniards justified killing and enslaving island Caribs by accusing them of being cannibals. Now it was the Spaniards who were cannibals, while it was the Indians who were appalled. The *Relación* comments, "At this the Indians were so startled, and there was such an uproar among them."[6]

Fewer than twenty of the original two hundred and fifty or so expeditionaries who'd set out in the boats were still alive after the first winter. Dorantes said they saw the wreckage of other boats and bodies on the beaches, and at some point they were joined by an Asturian cleric and an African man who were survivors of the boat commanded by Alonso Enriquez and Friar Juan Suárez.[7] That priest and black man were never mentioned again.

Believing that Cabeza de Vaca was dying, twelve still able-bodied men paid an Indian a fur cape so he'd take them to the sick Spaniard's village on the first day of April 1529. Cabeza de Vaca reported in the *Relación* that his visitors included Castillo, Dorantes, and "Estevanico, the Negro."[8] This was the first mention of Esteban's existence in seventy-three *Relación* pages. Giving Esteban's name indicated that the African was becoming included in a band of brothers among the dwindling number of survivors. Most of the time Cabeza de Vaca continued referring to Esteban as *el negro*, but Cabeza de Vaca referred to Esteban by name seven more times in the rest of his account. When they visited Cabeza de Vaca, the twelve decided they must try again to reach Pánuco because they could not survive much longer.[9] So many had already died from drowning, starvation, disease, Indian killings, and from just giving up. The close call from being blamed for the fatal stomach ailment also alarmed them.

Esteban was among the dozen expeditionaries Dorantes led down the coast that spring in another attempt to reach Pánuco, constructing rafts to cross four large rivers they encountered, sometimes with the help of Indians who were paid *ciertas cosas*, certain things. Two men drowned when their raft was swept into the gulf. Esteban and the others walked more than a hundred miles through coastal swamps, suffering great privations. They made it about a fifth of the way to Pánuco, but only Esteban, Dorantes, and Castillo survived to turn back.

By mid-1529, Indians decided the strange travelers might as well be of some use. Karankawas enslaved Cabeza de Vaca after he recovered from his illness on Malhado Island, while other Indians along the saltwater-flooded coast around Corpus Christi Bay made slaves of Esteban and the rest. Now began a wretched period of more than five years of slavery, beatings, near starvation, threats, and unrelenting work. Cabeza de Vaca and Dorantes both said all of them were worked to exhaustion. Because they were naked like the Indians, they suffered each winter. During the spring, summer, and fall they remained so sunburned that they shed their skin twice a year like snakes.[10]

Spanish historian Gonzalo Fernández de Oviedo y Valdéz retold Dorantes's testimony in his report to the king, writing about their captivity: "The Indians took [Esteban, Dorantes, and Castillo] as slaves, using them more cruelly. . . . At all times they had been naked and barefoot. This was in summer when that coast burned like fire. Now their function was nothing less than carrying loads of firewood close to their flesh, as well as everything else the Indians needed. In that heat, they also dragged canoes through those floodlands. . . . All this contributed to the greater fatigue of the Christians. . . . They feared everyone. Moreover, all treated them poorly by deed and by words. . . . The Spaniards were worthy men and gentlemen, who were new at such a life . . . to suffer so many and such intolerable torments."[11]

Esteban must have found it an interesting turn of events. Not many slaves have ever seen their masters also enslaved. Esteban remained a slave, but now with Spaniards toiling at his side.

Mexican historian Andrés Reséndez discusses the changed dynamics of Esteban's relationship with the three Spaniards:

> The man best able to cope psychologically with the adverse conditions was in all likelihood the African Estebanico. . . . Although it is possible that his subordination to Dorantes and the other Spaniards persisted in some fashion, the fact that the white Europeans were also enslaved must have reduced the disparities. Indians, not Spaniards, exercised the ultimate authority now, a fact that must have complicated immensely Dorantes's ability to enforce his authority over the African.[12]

Dorantes managed to escape from his first captors on the islands and make it to a tribe of mainland Indians in August 1530. It was the first time he and Esteban were separated. But Dorantes went from bad to worse. The mainland Indians treated him so roughly as a slave that he later said he feared for his life. Three months later, Esteban also escaped and rejoined Dorantes, leaving Castillo alone. When Castillo escaped a year and a half later, he found Esteban, but Dorantes had moved on again and was enslaved by a third tribe, the Mareames.[13]

As for Cabeza de Vaca, he wrote about his recovery from his illness: "So great was the lack of food then that I often remained without eating anything whatsoever for three days, and [the Indians] were in the same plight, so that it seemed impossible for life to last, although I afterwards suffered still greater privations and much more distress. . . . I had to remain with those same Indians of the island for more than one year, and as they made me work so much and treated me so badly I determined to flee and go to those [the Chorruco tribe] who live in the woods on the mainland."[14]

He said he tried three times to escape, but the island natives caught him every time.

Who Was the Trader?

Then Cabeza de Vaca wrote that he came up with the ingenious plan of becoming a trader, traveling as a neutral person between hostile tribes and supplying their needs. The Indians thought he could be more useful that way, he wrote, so they allowed him to be a trader, which "improved my condition a little."[15] He wrote that he traveled far inland and forty to fifty leagues, a hundred and thirty miles or more, along the coast. His pack was filled with trade items that each tribe wanted from the other. They dared not go themselves because of constant warfare, but all tribes granted safe passage to traders.

Unlike the *Relación*, which contains Cabeza de Vaca's views, historian Oviedo was able to add Dorantes's observations and maybe also Castillo's in the Joint Report portion of his *Historia*. One contradiction between the two accounts concerns Cabeza de Vaca's claim that he was the trader. For example, Oviedo's *Historia* states that Cabeza de Vaca spent the entire five-plus years on and around Malhado Island, digging edible roots along the shoreline for the Indians.[16] Oviedo went on to report that Dorantes was the trader, not Cabeza de Vaca.[17] English translators of that portion of his *Historia* routinely substituted Cabeza de Vaca's name, however, deferring to Cabeza de Vaca's *Relación* claim to have been the trader and thinking the historian Oviedo made a mistake.

Gerald Theisen is one of the few translators who point out that Oviedo seemed to be writing about Dorantes in the passage about a trader, although even he concluded Oviedo must have meant Cabeza de Vaca.[18] Researcher Robert Goodwin speculates that if the Indians had one non-Indian trader in the 1500s, Oviedo's mention of "Dorantes" was more likely a reference to Esteban de Dorantes. All the tribes considered Esteban to be more approachable and amicable than the Spaniards, and he learned to communicate with them.[19] The ambiguity in Oviedo's writing opens up that possibility and many others.

Dorantes told Oviedo that for five years Cabeza de Vaca "wore no clothing and was like a savage . . . and he served the Indians in this manner [digging roots and carrying loads of firewood on his back every day] and in other ways they ordered him."[20] Such a description did not fit the heroic leadership image that Cabeza de Vaca wanted to give readers in his account. He does not describe his situation that way, but the description does give insight to conditions endured by any survivors who were not traders. Coincidentally, Cabeza de Vaca claimed to be a trader during the time he was alone with no witnesses to refute him.

Even if Cabeza de Vaca is taken at his word that he was the trader, questions come up that seem to indicate he wasn't. For example, Cabeza de Vaca knew what tribes held Esteban, Castillo, and Dorantes, so why did he never see them in the years of travels he claimed as trader? Another question: If Cabeza de Vaca were an unsupervised trader, free to go anywhere, why didn't he keep heading southwest to Pánuco and bring back a Spanish force to rescue his boat-wrecked companions—or at least mention that he was tempted to do so, despite the risk? Instead, he insisted he stayed out of concern for another Spaniard. "The reason for remaining so long was that I wished to take with me [in an escape] a Christian called Lope de Oviedo, who still lingered on the island."[21]

Cabeza de Vaca reported that Lope de Oviedo kept refusing escape offers. In light of later events, perhaps Oviedo was not being as mistreated as the rest and saw no reason to leave. Or perhaps concern for his fellow expeditionary was not the real reason Cabeza de Vaca stayed. After all, Dorantes said Cabeza de Vaca was a slave doing hard labor the entire time. In 1532, Lope de Oviedo and Cabeza de Vaca managed to slip away, and the two of them traveled a hundred miles or more south to bays near Corpus Christi, Texas. But Oviedo felt threatened by the Indians they met, so he returned to Malhado with some Desguanes women despite objections by Cabeza de Vaca, who never saw Oviedo again.[22] Such self-sacrifice of waiting for years for Oviedo, and also not escaping while a trader, is not plausible, especially in light of other incidents in the *Relación* where Cabeza de Vaca confessed to plans for escaping alone. But the account is how Cabeza de Vaca wrote it. Those are a few of the details he put forth that are inexplicable but often reprinted as fact in history books.

Two days after Lope de Oviedo turned back toward Malhado, the natives arranged for Cabeza de Vaca to meet Dorantes, who was in the area with the Mareame tribe. It had been more than four years since landing at Malhado. "We gave many thanks to God for being together again," Cabeza de Vaca wrote.[23] This was near present-day Matagorda Bay. Dorantes had assumed Cabeza de Vaca had died from his earlier sickness. He managed to find a way for him and Cabeza de Vaca to meet with Esteban and Castillo, and they began plotting how they could escape. They'd need to wait several months, they decided, when the area tribes all went to harvest river-valley pecans or the fruits and pads of prickly pear cactuses, and when enemy tribes also would be present from whom their captors would not dare to retrieve them. In the meantime, Cabeza de Vaca stayed with the Mareames who held Dorantes, while Esteban and Castillo stayed with the neighboring Yguaze tribe.

Esteban and the others witnessed the use of hallucinogens or intoxicants among these Karankawa bands, which had been in use worldwide for thousands of years from fermented grains and fruits and various hallucinogenic substances. It's believed the Karankawas used the mescal bean, possibly peyote, and/or a marijuana-like substance or strong tobacco.[24] In his condescending Eurocentric tone, Cabeza de Vaca described the Indians as "great drunkards," as if Europeans were not subject to such temptations.[25] Also during this time, Cabeza de Vaca, and likely Esteban and the other two Spaniards, were the first non-Indians on the continent to see buffaloes, also known as American bison, during their captivity. All assumed the expeditionary

Oviedo must have perished after leaving Cabeza de Vaca to return to Malhado Island, so the *Relación* never again mentioned Oviedo.

Other Survivors
JUAN ORTIZ

While Esteban and others were stranded on the Texas coast after the expedition had landed in Florida, a small Spanish ship called a "pinnance" appeared along Florida's west coast.[26] Upon reaching Tampa Bay, the pinnance approached the village of Hirrihigua, whose nose had been cut off by Narvárz's order in 1528 a year or more earlier. By then Hirrihigua's village was called Uçita, Uzita, or Oçita and located at either the southern tip of today's St. Petersburg or across the bay near Rushkin, Florida. Hirrihigua saw the ship's arrival as his chance for revenge.

According to an account about a decade later by one Soto chronicler, when Juan Ortiz returned to Cuba on Miruelo's brigantine he'd called on Narváez's wife in Cuba as a courtesy, and she asked him to return to Florida and find her conquest-minded husband.[27] Eighteen-year-old Ortiz was adventurous, and he agreed to go back.[28] She bought a pinnance, on which Ortiz and about twenty sailors sailed back to Florida.[29] When Soto's men came across Ortiz in mid-1539, he told them what he'd endured since being captured. And it was not until years later that his story was published.[30]

Secondhand accounts many years removed from the incident resulted in several contradictions in the record, and time can widen the gap between facts and good storytelling. There are two main accounts of Juan Ortiz's misadventures. One is by an anonymous Portuguese nobleman known as the Gentleman of Elvas, who participated in the Soto expedition and published his account in 1557. The other is by Garcilaso de la Vega, a man of half-Inca ethnicity who completed his history of the Soto expedition in 1599, basing his account on interviews with survivors and now-lost writings. The Elvas account is brief and generalized. In contrast, *The Florida of the Inca* provides seven chapters full of details about Ortiz. Like numerous conquistador narratives, the Inca Garcilaso's more entertaining fabrications developed into legend mixed with fact.

In both accounts, Hirrihigua lured the Spaniards off the Spanish ship with promises he would give them news about Narváez. Elvas said Juan Ortiz and one sailor got into a boat and paddled to shore. Indians seized both men, killing one in a brief struggle, and took Ortiz away.[31] The Inca, as he has become known, wrote that three sailors rowed ashore with Ortiz, and all were seized. The sailors were killed, but Ortiz was allowed to live as a slave with the Tocobagas.[32] Both accounts say the sailors still on the pinnance sailed away, making no attempt to rescue Ortiz on shore.

One day, according to both accounts, Hirrihigua tied the teenager to a wooden grill built a few feet above a bed of hot coals, planning to burn Ortiz alive. At the youth's shrieks of pain, however, Hirrihigua's wife and daughters rushed up and convinced the chief to take the blistered Ortiz off the grill. The Inca claimed Ortiz and one daughter fell in love, and that she took him to a neighboring chief, who sheltered him from her father's wrath. Florida folklore likes to refer to the chief's daughter as Princess Uleleh.[33] All of this happened almost eighty years before John Smith wrote his famous Virginia story about Pocahontas saving him from her vengeful father. He might have gotten the idea from reading the Inca's story about Juan Ortiz.

Ortiz was adopted into the second tribe, and Soto's men found him in 1539 with a group of Indians. According to one of Soto's chroniclers, when lancers on horseback attacked the Indians, one who looked like an Indian came forth and cried out in Spanish, "Sirs, for the love of God and of Holy Mary, slay not me. I am a Christian like yourselves and was born in Sevilla, and my name is Juan Ortiz."[34] Another chronicler reports that Ortiz said, "Sirs, I am a Christian. Do not kill me. Do not kill these Indians, for they have given me my life."[35]

Actually, Ortiz said none of that. Both quotations are good examples of fables that Spaniards concocted about themselves that now masquerade as history. The most reliable of Soto's chroniclers, because his report to the king was written the earliest in 1544 and the least corrupted by editors, was the king's agent, Luys Hernández de Biedma. When the lancers found Ortiz, Biedma wrote, they "easily might have killed the Christian, because he knew little of our language, since he'd forgotten it. He remembered how to call to Our Lady, and by this he was recognized to be a Christian."[36]

After a decade with the Indians, Ortiz spoke so few words in Spanish that he was unintelligible when taken to Soto's camp. Biedma explained, "He was among us more than four days before he could join one word with another, since upon saying one word in Spanish, he would say another four or five in the language of the Indians."[37] After Ortiz reacquired Spanish, Soto used him as an interpreter because of his knowledge of the region's languages and mutually intelligible manual gestures. Ortiz died of an illness in the winter of 1541–1542 in the Coosa chiefdom's town of Utiangue, possibly near present-day Newport, Arkansas, west of the Mississippi River.[38]

LOPE DE OVIEDO

Another survivor of the Narváez expedition was Lope de Oviedo.[39] Very little is known about him after Cabeza de Vaca dropped the man from his account when Oviedo turned back from their escape attempt in 1532.

Members of the Soto expedition learned about Oviedo in 1543, a year after Soto died by the Mississippi River. The expedition's remnant under the command of Luis de Moscoso Alvarado traveled into Texas in a futile bid to walk to Mexico, then headed back to the Mississippi River after deciding it was the best escape route. An expedition member's account described how Indians told Moscoso that a white man lived in a village named Chaguate, which was on the route back to the Mississippi River.[40]

Spaniards went to the village to retrieve their countryman, but upon arrival they learned he'd fled. Bewildered, Moscoso wrote a letter for the Indians to take to the man. "[Moscoso] put him in remembrance that he was a Christian, that he should not remain in the subjection of infidels [and] that he should come to him," an expeditionary member wrote.[41] Lope de Oviedo wrote his name on the back of Moscoso's letter to prove he was alive. But he refused to join the expedition. "[Moscoso] sent twelve horsemen to seek him. But he, who had his spies, so hid himself that they could not find him. For want of corn, the governor could not stay any longer to seek him."[42]

Lope de Oviedo was left there, never to return to European society. Later the phrase "gone native" expressed Oviedo's preference for Indian society and his refusal to return to the world of Europeans.

Escape from Slavery

Even if captivity and slavery were not that oppressive for Oviedo, misery and hardship remained for Esteban and the three Spaniards with him.

As Cabeza de Vaca admitted, however, he suffered starvation and from the elements no worse than the Indians did. And as a slave he did the same work that all tribal women were required to do every day of their lives. To a Spaniard accustomed to easy living, however, being subjected to slavery and a lesser station in life was insufferable. He recalled, "The men do not carry burdens or loads—the women and old men have to do it . . . the women are compelled to do very hard work . . . for out of twenty-four hours of day and night they get only six hours rest."[43] Esteban and the three Spaniards were required to work the same way, and they also suffered beatings and threats against their lives—just as women often did.

Esteban adjusted better than the others. He knew how to get along with Indians and was used to being ordered around. He'd spent years doing work that his masters from privileged Spanish families refused to do.

The tribes holding Esteban and the Spaniards converged in the fall of 1533 in a distant area to harvest the purple fruits and green pads of prickly pear cactus. Prickly pear still grows throughout Mexico and the Southwest United States but usually in small clumps. However, early settlers reported there once were "vast ramparts and towers of prickly pear that seemed to form walls and mountains in their terrible array" and acres of "thickets higher than a man on horseback" that produced "an immense quantity of fruit."[44] Those formidable stands of prickly pear cactus in the southern Texas counties disappeared after a killing frost in 1899.[45] Although covered with inches-long thorns on the pads and clusters of small spines on the fruits, all parts of the prickly pear cactus are nutritious. Many people still skin and roast the pads, while they cut apart the fruits resulting from the flowers and scoop out the seedy and juicy pulp inside. Prickly pear jam is sold throughout the Southwest still today.

During the harvest, Esteban and the Spaniards abandoned any plan to escape when members of different tribes became mad at one another, packed up, and left. But the four of them promised to look for one another again during the next year's visit. In the fall of 1534, the castaways returned with their tribes to harvest the prickly pears in southern Texas. Some researchers put that harvesting location near present San Antonio, and others farther south near Corpus Christi. Regardless, the four needed to find a way to link up without their captors becoming suspicious.

Dorantes told the historian Oviedo how all four arrived separately at the

Figure 10. The fruits of the prickly pear cactus shown here were an important food source for Natives in the arid areas of the United States and Mexico. Even the pads were eaten—after the spines were removed, of course. The fruits are still used to make jellies and jams in parts of both countries. Photo by Dennis Herrick.

prickly pear harvesting sites, and each managed to sneak away from their tribes with plans to meet at another well-known area that would no longer have fruits because it was always picked first. Dorantes was the first to arrive at the harvested site. "By chance," Dorantes reported, he "encountered some Indian people who had come to that place the same day." Those Indians were Anagados, who were "great enemies" of the coastal tribes who had enslaved the four expeditionaries, so they knew about the four captives and treated Dorantes well.

Dorantes said "the black man" arrived on his trail three or four days later, leading Castillo. When they saw columns of smoke in the distance, they guessed Cabeza de Vaca might be found there. They decided one of the three had to stay behind to assure the Anagados that the other two were going forward and would return with the fourth expeditionary. In the past, the African probably would have been the one left behind while the two Spaniards went forward to join the other Spaniard. However, all three Spaniards had come to value Esteban as a companion, and old prejudices no longer held. Thus it was Esteban and Dorantes who went ahead to find Cabeza de Vaca while Castillo remained behind with the Anagados as a hostage.

Esteban and Dorantes walked until nightfall, when they met an Indian who took them to Cabeza de Vaca. In the *Relación*, Cabeza de Vaca made it clear that he intended to escape alone if the other three did not show up at the full moon. Again the question arises: why didn't he flee during the time he claimed to be a roaming trader? But on the day he planned to make a break for it, he wrote, "there came to where I was Andrés Dorantes and Estevanico." On the following day, the Indians at that place moved toward the Anagado tribe. "So we got Castillo also," Cabeza de Vaca wrote, adding: "Two days after moving [to the Anagado camp], we recommended ourselves to God, Our Lord, and fled, hoping that, although it was late in the season and the fruits of the [prickly pears] were giving out, by remaining in the field we might still get over a good portion of the land."[46]

It was September 8, 1534.[47] That fall's flight from the Anagados, who also intended to enslave them, was fraught with panic. Two days after they left the Anagado camp, they were still on the run. The *Relación* told how Esteban saved them:

> As we proceeded that day, in great fear lest the Indians would follow us, we [saw] smoke and, going toward it, reached the place after sundown, where we found an Indian who, when he saw us coming, did not wait but ran away. We sent the Negro after him, and as the Indian saw him approach, he waited.[48]

The Indian was armed because no warrior would venture out alone without weapons. The *Relación* implied that the Spaniards ordered Esteban to go after the Indian and face that danger alone. But it's more likely that Esteban had become a brother in survival. Esteban was braver, confident in his ability to communicate with Indians, and in better physical condition than the Spaniards. He chased after the Indian because he was willing to do so, and he knew he could succeed because he'd learned some Indian languages.[49]

The Indian was an Avavare who traded wood for bows to the coastal tribes and, as usual for a trader, was multilingual. Esteban was able to talk to the Indian in the Mareame language and told him they were searching for a tribe where they would be safe. Some researchers theorize that the four escapees had pre-arranged sanctuary among the Avavares during more than a year of planning, and that the smoke plume was a signal to help them find the tribe.[50] Whether that's true, the native whom Esteban met agreed to guide all of them to his village in what is now southern Texas.

Esteban returned to the three Spaniards to assure them there was no danger, and the Avavare led them to his village. The Avavares housed Esteban and Dorantes in the lodge of a medicine man, while Cabeza de Vaca and Castillo stayed with another. The Avavares treated them kindly instead of as slaves, Dorantes reported, describing the Avavares as gentle people.[51] Although the escapees lived freely among the Avavares, they suffered great hunger over the next winter just as the Indians did.

With their escape from the coastal tribes, wrote Terrell, "The most remarkable overland journey in the history of American exploration had begun."[52]

CHAPTER 12

Faith Healing and Proselytizing

THE AVAVARES HAD looked on with surprise that fall day in 1534 at the appearance of four gaunt, bearded men at their camp. One was burned jet black by the sun, and the lighter-skinned ones were red with sunburn. The Avavares had heard about the four strangers, and many had seen them on trading missions to the coastal tribes.

Both the *Relación* and the Joint Account reported how the Avavares danced all that night until sunrise and for three days, one of several times the travelers witnessed Indians dancing. The egocentric Spaniards always thought the dances were to celebrate their arrival.[1] Accounts indicate that Esteban joined the Indians, resulting in them feeling closer to him as a friend and building goodwill toward them all.

From this point on, both the *Relación* and the Joint Account focus on the humanity of Indians rather than their cruelty, a change of heart that would continue for the rest of their journey. The tribes north of the Spanish-occupied portion of Mexico would give Esteban and the Spaniards safe passage from tribe to tribe as wandering guests, greeting them with curiosity and hospitality at first, and then as healers.

Faith Healing

Cabeza de Vaca claimed the reputation of all four travelers as healers took hold while they were with the Avavares. The Joint Account with Dorantes's interview maintained that the first faith healing did not take place with the Avavares but instead took place a few tribes and weeks later while with the Coahuiltecans in Mexico. That disparity is another indication of how Dorantes and Cabeza de Vaca differ in certain places in their accounts.

Also, the *Relación* claimed Cabeza de Vaca earlier performed the first healing on Malhado Island. The omission of any other Spaniards' names assisting him on Malhado is another reason many historians do not believe Cabeza de Vaca performed healing there. During that time, Esteban, Dorantes, and Castillo were slaves with the Han Indians and out of touch with Cabeza de Vaca, who was enslaved on Malhado Island.

Some researchers think Cabeza de Vaca's publisher moved faith healing to sooner in the *Relación* to grab readers' attention.[2] Skeptics note that Cabeza de Vaca wrote about cure after cure starting in 1534, but on Malhado Island his *Relación* mentioned just one faith-healing incident. The Karankawas remained so unimpressed that they continued to enslave him anyway. Later in the *Relación*, Cabeza de Vaca contradicted himself by giving Castillo credit for being the first to treat Indians, starting with the Avavares in 1534. Cabeza de Vaca reported the first healing, whether on the island or with the Avavares or with the Coahuiltecans, with the *Relación*'s single hint of humor, writing, "They wanted to make medicine men of us without any examination or asking for our diplomas."[3]

Whenever and wherever it was that faith healing was first practiced, the *Relación* mentions that the Spaniards at first declined to treat the Indians' illnesses, saying they possessed no such ability, fearful they might be killed if they tried and failed. When the Indians withheld their food, the Spaniards decided there was no choice but to try.

Cabeza de Vaca explained that Indian medicine men "cure diseases by breathing on the sick, and with their breath and with their hands they drive the ailment away." They also might make an incision and suck out blood and then cauterize the wound." He goes on: "The way we treated the sick was to make over them the sign of the cross while breathing on them, recite [the Our Father and Hail Mary prayers], and pray to God, our Lord, as best we could to give them good health." The quackery worked. "All those for whom we prayed, as soon as we crossed them, told the others they were cured," Cabeza de Vaca reported.[4] Food, when it was available, was provided again. In Cabeza de Vaca's account about the Avavares, he said the first ailments were headaches. "As soon as [Castillo] had made the sign of the cross over them and recommended them to God, at that very moment the Indians said that all pain was gone."[5]

The Indians expressed their thanks by giving Castillo chunks of venison, the taste of which the famished travelers had almost forgotten. Cabeza de Vaca wrote that more "sick Indians" came to Castillo for treatment, and they also paid with so much venison that the travelers struggled to find ways to store the meat. It occurred to them that they might be on to something.

Cabeza de Vaca took care in his account to placate fanatical priests of the Inquisition who would read his account. Once he returned to Mexico, it had to occur to him that taking on priestly roles of that time such as healing the sick might get him in trouble. So he wrote at one point that it was the Indians who forced them to act like shamans, and it was the Indians who insisted, "We were children of the sun and had the power to heal the sick and to kill them, and other lies even greater than these."[6] Perhaps the Holy Office of the Inquisition gave them a pass because they returned as heroes. Also, Viceroy Antonio de Mendoza and Bishop Juan de Zumárraga had special plans to use one of them as a guide to the north, as will be seen in chapter 14. That might be what spared Esteban, who as a slave and former Muslim was the most vulnerable to suspicion of heresy.

Early in their journey, the survivors learned that Indians referred to things they did not understand as coming from the sky—heaven, to the Spanish way of thinking. Thus the one black and three white expeditionaries often described themselves as Children of the Sun, hoping to awe the Indians into treating them well by saying they came from heaven.[7] And it must have seemed true in southern Texas and northern Mexico, just as it might to some people today if green and blue people suddenly appeared. Spaniards attributed the cures to miracles performed by God through the four travelers' hands. Indeed, all four of them also believed the cures to be religious miracles that God for some reason chose them to perform.

The supernatural aspects could be explained by the likelihood of the Indians suffering from psychosomatic illnesses. Such ailments were not recognized in sixteenth-century Europe, but they were seen as real by tribes in the Americas. Psychosomatic illnesses can be mental or emotional in nature, but they also can be psychiatric disorders manifested through physical problems. Or, put another way, the physical symptoms of illness can be due to psychological problems. If you think you're sick, you might very well make yourself sick. If the patient's confidence is strong enough in the healer, psychosomatic illnesses can be effectively *cured* by means ranging from placebo medications to faith healing through belief systems.

Faith healing is explained by French anthropologist Claude Lévi-Strauss's proposition that it is shamanism, which he describes as a kind of collective reality-altering experience. The most important factor isn't what the shaman does by way of treatment, he explains. Instead, it is that their patients believe the shaman has medicinal power.[8] Tanya Luhrmann, a Stanford University anthropologist, says faith-healing results can be "astounding," but it requires a shaman's convincing performance and a patient with the ability to make what is imagined seem real. "Belief is natural," she says. "It comes partly from the way our minds are hardwired."[9]

Researchers into the phenomenon have learned that a patient's expectation of relief triggers the release of endorphins in his or her body, and those endorphins reduce the sensation of pain. The patient self-medicates, literally, by expecting the relief to occur. When a person's belief is shared with a like-minded group of people, faith healing becomes even more effective.[10] It's important that the healer/shaman believes he or she has medicinal power.

Through his religion, Cabeza de Vaca believed. God becomes almost a physical companion in Cabeza de Vaca's way of thinking, granting favors when pleased with Cabeza de Vaca, and punishing him with great ordeals when not pleased.

Onward to Mexico

The foursome spent a difficult, starving time with the Avavares the first winter after escaping the Karankawas. After spending the winter amid growing impatience with the delay in looking for Spanish settlements, the four agreed to strike out on their own despite requests by the Avavares that they stay. It's not certain whether this happened near the end of May or in early June 1535, but it might have been near today's Freer, Texas.[11] Esteban and the three Spaniards walked southward toward their long cherished goal of Pánuco. They would end up covering a distance they could not imagine.

At some point, Cabeza de Vaca wanted to contact a band of Indians about twenty miles away. The ever-reliable Esteban was the only one who would go with him. After they found the camp, Esteban retraced his steps for three days and brought Dorantes and Castillo so they could be together at the new Indian camp.

All the native groups they met treated them well but were so deprived of food themselves that the Narváez survivors suffered from constant hunger. Because the Indians were so busy hunting for food all day, the four travelers volunteered to stay in villages making needed articles and building lodges. They would stay awhile with each tribe, and then move on to the next.

The *Relación* reported that after several days the travelers crossed a "big river coming from the north. Later they "forded a very big river with its water reaching to our chest."[12] At some point, without knowing it, they were in Mexico.

Little Agreement on Route

Cabeza de Vaca's descriptions of distances and directions are so vague that there are many ideas about their eventual route after they left the Texas coast. Each scholar has put forward his or her proposal for the path that Esteban and the three Spaniards traveled after leaving the Galveston area. Anthropologist Alex Krieger estimates that his book was one of about sixty written between 1871 and 2002 that tried to determine the route from the maddening ambiguity and incompleteness of Cabeza de Vaca's descriptions. Most early route proposals suggest a northern trek across the Texas Great Plains, while more recent ones advocate a southern alternative through Texas and into Mexico.[13]

The distance between the most north and south routes put forth over the years is about seven hundred miles, which gives an idea of the scholars' differences. Some routes eventually dip southwest until crossing the Rio Grande in southern Texas before continuing westward across Mexico. Others march the survivors across New Mexico and Arizona, but modern researchers no longer think the travelers went far enough north to be in New Mexico or Arizona, or even through El Paso.

Academics Roleno Adorno and Patrick Charles Pautz, who wrote a three-volume biography of Cabeza de Vaca, send the travelers down the Texas

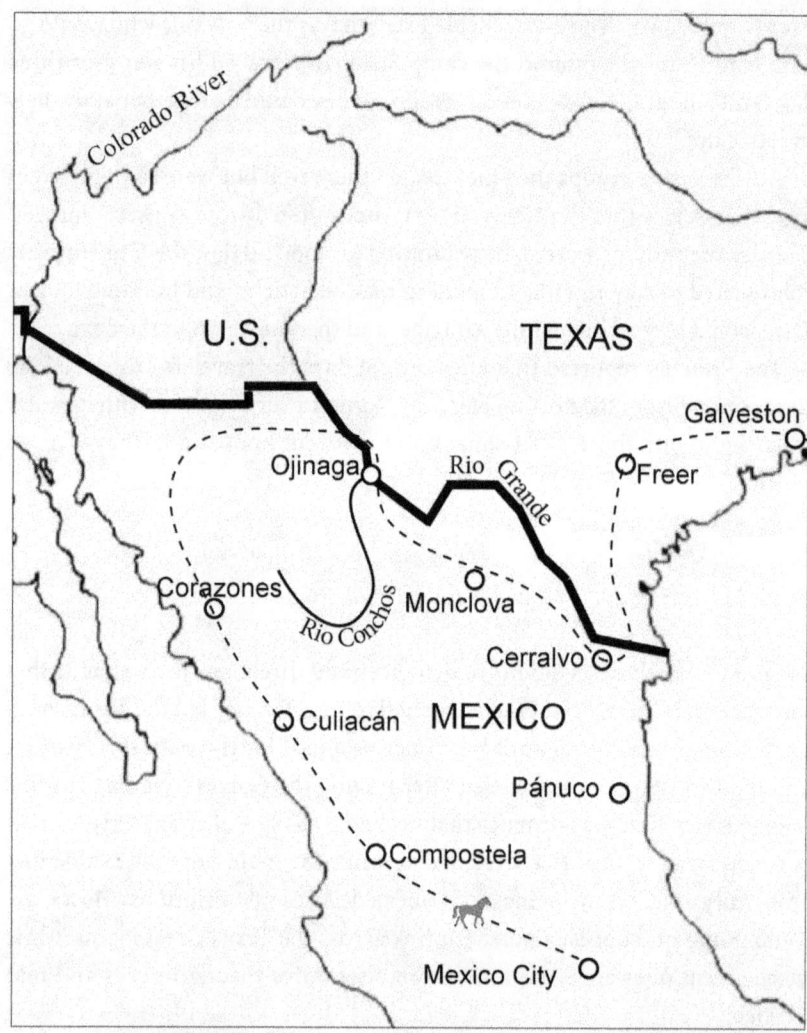

Figure 11. Approximate route on which Esteban and Indian guides led the Narváez survivors across most of Texas and northern Mexico from Malhado, the island near Galveston where the travelers spent six years in slavery. This generalized route is based mostly on the research by Alex D. Krieger in his *We Came Naked and Barefoot*, adapted from maps on pages 70, 109, 137, and 145. Composite map by Dennis Herrick.

coast. Krieger has them descend farther inland instead, almost to Laredo, Texas, entering Mexico more than a hundred miles west of Adorno and Pautz's entry point.

Researchers now seem to have settled on the four travelers' route after they left Velasco Peninsula, at that time Isla de Malhado, near today's Galveston. That route has the expeditionaries going west across southern Texas, bending south into Mexico near Cerralvo, and then traveling west far enough so that they are on the Mexican side of the Rio Grande. Then their route travels north past Monclova before turning west across northern Mexico, and then southerly parallel to the coast on their way to Mexico City.

Change of Mind

Esteban and the three Spaniards had long intended their ultimate goal to be Pánuco. The *Relación* and Joint Report both mention the Pánuco goal several times. When the travelers decided to leave the Avavares, they headed south because their sights were still locked on reaching Pánuco.

Near today's Cerralvo, Mexico, just south of today's Texas border, the four of them made a momentous decision. They might not have known the name of Cortés's Spanish settlement of Santiseban del Puerto, but they knew it was an unknowable distance away near the mouth of the Río Pánuco. Some researchers believe they made a bizarre decision to turn northwest when they knew they were as close to Pánuco as they'd ever been. However, their fear of the Karankawa tribes along the coast where they had suffered for so long gave them second thoughts about taking a route to Pánuco that followed the coast south to the Río Pánuco. Dorantes testified, "These Christians did not want to go in any direction but inland . . . because they had experienced painful mistreatment of those people of the coast."[14] Going north to get around the worst part of the mountains and then west was safer, they decided, even if it meant abandoning their original search for Pánuco. Indians with them also gave assurances that tribes were better natured and there was more food and water that way.

Cabeza de Vaca came up with a more patriotic reason. He claimed in the *Relación* that they decided to travel the much longer way through northern Mexico so they could give helpful advice to future Spaniards who would conquer those regions: "We were doing this because in crossing the land we would be seeing many features of it, for if God our Lord would be pleased to save one of us and carry him to the land of the Christians, he could give information and an account of it."[15] It's not likely that was a major motivation at the time. It sounds more like an afterthought by Cabeza de Vaca to ingratiate himself to the king in his *Relación*, when all three Spaniards were hoping for royal honors and appointments. Cabeza de Vaca also explained the decision by writing that they wanted to go west toward reports of maize being grown in that direction. That would return them to Spanish-held Mexico—New Spain, as they thought of it.

If they'd had a guide who knew the way, from Cerralvo it would have been about three hundred miles in a straight line heading south-southeast to reach the Cortés settlement. From Pánuco, it would have been less than two hundred more miles southwest to reach Mexico City. That's if they could survive and not get lost. By turning north and then walking west across the top of Mexico, and then turning south along the coastline before going east again, they would end up traveling about two thousand miles—about four times farther to reach Mexico City. But they couldn't know that because they had no sense of the continental geography. After deciding against Pánuco, their need to keep near rivers for water and to look for ways to cross the mountains influenced their decisions on where to travel.

Reports of Their Visits

Their journey would leave stories about their passing among generations of Indians. In 1643, more than a hundred years after Cabeza de Vaca's account was published, Captain Alonso de León claimed that Indians near Cerralvo, Mexico, told him about a white man who had passed through there long ago and performed miraculous cures.[16] Oddly, the reference was to just one man. If true, it's presumed that white man was Cabeza de Vaca, Castillo, or Dorantes.

Francisco Vázquez de Coronado heard about them earlier as his expedition's advance force spent the summer of 1541 finding its way across the Great Plains while traveling to Kansas. Juan Jaramillo, one of Coronado's captains, described an encounter with Indians who probably were Teya, a Plains

Apache tribe. The meeting took place in present-day New Mexico or Texas. "Among them was an old, bearded, blind Indian," Jaramillo wrote, "who made us understand through signs he made to us that many days before he had seen four of us. And he indicated he had seen them near there and closer to New Spain [Mexico]. Thus we understood and assumed they were Dorantes and Cabeza de Vaca."[17] Esteban and Castillo would have made up the rest of the foursome.

Pedro de Castañeda de Nájera, a horseman on Coronado's expedition, also described an Indian memory of the four travelers. When Coronado's expedition reached Blanco Canyon in west Texas, Castañeda concluded from what he was told that "Cabeza de Vaca and Dorantes passed this way."[18] Castañeda did not realize the Indians had encountered the Spaniards two hundred miles farther south in their seasonal, nomadic rounds. The Plains tribes covered vast distances in their wanderings, and they would not have thought two hundred miles worth explaining. Similar is the blind Indian's comment, in which six years were passed off as *many days*.

Forty years later in 1581, the friars in the Chamuscado-Rodríguez expedition, which was the first to return to New Mexico since Coronado, reached the junction of the Conchos and Rio Grande Rivers in Mexico. They were surprised by the respect and homage the Indians there extended to them. When the friars asked if the Indians had ever seen people like the Spaniards, they answered that several years before they had been visited by four bearded men, undoubtedly Esteban and his three Spanish companions.[19]

The following year, wealthy Spanish rancher and escaped murderer Antonio de Espejo ventured north from Mexico with a friar and fourteen men-at-arms. He reported Indians living in five pueblos of permanent houses along the Rio Grande upriver from its junction with the Río Conchos. The villages were on both sides of the Rio Grande near the Mexican town of Ojinaga, about 150 miles southeast of El Paso, Texas. The Indians greeted the expedition with food, tanned deerskins, and buffalo hides. Espejo wrote in his report: "These Indians appear to have some light of our holy Catholic faith, because they point to God our Lord, looking up to the heavens. They call him *Apalito* in their tongue, and say that it is He whom they recognize as their Lord and who gives them what they have."[20] The Indians went to Espejo's friar and asked for blessings. When asked where they'd received knowledge of God, Espejo reported the Indians replied through interpreters that they learned from "three Christians and a Negro [who] had passed through there."²¹ Espejo named the three Spaniards but omitted Esteban's name, identifying him simply as a Negro.

In the *Relación*, Cabeza de Vaca had revealed the travelers' contact with these same Indian people in 1535 near the junction of the Río Conchos and Rio Grande. After fording the wide and deep Río Conchos, Esteban and the three Spaniards waited with their accompanying Indians for two women to scout ahead "because these can trade anywhere, even if there be war."²² The women returned after five days and said they hadn't seen many people because the tribes were out hunting for buffalo.

Eager to resume travel, Cabeza de Vaca called upon Esteban and Castillo to go back with the women for a better idea of what lay ahead. In three days the women took the pair to a village, evidently one of the villages that Espejo would visit fifty-four years later. Cabeza de Vaca wrote:

> Alonso del Castillo and *Estevanico el negro* left with the women as guides ... [who] took them to a river [the Rio Grande] that flows between mountains ... and these were the first abodes we saw [since Florida] that were like real houses.²³

Esteban stayed in the village. With his knowledge of sign language and ability to pick up languages, he was to learn what he could from the Indians, negotiate for the travelers' safety, and build good relations. Castillo returned to Cabeza de Vaca and Dorantes to report that he and Esteban "had found permanent houses, inhabited, the people of which ate beans and squashes, and that he had seen maize."²⁴ Cabeza de Vaca would later write about this news of what seemed to be an agricultural village: "Of all things upon Earth this caused us the greatest pleasure, and we gave endless thanks to our Lord for this news. Castillo also said that the Negro was coming to meet us on the way, nearby, with all the people of the houses. For that reason, we started and ... met the Negro and the people that came to receive us, who gave us beans and many squashes to eat, gourds to carry water in, robes of [buffalo] hide, and other things."²⁵

Cabeza de Vaca wrote that he and most Indians with him went north where the women had taken Esteban and Castillo. The trip would have taken them longer than the three days that Esteban, Castillo, and the women required, because there were hundreds of people camping with them. This is the first indication that not all the healers' patients were cured. The major reason the four travelers had paused in their journey and sent Esteban and Castillo ahead was that they needed to continue treating Indians who'd come to them for cures. Dorantes testified that the Indians believed the Christians could heal them, even if they weren't able to cure all.[26] When the women offered to guide them to the village near today's Ojinaga, Mexico, Cabeza de Vaca admitted that some "sick were on the way to recovery" but were not well enough to travel, and so he "ordered those who had been sick to remain and those who were well to accompany us."[27]

It also might have taken a day or more to prepare for departure because they needed to motivate and organize the Indians they'd been caring for to go with them. They eventually left to rejoin Esteban, deciding to leave some Indians behind because they were still not recovered from their real or perceived ailments. During that unspecified period, Esteban remained alone with the villagers.

A time lapse occurred here in the *Relación*, with Cabeza de Vaca never referring to the additional days it took to travel northward. He must have thought it too obvious to mention. So his account should be understood to mean that Esteban and the villagers came forth and met the Spaniards several days after Castillo's return. When they reached the village, the Indians "received us with great ceremonies," which resulted from Esteban's building of goodwill. Although the villagers grew some crops, Cabeza de Vaca and Dorantes did not think they made pottery. Both reported the Indians put heated stones into gourds to cook, bringing the water to a boil and then adding food. They didn't realize these Indians did have pottery, as proved by modern excavations that turned up centuries of pottery near the junction of the two rivers.[28]

These Indians were seminomadic hunters of the bison on the Texas plains. The village Espejo encountered was a base to which the men returned each year when the buffalo herds receded. That village was one of the few places described in the *Relación* where Cabeza de Vaca did not reveal the natives' tribal name. He just called them "people of the cows" because of their dependence on buffalo hunting. Historians have been wondering about their tribe ever since.

The Indians told the travelers that they hadn't grown any corn-like maize for a couple of years because of so little rain, but they showed some that came from people far to the west and north. That was the first maize the four survivors had seen since Florida.

Indian Conversion

No healing is discussed among these Indians, although Cabeza de Vaca reported, "They also begged us to ask heaven for rain, which we promised to do."[29] For such a request to be made, the four travelers must have convinced the Indians that they were blessed with access to a powerful deity. This brief reference to evangelism by the four travelers left the Indians with a familiarity with Christianity that survived for forty-seven years until Espejo's arrival. This encounter is when the villagers came away with the idea of Apalito that Espejo later described.

Because the travelers left the village the very next day, a reasonable conclusion is that the villagers received much of their concept of a new religion from the former Muslim Esteban, not so much from the Spanish Catholics. Therefore, it becomes clearer why their idea of an all-powerful God named Apalito, like the Christian God, could blend with the Muslim practice of prayers celebrating each sunrise and sunset, which Espejo reported.

The three Spaniards were together at the village for just a few waking hours, but Esteban had spent time with them for several days to a week or more. His exotic skin color and powers of persuasion mixed with his sincere sense of friendship must have been compelling, which could have resulted in a syncretism of Islamic and Christian ideas of religion staying with the Indians for decades to come. However, one could argue that the villagers' idea of religion resembled sun worship more than either Christianity or Islam. Espejo's conclusion that their behavior was evidence of Christianity might have been influenced by the Indians mentioning their remembrance of the black man and three white men.

Evangelism

Other episodes describe the travelers' evangelism wherever they went. Cabeza de Vaca wrote: "We told [tribes] by signs which they understood that in heaven there was a man called God by us, who had created heaven and earth, and whom we worshipped as our Lord . . . all good things coming from His hand, and that if they were to do the same thing they would become very happy . . . all this we gave them to understand as clearly as possible."[30] The Spaniards would have relied upon Esteban to deliver that religious lesson because the Spaniards held themselves aloof and Esteban could communicate the best. That message reinforced the idea the travelers tried to always convey—that they were Children of the Sun and merited respect and good treatment.

After the short visit near the Río Conchos and Rio Grande, the African and three Spaniards left to find the maize growers, walking north for two weeks along the Rio Grande to get beyond the most rugged of the Sierra Madre mountains before turning west. The land from that village onward was described as well settled. Agricultural produce became available with beans and squash—and the corn-like maize.

Faith healing of Indians returned then to the forefront of the *Relación* and Joint Report narratives.

Religious Fervor

Thinly disguised biblical references started popping into Cabeza de Vaca's account while he was still in Texas. He believed he healed the sick, was saved by a burning tree in the desert, raised a man from the dead, and was rescued by divine intervention.

Cabeza de Vaca became lost on the plains. Religious before, now Cabeza de Vaca became mystic. Although naked and lost, he said he was saved when he found a burning tree. A lightning strike? He wrote only that "it pleased God" to let him find it. The tree burned all night, he reported, keeping him warm and enabling him to travel with burning sticks for five days until he found his way to the Avavare camp from which he'd strayed.

At the Avavare camp, according to Cabeza de Vaca—or later in Mexico, according to Dorantes—several Indians brought five natives who were ill and asked Castillo to cure them. Some translators said the Indians had headaches, but the afflictions are never described in detail. The travelers prayed for Castillo's cure to help the Indians. They might have prayed even harder to avoid having the Indians become disappointed or angry if Castillo failed. "And [God], seeing there was no other way of getting those people to help us so that we might be saved from our miserable existence, had mercy upon us," Cabeza de Vaca recalled. "And in the morning all woke up well and hearty and went away in such good health as if they never had any ailment whatever."[31] Word of the successes spread to other tribes. Cabeza de Vaca wrote that "nothing was talked about in this whole country but of the wonderful cures which God, our Lord, performed through us, and so they came from many places to be cured."[32] The four of them traveled from tribe to tribe as healers.

Cabeza de Vaca raised a man in a Sausolas village in Mexico from the dead. So it seemed at least. Castillo feared he might be pressing his luck on that case. So Cabeza de Vaca, always the brave and confident one in his account, wrote that he went to the man's village with Esteban and Dorantes. When they arrived, the Indians were in mourning and said the man had died. Esteban and Dorantes agreed it appeared the man was lifeless. Undeterred, however, the self-styled hero Cabeza de Vaca reported he made the sign of the cross, prayed, and breathed on the man many times. Esteban and the two Spaniards must have been a bit unnerved when the man still appeared to be dead. They knew Indians could turn vengeful if they decided the travelers were charlatans.

However, the Sausolas Indians paid Cabeza de Vaca with the man's bow and some prickly pear cactus fruits. Fear of failure before had brought fear of punishment, but the Spaniards' fame as shamans now appeared to be so great that Indians accepted occasional failure. Cabeza de Vaca said the Sausolas then sent him to treat many others who suffered from dizziness. That night Indians ran to them and said the man who was thought to have died had revived and was talking, walking, and eating. As expected, the man's recovery "caused great surprise and awe," Cabeza de Vaca recalled, "and all over the land nothing else was spoken of."[33] More Indians came with ailments including headaches, other pains, cramps, and dizziness, paying for their treatment with food. Many were not cured until after eating and a night of rest, but that never seemed to raise doubts among the natives. Nor did it shake the confidence of the Spaniards and African. Cabeza de Vaca wrote:

Until then Dorantes and the Negro had not made any cures, but we found ourselves so pressed by the Indians coming from all sides, that all of us had to become medicine men.[34]

Castillo worried that his sins might make his cures ineffective. And Dorantes might have shared the same concern about himself. All three Spaniards must have been concerned whether God would assist a mere African slave. After all, Esteban converted from Islam, which good Catholics then considered to be as heretical as Judaism and deserving of the Inquisition's torturous deaths. But all four worked as healers because they saw shamanism as their salvation. More Indians showed up as the Spanish Catholics and Esteban the former Muslim were put into service. The demands of impressionable Indians to be cured by these strangers continued. "I was the most daring and reckless of all in undertaking cures," Cabeza de Vaca boasted.[35]

From that point on, Esteban and the three Spaniards were welcomed and treated well as they went mostly westward and sometimes northward in following rivers and mountain passes. Along the way they treated Indians in tribe after tribe. More than a century later, a Spanish judge cited what he called the four travelers' "miraculous cures" as proof that God wanted Catholics to dominate the Americas.[36]

Spaniards who read Cabeza de Vaca's account afterward were divided. Were the healing powers God's divine intervention? Miracles, in other words, manifested through the four naked or nearly naked travelers?[37] Or were they fantasies? Fantasy or not, the Indians continued believing cures were being performed. The curing ability, real or perceived, turned the four travelers into celebrities. Indian treatment of them improved so much that faith healing saved their lives.

Cabeza de Vaca claimed that unspecified medical skills enabled him to perform surgery. The one example he described occurred when he was with a tribe somewhere in eastern Mexico. "Here they brought to me a man who . . . a long time ago had been shot through the left side of the back with an arrow, the head of which stuck close to his heart. . . . So with a [stone] knife I cut open the breast. . . . By cutting deeper and inserting the point of the knife, with great difficulty I got [the arrowhead] out. It was very long.[38] Then with a deer bone, according to my knowledge of surgery, I made two stitches. . . . The next day I cut the stitches, and the Indian was well."[39] Such unsanitary stone-knife success and rapid recovery must give modern surgeons pause.

Regardless, more fame resulted. Large groups of Indians followed them as they traveled to other tribes, hailing the curing abilities of the African and Spaniards. As historian John Upton Terrell puts it, "It was a supreme demonstration of positive thinking; a moving testament to the power of faith."[40] Another historian, the late David J. Weber, wrote that the travelers succeeded in "posing as holy men who possessed the power to heal more through power of suggestion than medicine."[41]

Despite more time in the Americas in later years, Cabeza de Vaca never again mentioned his healing ability except for the Indians on this journey. His later account of his governorship in South America refers to illness among Indians and Spaniards several times, but his only reaction was the hope that "God would give them back their health."[42]

Toward the Maize

After Cerralvo and Ojinaga, the *Relación* related that the travelers kept hearing more stories of maize and even cotton blankets far ahead. This would have been almost unbelievable news for the shamans, who had seen naked and half-starved Texas Indians surviving on whatever they could hunt or dig up to eat. Fields of maize and other crops, cotton blankets and clothes, plus permanent villages indicated the advanced culture of the Pueblo tribes to the north and also what would turn out to be the Ópata and Pima-related people to the west, none of whom the travelers had ever heard of until then.

They are believed to have walked to within seventy-five miles south of El Paso when Cabeza de Vaca said they thought for two days about what to do. They decided to turn west "in search of the maize" and not travel farther north toward the sure food of the buffalo herds, "as we held it always certain that by going toward sunset we should reach the goal of our wishes."[43]

Esteban advanced westward ahead of them, meeting and making friends with different tribes as they searched for the maize growers. Upon nearing the coast at the end, they veered southeast to follow the coastal plain. Cabeza de Vaca conceded that they depended upon Esteban to guide them forward safely.

"It was the Negro who talked to [the Indians] all the time," Cabeza de Vaca wrote. "He inquired about the road we should follow, the villages—in short, about everything we wished to know."[44]

There are numerous indications in the *Relación* that affirm that the Spaniards never deigned to be as sociable as Esteban. The privileged Spaniards feared familiarity might lower their esteem in the eyes of others, resulting in them being thought of as just ordinary men, which they could never tolerate. "We exercised great authority over them and carried ourselves with much gravity, and, in order to maintain it, spoke very little to them," Cabeza de Vaca wrote, in explaining why they left it up to Esteban to talk with the Indians.[45] That attitude ensured Esteban's role as the survivors' most important member. As author Laila Lalami points out, "The translator is the person who holds all the power: he can decide what, and how much, gets said to either side."[46] The result was that the Indians grew close to Esteban, who talked, laughed, and became their friend.

Cabeza de Vaca attributed their success to God. However, he could just as well have been referring to Esteban as being God's instrument for "opening roads for us through a land so deserted, bringing us people where many times there were none, and liberating us from so many dangers and not permitting us to be killed, and sustaining us through so much hunger, and inspiring these people to treat us well."[47]

The general route across southern Texas and northern Mexico as described in this book meets the consensus of several leading modern researchers.[48] But as a biography of Esteban, only a general route is needed to show where he and the Spaniards traveled. The route details are not as important as the fact that it was Esteban who communicated with the tribes and led the way.

CHAPTER 13

Esteban's Rise and Fall

ONCE ON THE Mexican side of the Rio Grande, with the four shamans now assured safe passage because of their esteem as traveling healers, Esteban's role increased. Charles C. Mann in his book *1493* writes that "by some measures" Esteban became the group's leader. It was Esteban who ventured forth as scout and forward ambassador to the natives as the four of them walked across the continent, then down between the Gulf of California and the Sierra Madre Mountains and into central Mexico. "He certainly held the Spaniards' lives in his hands every time he encountered a new group and, rattling his shaman's gourd, explained who they were," Mann wrote.[1]

Without Esteban, it's doubtful the Spaniards would have survived. That in effect made him the leader, despite Cabeza de Vaca's effort to write himself into that role. Esteban began being mentioned often in the *Relación* and Joint Report, appearing in the kinds of leadership roles that Cabeza de Vaca once reserved for himself. The name "Dorantes" is present in almost every important event Cabeza de Vaca described in crossing Texas and Mexico. From the context, it's often uncertain whether the acts involve Andrés Dorantes, or Esteban de Dorantes, or both, or either, because a slave's achievement was routinely credited to the slaveowner. It can be certain, however, that wherever Andrés Dorantes was, Esteban would almost always be by his side.

In one surprising incident near today's Monclova in northeastern Mexico, the *Relación* reported that a group of Indian traders from farther west gave a large copper rattle with a facial image to Andrés Dorantes.[2] One could ask, however, which is more likely: (1) Indians gave the metal object "which they held in great esteem" to a Spaniard, or (2) they gave it to Esteban, whom they liked, respected, and socialized with, who then handed it over to his slaveowner?

Richard R. Wright Sr., a former slave and the highest-ranking African American officer as a major during the Spanish-American War, addressed this point in a 1902 article. He asked why Esteban "remained practically in obscurity for more than three and a half centuries?" In answering his own question, Wright explained that "historians were not careful to note with any degree of accuracy and with due credit the useful and noble deeds of the Negro companions of Spanish conquerors, because Negroes were slaves, the property of masters who were supposed to be entitled to the credit for whatever the latter accomplished."[3] Therefore, Spanish chronicles were faithful to the way slaves were ignored in the 1500s, crediting his or her owner for any positive thing that was done by a slave.

Although Cabeza de Vaca said the metal object with a facial image was given to Andrés Dorantes, that's not what Dorantes reported in the account he told to historian Oviedo for the Joint Report. Dorantes made no claim for the gift, Oviedo writing only that Dorantes said the Indians gave a brass rattle to the shamans.[4] The metal object was a remarkable discovery and was presented with the first cotton blankets the travelers had seen since at least 1528. Cabeza de Vaca mentions the metal artifact one more time, when Indians told him it came from the western coastal area. This first reference to the Pacific Ocean must have excited the travelers and given them a false impression that the ocean could not be far away. They could not realize how far trade goods traveled in northern Mexico and the American Southwest.[5]

The four shamans believed they were heading toward the Pacific. It would be three more years before anyone realized that the Baja Peninsula and a gulf separated the ocean from that portion of the Mexican coast.[6] The gulf was known as the Sea of Cortés for more than three hundred years, but it has become better known as the Gulf of California.

"After leaving these people, we traveled among so many tribes and languages that nobody's memory can recall them all," Cabeza de Vaca wrote. "The number of our [Indian escort] became so large that we could no longer control them."[7] Cabeza de Vaca estimated that the Indians accompanying them were in the hundreds and at times in the thousands. Regardless of whether such totals were exaggerated, the masses of people were so large that Cabeza de Vaca complained, "It was very tiresome to have to breathe on and make the sign of the cross over every morsel they ate or drank."[8]

Nevertheless, Esteban and the three Spaniards blessed everyone's food and water as well as continued their healing activities to maintain the Indians' belief in their spiritual powers. It would have been an astonishing sight if any European had seen a black man and three Spaniards leading such a large contingent of Indian admirers across Mexico.

A Mystery of Language

Manual gestures of sign language were a means of communication among the many tribes of Native Americans then as it is now for members of the deaf community.[9] Esteban became skilled in the sign language used by tribes across America and Mexico, and combined that with the words he learned in several spoken languages.

Esteban's fluency in both signs and languages enabled him to lead the three Spaniards through numerous tribes across northern Mexico, where Cabeza de Vaca said the travelers encountered many tribes, which he lumped together as Primahaitu because they spoke one language. Cabeza de Vaca reported, "For more than four hundred leagues . . . we found this language in use, and the only one among them over that extent of the country."[10] That distance would be more than a thousand miles if his estimate was correct.[11] However, the distance probably was more like eight hundred or so miles, which is still close for any rough calculation by someone who had only a faint idea of where he was, knowing little more than that he was somewhere north of Mexico City.

Primahaitu seems to have been a transregional trade routes language used by related tribes.[12] The nineteenth-century anthropologist T. Buckingham Smith theorized it could have been a reference to the language of the Pima Indians, also known as the O'odham, who in the sixteenth century occupied the Sonoran Desert and Sonoran Ecoregion, stretching across northern Mexico and south to Sinaloa as well as north to above today's Phoenix in what is now Arizona.[13] Mutually intelligible Pima language dialects were spoken by the Sobaipuri and several tribes along the four travelers' route. "All these nations . . . excepting the Apaches," Smith suggests, "speak the same language, with so slight differences, say the missionaries, that they who shall have attained the one . . . with little difficulty will master the rest."[14] That must have been the Primahaitu that Cabeza de Vaca wrote about. Esteban would have become fluent in Primahaitu over the months of travel through Mexico.

There continues to be confusion about Primahaitu, resulting in many respected historians as well as other writers avoiding the issue by omitting any reference to it. For example, there is no mention of such a widespread idiom in Oviedo's Joint Account, influenced by Dorantes and Castillo.[15] Cabeza de Vaca did refer to it again in his 1555 *La relación y comentarios*.[16]

In the *Relación*, Cabeza de Vaca mentioned a Primahaitu-Spanish interpreter for the Christians. Was that person an Indian who spoke Spanish and Primahaitu? Was it a Spaniard who had learned Primahaitu or could understand the language of an Indian who also knew Primahaitu? Or was it the converted Christian who was fluent in Spanish and Primahaitu—Esteban? From what little is known, that interpreter could have been Esteban, which would have been in keeping with his role as communicator between Spaniards and Indians. Cabeza de Vaca was probably marginal in understanding the language. Esteban would have been the primary person using Primahaitu to talk with the Indians, not Cabeza de Vaca, who admitted he spoke very little with them.

Showing the Way

Because Cabeza de Vaca reported the language being used as far south as Culiacán, Esteban would have used the language three years later, finding it spoken almost all the way to Hawikku. Esteban's ability to learn signs and Indian languages would enable him to earn the Indians' trust, respect, and most important of all, the cooperation that the travelers, and later Friar Marcos, needed.

Esteban learned what it was like to be an independent person in the eight years spent in Texas or Mexico. This was especially true in the last year and a half, when the three Spaniards with him depended on him to make friends and communicate with the tribes they encountered. Terrell's 1968 description of

Esteban illustrates how the three Spaniards began to realize Esteban's importance. Terrell concludes:

> If legally he remained a chattel of Dorantes, in reality he was a partner. ... The *Relación* gives the impression that he was big and powerful, that he had the cunning of a panther and the heart of a lion. ... He had a greater facility for learning tongues than the others, and he was a master of the sign language. He had already shown a diplomatic ability. ... In the face of perilous situations he displayed a calmness and wisdom that made him not only reliable but a force to be heeded and admired. He marched on through the wilderness, defying the elements, cursing the dangers and hardships, a pillar of strength, and a monument to the brave of the world.[17]

Robert Goodwin points out that, as always through their journey out of Texas and across Mexico, "Cabeza de Vaca is ever the hero of his own story, but Esteban is never far away."[18]

Esteban, Castillo, and Dorantes deferred to Cabeza de Vaca and obeyed him because they respected him, and also because as a royal official he outranked them even though they were lost together in the wilderness. They also seemed to have recognized that Cabeza de Vaca displayed leadership qualities they lacked, and they realized someone must be in charge if they were to survive. Time after time, however, the Spaniards turned to Esteban when they needed help from Indians. That had been true since their escape from the Karankawas, and his essential role increased soon after crossing into Mexico in the late summer of 1535.

Pueblo Influence

After entering Mexico, the travelers kept hearing more stories of rich Indian cities to the north, which they would report after arriving in Mexico City. Although the term "Pueblo Indians" had not yet been conceived, the *Relación* told about "many good turquoises, which they get from the north."

Esteban led them to the land of the Sobaipuri people. The Sobaipuris occupied northern Sonora and southern Arizona when Europeans first entered the area. The travelers reported villagers showed them gourds that they said came from heaven, "because in that land there are none nor do they know where there are any, except that the rivers bring them when they flood [from Pueblo territory in the north]."[19]

After a bit more than a month of travel through the mountainous terrain of the Sierra Madre with its snowy peaks, they reached the land of maize they'd heard about, the villages of the populous Ópata tribe on a plain extending to the ocean and as yet untouched by Spanish invasion. The Ópatas lived in small adobe houses instead of brush shelters. Dorantes later estimated they traveled more than two hundred leagues from there to the northernmost Spanish town of Culiacán, a distance of more than five hundred miles.[20] If his reckoning is correct, the first Ópata towns would have been a few days walk west of the ancient Casas Grandes ruin, halfway across northern Mexico.

"Among those people we found the women better treated than in any other part of the Indies as far as we have seen," Cabeza de Vaca recalled.[21] He reported that Ópata men were naked but the women wore deerskin clothes, cotton blankets, and buffalo robes and lived in villages of permanent, flat-roofed houses of adobe similar to what Spaniards would find a few years later in the Pueblo country.[22] Dorantes concluded that the clothing and flat roofs were the influence of trading with villages to the north where the still mysterious Pueblo Indians lived in New Mexico.[23]

All across the Ópata homeland they were fed maize, toasted flour (tortillas), beans, and squashes. They saw beads of coral from the Pacific, which told them they were approaching the continent's western boundary, as well as turquoises, cotton blankets, and buffalo robes that the Ópatas traded for in the north. The *Relación* then reports additional gifts. In another village, as with the metal object that had a human face on it, Cabeza de Vaca reported that Indians gave another prized possession to Dorantes, describing "emeralds shaped as arrow-points."[24]

In the Joint Report, Dorantes never mentioned the green arrowheads, which are now believed to have been malachite. That opens the possibility that the arrowheads were given to Esteban de Dorantes, not to the Spaniard. Esteban seems the most probable original recipient because Dorantes didn't think them worth mentioning, or if he did, Oviedo didn't announce a discovery of what Spaniards would have considered valuable gems.

Cabeza de Vaca's continual mention of emeralds in the *Relación* reinforced rumors about riches in the Indian cities to the north, which would later be revealed as Zuni towns and be called the Seven Cities of Cíbola. "I asked whence they got them from," Cabeza de Vaca wrote, referring to the arrowheads and turquoise jewelry. "They said it was from some very high mountains toward the north where they traded for them with feather-bushes and parrot plumes, and they said also that there were villages with many people and very big houses."[25] This is a clear description of the Pueblo villages and the trade networks circulating in and out of today's New Mexico.

Esteban and the Spaniards walked on for at least two hundred more miles, always in Ópata territory, until they arrived at a cluster of three towns. Dorantes said Indians from the Pacific coast met them there, and from what they said, Dorantes concluded the coast was about forty or so miles westerly.[26] It might have been farther because Dorantes based his estimate on how fast Indians traveled instead of the pace conquistadors walked.

At the three towns Ópatas presented still another major gift, this time of dried deer hearts to feed them and their Indian escorts.[27] Once again, Cabeza de Vaca said the gift was given to Dorantes, while the Joint Report quoted apparently Dorantes as saying that "the natives there gave them more than six hundred deer hearts."[28] One could wonder why Cabeza de Vaca reports that no one except Dorantes ever receives valuable gifts such as a metal rattle or bell, five so-called emerald arrowheads, and finally six hundred deer hearts. Dorantes never takes personal credit for the gifts, so it seems likely they were given to Esteban, who turned them over to his owner, Andrés Dorantes. The gift of deer hearts was so staggering in its generosity to men enduring desperate years half-starved that they named that town and others around it Pueblo de los Corazones, the Village of the Hearts.

The Los Corazones name stuck for long after, and many researchers believe the travelers were at or near the village of Ures, in Sonora's Corazones Valley, about 130 miles south of today's Mexico-US border. William and Gayle Hartmann conclude that Los Corazones might have been at Ures but also might have been about eighteen miles farther northeast at Mazocahui. Anthropologist Alex Krieger concludes the Village of the Hearts was just south or southeast of today's Hermosillo, fifty miles farther southwest from Ures.[29] Researchers Rolena Adorno and Patrick Pautz believe the Village of the Hearts was even farther from Ures, pointing to a site far east-southeast of Hermosillo in the mountains at today's Onavas, Mexico, although that is an unlikely location for Los Corazones because it is about 120 miles from the coast.[30] The disagreement among scholars indicates how difficult it is to be precise in dealing with the travelers' locations, which were described so vaguely because Cabeza de Vaca and Dorantes didn't know where they were.[31]

Four years later, Coronado established his first rear base at Los Corazones to protect his supply and communication lines.[32] Coronado, who arrived in 1540 and knew his location, estimated the distance from Los Corazones to the coast was five days' travel, or about 75 or so miles by trail.[33] Krieger's proposed site near Hermosillo for Los Corazones at 70 miles due west from the coast is closest to Coronado's estimate, while Ures and Mazocahui villages are too far at 112 and 136 miles due west, respectively.[34] Somewhere in between?

The location of Los Corazones was well known into the seventeenth century and only lost in modern times.[35] After Los Corazones, wherever it was, Indians escorted the four travelers southward and entered the territory of the Yaqui tribe in southern Sonora. Although the travelers might not have known it, the powerful Yaquis had driven away a Spanish invasion force just four years earlier.[36] Conquistadors were never able to permanently subdue the Yaqui tribe, a proud and numerous people. The Yaquis and later the Mexican government fought sporadically, with the last major battle in October 1927.

The Yaqui territory also marked a major cultural boundary. To the north were the tribes influenced by the Pueblo culture of today's New Mexico. Beginning with the Yaquis, the people lived in houses of mat and straw and did not wear cotton clothes.[37]

Slave Hunters

On the best southward trail, Esteban and the rest were forced to wait for about two weeks near present-day Cócorit before crossing a river running high and fast with spring flooding from mountain snowmelt. It was there they received their first glimpse of Spanish presence.

Hundreds of Indians visited their camp beside the river, and one day

Castillo recognized a sword belt buckle hanging on a thong around one warrior's neck. Tied to the belt was a horseshoe nail. He ran to tell Cabeza de Vaca, taking the Indian with his buckle and nail with him. "We asked what it was," Cabeza de Vaca wrote. "They said it had come from heaven. We further asked who brought it, and they answered that some men like us, with beards like ours, had come from heaven to that river. That they had horses, lances, and swords, and had lanced two of them. As cautiously as possible, we inquired what had become of those men. They replied they had gone to sea, putting their lances into the water and going into it themselves, and that afterward they saw them on top of the waves going toward the sunset."[38] Cabeza de Vaca recalled that the Spaniards' joy at hearing about the presence again of Europeans was balanced against fear that the Indians with them might be killed or enslaved. As they ventured farther south, discovering more traces of Europeans and horses, they assured the Indians with them that they would not allow the Christians to harm or enslave them.

A contingent made up of Ópatas, Upper and Lower Pimans, and now Yaquis and probably also Mayos guided them about eighty more miles southward, staying close to the game-rich mountain chain and avoiding poorer areas toward the Pacific coast. "We traveled over a great part of the country and found it all deserted, as the people had fled to the mountains, leaving houses and fields out of fear of the Christians," the *Relación* reported. "This filled our hearts with sorrow, seeing the land so fertile and beautiful, so full of water and streams, but abandoned and the places burned down, and the people so thin and wan, fleeing and hiding."[39] Perhaps their own years of enslavement had given the three Spaniards a better ability to understand the consequences of slavery on other people.

At first, the three Spaniards feared that the Indians would take vengeance on at least them for the Spanish slave hunting. But when they climbed a steep trail to the top of a mountain where local people hid as refugees, those victims of aggression shared maize with all four travelers and the hundreds of famished Indians accompanying them. The *Relación* reported: "They brought us blankets, which they had been concealing from the Christians, and gave them to us, and told us how the Christians had penetrated into the country before, and had destroyed and burnt the villages, taking with them half the men and all of the women and children, and how those who could escaped by flight."[40]

Esteban was traveling through the area he would revisit three years later when he guided Friar Marcos de Niza north to find the fabled "Seven Cities," a term used since at least 1530 by Spaniards who'd heard tales of rich Indian towns to the north.[41] Well remembered by the region's Indians, Esteban's reputation for friendship and honest relations with them would ensure safe passage for both him and the friar. News of Spanish slave hunters must have stirred great anxiety in Esteban. The African could envision a future for himself in which the Spaniards might thrust him down into harsher and deadlier servitude. He could sense his camaraderie with the three Spaniards ebbing away.

Dorantes said they'd traveled about 260 miles from Los Corazones when Indian runners told how they'd seen from their hiding places a group of Spaniards who'd captured Indians and shackled them in chains. "At this," Cabeza de Vaca wrote, "the people who were with us became frightened, and some turned back to give the alarm throughout the land that Christians were coming."[42] To keep more of their Indians from deserting, the Spaniards kept promising them they would be safe. Esteban must have considered deserting as well.

Cabeza de Vaca wrote that he entreated Castillo and Dorantes to go forward to find the Spanish horsemen. Both refused. "Seeing their reluctance, in the morning I took with me the Negro and eleven Indians and, following the trail, went in search of the Christians."[43] Cabeza de Vaca, now seeing himself close to being rescued by Spaniards, no longer seems to consider Esteban one of his *companions*, if he ever did. However, Esteban had again demonstrated he possessed more courage and fortitude than Castillo or Dorantes by agreeing to go. Historian Paul Schneider sums up Esteban's situation:

> Esteban the enigmatic—black-skinned Moroccan, Arabic speaking, Christianized, slave of Arabs perhaps, slave of Spaniards, slave of [different Indian tribes], front man and translator for the wandering faith healers. He is the least discussed yet most intriguing character in the entire expedition.[44]

They found the Spaniards on the second day. No one can know what Esteban thought as he accompanied Cabeza de Vaca to find the Spanish slavers because no one recorded his thoughts. It was late March 1536 when four Spanish horsemen were startled to see two thin and mostly naked men, one an African slave and the other a Spanish nobleman, step out of the thickets. Esteban and Cabeza de Vaca were back among conquistadors for the first time in almost eight years. The horsemen comprised one of Governor Nuño Beltrán de Guzmán's slave-hunting patrols scouring the region. Linking up with the raiders took place in today's state of Sinaloa, Mexico. Cabeza de Vaca estimated the encounter occurred about seventy-five miles north of Spanish-held Culiacán.[45] By his estimate, the event would have taken place within a few miles of Guasave, Mexico.

Cabeza de Vaca reported that the slave raiders were dumbstruck by the sight of him and Esteban when he greeted them in Castilian Spanish. He wrote, "I [and Esteban, who abruptly ceases to be mentioned] came upon four Christians on horseback, who, seeing me in such a strange attire, and in company with Indians, were greatly startled. They stared at me for quite awhile, speechless. So great was their surprise that they could not find words to ask me anything."[46]

Upon the horsemen's appearance, Esteban's status plummeted. For at least the past year and a half, he'd been the most vital member of the four survivors' troupe. He'd opened the way westward for the others through the territories of tribe after tribe, ensuring their safety, good treatment, and continued travel. Esteban knew in that instant that his dark skin doomed him to renewed slave status. If he dared to disobey or speak back, he would be beaten or even executed. Cabeza de Vaca reported he told the horsemen to take him to their captain.[47] The captain would turn out to be Diego de Alcaraz.

Alcaraz was notorious for his brutality and raiding for slaves. Years later he joined the Coronado expedition and was left behind at San Gerónimo III in northern Sonora to guard Coronado's rear area. Ópata Indians told a Spanish expedition two decades later that Alcaraz and his men seized "wives and daughters to use for dishonorable purposes," so they retaliated in 1542, killing Alcaraz and forcing abandonment of Coronado's rear garrison.[48]

The horsemen took Esteban, the Spaniard, and the Indians a short distance to where Alcaraz was camped with more of his men and Indian guides on a river. Historian Cyclone Covey believes Alcaraz's camp was near present-day Ocoroni, Mexico, on the Sinaloa River near the mountain foothills. However, he also indicates that the site was thirty leagues from

Culiacán, but Ocoroni is about thirty-eight leagues away, whereas Cabeza de Vaca estimated the campsite was twenty-eight or thirty leagues from Culiacán.[49] If Cabeza de Vaca's estimates were accurate, it's more probable Alcaraz's camp was near today's river through San Rafael or the Sinaloa River through Guasave, both near the mountains.[50] In any case, Alcaraz would have been camped in today's wide and rich agricultural valley on Mexico's western coast that runs along the mountains north of Culiacán.

Esteban was not mentioned as attending any meetings with Alcaraz. Cabeza de Vaca was dark from sun exposure, and Alcaraz might have briefly wondered if he was a Spanish-speaking Indian. Confident he could protect his Indian companions, or perhaps intimidated by unreported Alcaraz threats, Cabeza de Vaca exposed the location of his Indian escort. "I stated to [Alcaraz] that, in the rear of me, at a distance of ten leagues [about twenty-six miles], were Dorantes and Castillo, with many people who had guided us through the country."[51] Alcaraz dispatched three horsemen and fifty Indian allies to look for Dorantes and Castillo. "The Negro went with them as guide," Cabeza de Vaca noted, bringing Esteban back into the account.[52]

Five days later, Esteban returned with Dorantes and Castillo as well as "more than six hundred Indians . . . which the Christians had caused to flee to the woods and who were in hiding about the country."[53] In the later Joint Report, the chronicler Oviedo wrote that the Spaniards "were much more amazed upon hearing [Cabeza de Vaca] tell how he had passed through so many lands with different peoples and languages." The three Spaniards were told to give a sworn statement about their experiences.[54] Esteban was not included.

After the surprise wore off about finding four survivors of the long-lost Narváez expedition, Alcaraz realized that six hundred potential slaves were within his grasp. Cabeza de Vaca's account passed over two big questions. Why would he be so naïve as to think he could protect Indians from such marauders, and why were the Indians so reckless to think he could protect them?

Cabeza de Vaca wrote that he told his Indians to go back to their tribes and plant their crops. But it was too late to think of that by then because Alcaraz would have stopped them. They replied they wanted to stay until they could be sure that Esteban and the three Spaniards were safe, adding that "as long as we were with them, they had no fear of the Christians and of their lances."[55] Alcaraz's interpreter told the travelers' faithful Indians that

Cabeza de Vaca, Dorantes, and Castillo were Spaniards just like the slave hunters. But he said they were unlucky and lost for a long time and were now returned along with the Negro to Alcaraz and his men, who were lords of the land. The Indians didn't believe it.

Cabeza de Vaca's next entry in his account became one of the great passages in history, where the emotion of a people usually with no voice resonates across centuries. What the Indians said reveals how devoted they felt toward the four shamans. It also provides an insight into how Cabeza de Vaca's own years of living among the Indians changed his original way of thinking about them. It was a daring message he sent to his own countrymen when he wrote:

> [The Indians] parlayed among themselves, saying that the Christians lied, for we had come from the sunrise, while the others came from where the sun sets; that we cured the sick, while the others killed those who were healthy; that we went naked and shoeless, whereas the others wore clothes and went on horseback and had lances. Also, that we asked for nothing, but gave away all we were presented with, meanwhile the others seemed to have no other aim than to steal what they could and never gave anything to anybody.[56]

Michael Wood points out that Cabeza de Vaca must have chosen his words carefully and also with trepidation about how his Spanish audience would receive that passage. "All conventional categories of the Age of Conquest seemed to slip," Wood wrote in his book, *Conquistadors*. "Even though [Cabeza de Vaca] took pains elsewhere in his book to emphasize how he had not lost his Christian faith, was he saying he was now not quite the same as the Christians? Was he being ironical? Or was he asking his audience to see the Christians as a stranger might?"[57]

The *Relación* reports, "We never could convince the Indians that we belonged to the other Christians. . . . We gave the Christians a great many [buffalo] robes and other objects and had much trouble in persuading the Indians to return home."[58] Cabeza de Vaca continued: "We had many and bitter quarrels with the Christians, for they wanted to make slaves of our Indians, and we grew so angry at it that at our departure [to go to Culiacán and then on to Mexico City] we forgot to take along many bows and arrows, also the five emeralds, and so they were left and lost to us."[59] A Spaniard expressing opposition to enslaving Indians made Alcaraz suspicious. He arrested Esteban and all three Spaniards.[60]

Cabeza de Vaca's concern for the Indians signified that he now felt some degree of kinship with them. For the rest of his life, his experiences in the Americas would make him an advocate for better treatment of Indians. His advice to the king echoed the lifelong commitment of Friar Bartolomé de las Casas when he wrote, "To bring those people to Christianity and obedience unto Your Imperial Majesty, they should be well treated, and not otherwise."[61] His more enlightened attitude resulted in Baker H. Morrow stating that Cabeza de Vaca became "the greatest secular champion of the Indians in the sixteenth century."[62]

Alcaraz decided to let Culiacán's Spanish commander, Melchior Díaz, sort out what to make of this Spaniard who seemed so unorthodox. Alcaraz didn't make the trip to Culiacán easy for the weary travelers, sending them on a roundabout route through trackless wilderness. If he hoped they would perish on the dangerous trip, he underestimated the toughness of Esteban and the three Spaniards, who'd managed to survive years of incredible deprivation and exertion.

Alcaraz assigned a man named Cebreros, two other horse-mounted slave hunters, and several Indian allies to go with them. Cabeza de Vaca complained, "He took us through forests and uninhabited country in order to prevent our communicating with the Indians . . . to prevent us from seeing or hearing what the Christians were carrying on."[63] He continued, "[Cebreros] took us through the timber for two days, with no trail, bewildered and without water, so we all expected to die from thirst." Seven Indians did perish on the trip, their bodies left in the woods.

According to the Joint Report, Spanish commander Melchior Díaz met them about twenty-one miles north of Culiacán. Díaz treated them well and gave thanks to God for the survival of these "gentlemen."[64] Esteban was not included in that honorific. When chronicler Oviedo named the *gentlemen*, he listed just the three Spaniards. Their treatment improved because Díaz realized these four Narváez survivors were heroes. "He was deeply moved and praised God for having delivered us in His great pity," Cabeza de Vaca wrote. "He appeared much grieved at the bad reception and evil treatment we had met at the hands of Alcaraz and the others."[65]

In his 1555 revision of the *Relación*, Cabeza de Vaca explained what happened to the Indians who'd accompanied him, writing, "We wanted only to seek freedom for the Indians, and when we thought we had done so the exact opposite occurred, for the Spaniards had agreed to fall upon those whom we had sent away reassured and in peace."[66] He learned that Alcaraz detained as many as he could catch of the six hundred Indians so he could sell them as slaves, especially to silver mines, which always needed more slaves because of high fatality rates for African and Indian miners.

Díaz heard their story of survival and cross-continent travel. Díaz and Viceroy Mendoza would have recognized the value of the information the Narváez survivors knew about the unexplored areas to the north. For the next few days in Díaz's forward camp something happened that no one expected. It started when Díaz announced his sudden revelation. One of history's great omissions is why he took a stand against enslaving Indians after talking with the Narváez survivors.

Díaz had been disturbed since his recent arrival in Culiacán at how the land had been abandoned since Guzmán had illegally reinstated slave raids earlier that year.[67] He had come to realize, as Morris Bishop observes, "An uninhabited land is valueless to any conqueror. The only salvation . . . lay in the suppression of slavery and the tempting back of the people from their mountain refuges."[68] Did talking to the three Spaniards, with their perhaps altered view of slavery, lead him to make his decision? Neither Cabeza de Vaca nor Dorantes take such credit, and they narrated the event matter-of-factly in their accounts. Díaz asked the three Spaniards to urge Indians hiding in the mountains to come to Díaz's camp. How the hidden Indians were found is not revealed, but it's possible that Esteban was sent to fetch them. When a delegation of Indians arrived, according to the Joint Report, "[Díaz] informed the Indians that they would not be molested so long as they would remain in their settlements, believe in God, and build churches where He might be served. The Indians . . . said they would act thusly, and they departed. Then they began to come down from the mountains to settle and to build churches. These people put crosses in the manner it had been ordered of them. Thus it was that all the land was populated in peace."[69]

Díaz then ordered Alcaraz to release the six hundred Indians who'd come with Esteban and the three Spaniards. The descendants of those far-away Piman peoples still live today in a linguistic island around Bamoa on the

Sinaloa River about eighty-five miles northwest of Culiacán.[70] Cabeza de Vaca calmed his earlier anger about Alcaraz's treachery after Díaz set the Indians free and resettled them in that area, now as nominal Catholics.

Although Esteban would remain a slave, the African nevertheless must have been pleased to witness hundreds of Indians freed from the threat of slavery.

On April 1, 1536, Díaz took Esteban and his three Spanish companions the rest of the way to Culiacán and they stayed with him until May 15, when twenty mounted horsemen were assembled to escort them three hundred miles through the war-torn countryside between Culiacán and Compostela, the capital of Nueva Galicia province.[71] Six other Christians from other areas joined them on the way with five hundred Indians they'd captured for slaves and chained together by the necks. Despite his earlier actions near Culiacán, Díaz did not free those five hundred unfortunates, who would be branded on their faces and sold into slavery. Neither Cabeza de Vaca nor Dorantes had anything to say about those Indians' fate. Even though all four continued on together, the *Relación* and Joint Report also stopped referring to Esteban, except at the very end of Cabeza de Vaca's account when he named the four traveling healers.

Although not freed himself by Díaz's order freeing the Indians, Esteban had survived the invasion of Florida and the cross-continent escape. Andrés Reséndez explains why Esteban's survival was a miracle:

> All the other castaways were elite Spaniards who were likely to outlast Africans, simply because they were better nourished and their bodies had been less exposed to the ravages of punishing physical labor.... and able to use their authority in ways that shielded them from danger and maximized their chances of survival. And yet Estebanico managed to outlive dozens of Spaniards who could have reasonably expected to be among the last men standing. By all accounts, he was the ultimate survivor. He had experienced the life of bondage on three different continents and had been forced to face incredible perils and adventures. Against astonishing odds, he had survived through it all.[72]

Journey's End

Treatment of the four kept improving. They arrived in Compostela in early June, where Esteban and the three Spaniards appeared before Nuño Beltrán de Guzmán, the province's governor and one of Spain's most vicious conquistadors. His slaughters and enslavements of Indians were extreme even by conquistador standards. However, Guzmán showed the greatest care and courtesy to the four survivors. "When we reached Compostela, the governor received us very well, giving us of what he had, for us to dress in," the *Relación* reported. By now news was spreading throughout Mexico that four men of the years-ago Narváez expedition had survived.

Not mentioned in Cabeza de Vaca's account is that Guzmán would be arrested in about eight months. He'd made enemies of his rival conquistador Hernán Cortés, Viceroy Antonio de Mendoza, and Bishop Juan de Zumárraga. Guzmán would be sent to Spain in chains, accused of treason and abuse of power, among other charges. Although he'd been one of the richest and most powerful men in Mexico, Guzmán would die impoverished in Spain in 1558.

But in 1536 Guzmán provided Esteban and his three Spanish companions with royal treatment in Compostela for two weeks. Goodwin says the three Spaniards were put up in a brick building and entertained lavishly. As for Esteban, he was lodged in Guzmán's palace, where Goodwin reported "he was feted as rarely a slave has ever been regaled."[73] Cabeza de Vaca wrote that at Compostela he—and presumably also Esteban, Dorantes, and Castillo—could hardly bear the touch of clothing and could not sleep in beds, choosing to lie on the floor instead.

The men still faced weeks of travel to Mexico City, but now all of them, including Esteban, would travel on horseback instead of walking. Guzmán accompanied them and provided a mounted and armed escort.

CHAPTER 14

Return to Slavery, but an Indispensable Man

WITHOUT ESTEBAN'S INTERCESSION with the Indian tribes, even the three Spaniards' shamanism might not have protected them, dooming them to perish or remain stranded in the wilderness. Despite his importance, Esteban was still legally Dorantes's slave. Esteban's slavery was made clear to him all the way to Compostela and then on to Mexico City. It's easy to see Spaniards ordering him about, Dorantes assigning him all the distasteful jobs he didn't want to do, people acting in a condescending way, and Nuño Beltrán de Guzmán segregating him from the others, albeit in comparable luxury. Esteban the slave had become, at best, a curiosity whose value was not yet certain.

Esteban was given credit for the men enduring the eight-year escape from Florida, but not like the three Spaniards, who were treated as heroes and given rewards. Esteban became an African celebrity, known across Spanish-held Mexico. Even so, he remained *just* a slave. He must have regretted not remaining behind in one of the Indian villages. Once again he was ensnared in a Spanish legal system that maintained he was a lesser being and the property of Dorantes. By Spanish law Esteban was bound to obedience and could be punished, or he could be sold to another slaveowner if Dorantes wanted to be rid of him.

CHAPTER 14

Tenochtitlan—Mexico City

Mexico's present name comes from the Mexica natives. Because it is the common term today, the original inhabitants of the Mexico City area are referred to now as Aztecs, even though Spaniards of Esteban's time called them Mexicas.

When Esteban arrived in 1536, Mexico City had surpassed Santo Domingo as the center of Spanish presence in the New World. The travelers must have been amazed at the change in organization and nomenclature. From an early base on the Mexican mainland in 1527, when Esteban had departed from Santo Domingo, Spanish officialdom had centralized its New World operations in Mexico City with Viceroy Antonio de Mendoza as the king's representative on the west side of the Atlantic.

Mexico City was emerging as a Spanish town atop the demolished ruins of the Aztecs' capital city of Tenochtitlan, built on islands in Lake Texcoco. Although Texcoco appeared to be one lake, it actually was two, with one made up of fresh water and the other saline.[1] This difference in salinity was the result of Mexica/Aztec engineering, with the lake system in the Basin of Mexico, considered to be five interconnected and separately named bodies of water: Lake Texcoco, Lake Zumpango, Lake Xaltocan, Lake Xochimilco, and Lake Chalco.[2]

Seventeen years earlier, when conquistadors first saw the island city of the Aztecs, it had a population estimated at hundreds of thousands. More people lived on the surrounding mainland in separate communities, which connected to the city with six causeways across the lake. It was reported that Tenochtitlan contained sixty thousand houses with two to ten people living in each.[3] It might have been one of the three largest cities in the world at that time, along with Paris and Constantinople.[4]

The sight of the city amazed the first conquistadors, who called Tenochtitlan the most beautiful city they'd ever seen. Fruit orchards and hunting preserves covered the countryside outside the city. Drinking water was delivered to the city through aqueducts from Chapoltepec west of the city. Tenochtitlan also had a sewer system, an aviary, and a zoo—none of which were common in the best European cities. In the zoo, Spaniards reported seeing what they called a Mexican bull. They described an animal that could only have been a bison, proving the Aztecs' knowledge of their world extended into at least northeastern Mexico and possibly what is now the United States.[5]

Conquistador Bernal Díaz would later write about the city: "We were amazed and said [Tenochtitlan] was like the enchantments they tell of in the legend of Amadis, on account of the great towers and [temples] and buildings rising from the water and all built of masonry. . . . Of all these wonders that I then beheld, today [1568] all is overthrown and lost, nothing left standing."[6] His reference to Amadis was to a popular 1508 book, *Amadis of Gaul*, which depicted a medieval knight Amadis as a courteous, gentle, sensitive, Christian who battles monsters and defends the honor of his twelve-year-old love, Oriana.[7] Cortés boasted to the king that Tenochtitlan was "razed and destroyed" after conquering the Aztec capital in 1521. But an illustration reveals that Mexico City was still a blend of Aztec and Spanish architecture when Esteban arrived in 1536.[8]

In 1524 Cortés commissioned a woodcut for a report to the king showing a bird's-eye view of the island city so the king could envision what Tenochtitlan looked like. His illustration is believed to have been based on a stylized, not-to-scale Aztec drawing.[9] A comparison with a view of Mexico City drawn in 1535, the year before Esteban's arrival, shows that the city still looked much the same as the preconquest Tenochtitlan in at least generalities of the two drawings.[10] Spaniards modified both drawings as mirror images of the original Aztec illustration.

The Europeans commandeered Aztec homes and the city, evicting most native residents to the mainland. Then they used Aztec and African slaves to remodel Tenochtitlan houses or demolish them and build new houses and other buildings in a European streetscape.

The Aztec historian Chimalpahin, writing in the Nahuatl language from an Aztec perspective, said the workers suffered much, explaining: "They worked hard, ate little, and fell ill. There was a pestilence, and an infinite number of them perished. The labor was considerable since they dragged or carried on their backs stones, earth, wood, lime, bricks, and other materials. . . . There was little to eat since the fields had not been sown due to the city's siege."[11] Friar Toribio de Benavente also described the rebuilding of Tenochtitlan into Mexico City, writing in 1541: "The building of the great city of Mexico, which, in the first years, employed more people than the building of the temple at Jerusalem . . . the Indians do all the work, get the materials at

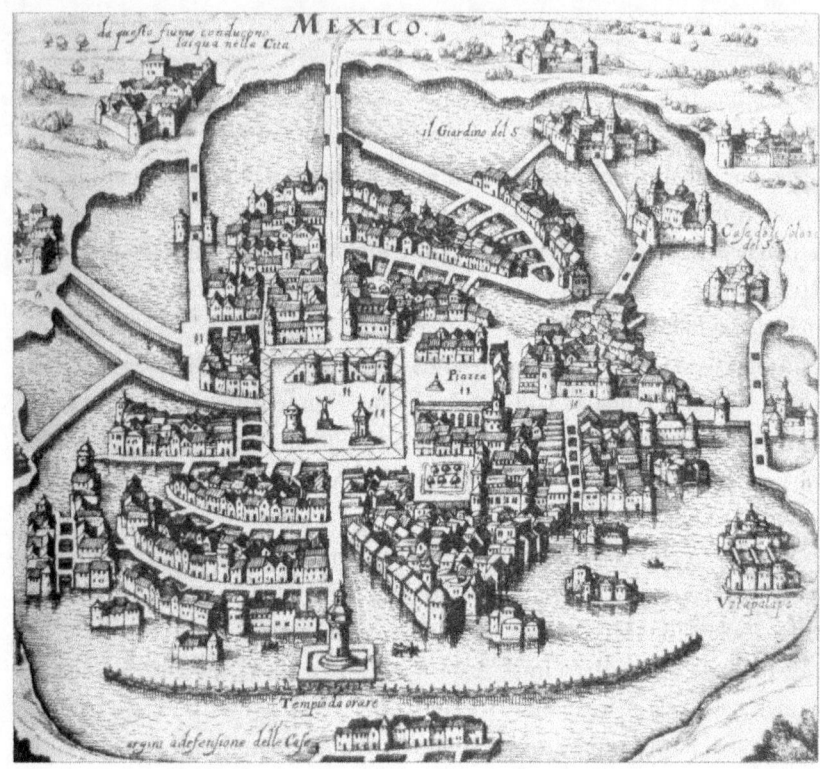

Figure 12. A view of Mexico City in 1535, rebuilt with Indian slave labor from the ruins of the Aztec city of Tenochtitlan. This not-to-scale drawing is how an artist envisioned it at about the time Esteban arrived. Since then the lake has been drained, and Mexico City now has a population of nearly nine million. In this drawing, west is to the top and north is to the right. The causeway at the top center is where Cortés suffered his greatest defeat in a fighting retreat on June 30, 1520—*La noche triste* (The Sad Night)—when several hundred Spaniards and their Tlaxcalan allies were killed. Published in Sebastian Münster's *Cosmographia*, 1544.

their own expense, pay the stonemasons and carpenters, and if they do not bring their own food they go hungry."[12]

Fourteen years after Tenochtitlan fell to the Spaniards, the city layout upon Esteban's arrival shows the same basic city layout and appears to still contain some Aztec buildings. The central square, which was Tenochtitlan's ceremonial plaza, continued with much the same layout and use, but with new Spanish buildings. The Aztec city's Grand Temple had been a flat-topped double pyramid about two hundred feet high that Chimalpahin said contained altars to Tezcatlipoca, the god of providence, and Huitzilopochtli, the god of war, surrounded by about forty smaller temples to other Aztec gods.[13]

Esteban would have seen the viceroy's castle-like palace, which had replaced the Grand Temple and was built of the same stones and in similar dimensions, except for the lofty height. The viceroy's palace was the heart of Spanish government in the Americas. Besides being Mendoza's residence, it also housed a busy collection of artisans and craftsmen, a post office with scribes to help the illiterate with letters and documents, and the Audiencia's legal court.[14] Esteban would have seen it teeming inside and out with colonists, Indians, merchants, officials, and people from other parts of Europe.

Esteban also would have seen a Catholic cathedral built with stone from demolished Aztec ceremonial buildings. It was erected beside the plaza to the square's north side, while Moctezuma's palace and gardens on the south side of the square were obliterated.[15] Two buildings at the bottom of the center plaza's square look similar to buildings in both the 1524 and 1535 maps.

There is a human sculpture in the middle of the plaza square in both drawings. The Cortés 1524 woodcut showed what was described as a stone idol there, representing the decapitated female deity Coyolxauqui.[16] In the 1535 drawing, that plaza's stone sculpture is replaced in the same location by another human figure in a similar pose with outstretched arms, but now complete with a head. It likely was a sculpture of the Virgin Mary. Whenever Spaniards came across a female figure in a native religion, they tried to substitute the Virgin Mary.[17] Aztec historian Chimalpahin referred several times in his account of the conquest to sculptures of the Virgin Mary on or near Mendoza's palace. Today, remnants of Tenochtitlan's Grand Temple foundations have been uncovered and can be seen in downtown Mexico City.

Procession of Heroes

It's impossible to know with any precision how far Esteban and the three Spaniards traveled from Florida to Mexico City because their route details are unknowable. Based on a measurement of straight-line distances, the four traveled 3,500 or more miles, if the distance is included that they walked in

Florida, the 800 miles they sailed and rowed across the Gulf of Mexico, and their travels following rivers and detours for mountain passes in northern Mexico. Just from Galveston's Malhado Island area to Mexico City, they traveled more than 2,500 miles in fourteen months, only the last 400 miles of that on horseback along the royal road, the Camino Real, between Compostela and Mexico City, going most of the way near the present route of Mexican Federal Highway 15D. "All along the way we were well received by the Christians," the *Relación* reported. "Many of them came out to the roads to greet us, giving thanks to God for having saved us from so many dangers."[18]

The arrival of Esteban and the three Spaniards was scheduled so they would reach Mexico City on July 23, 1536, two days before the major feast day of Santiago—Saint James in English—who was the patron saint of conquistadors and Spain.[19] Feast-day festivities included elaborate stages, war games, and a bullfight.

As they came out of the high hills west of the city and began to make their descent, they would have marveled at how Mexico City seemed to float on the waters of Lake Texcoco. A crowd of citizens, servants, and slaves welcomed them, and they were greeted "with joy and kindness" by Cortés and Viceroy Mendoza.[20] Richard Flint and Shirley Cushing Flint believe that Esteban and his Spanish companions most likely resided inside the viceroy's palatial mansion in the center of Mexico City, where they lived in almost regal splendor.[21]

The three Spaniards spent much of their time giving their testimony to Viceroy Mendoza, which later became the basis of both the *Relación* and the Joint Report chapters in Gonzalo Fernández de Oviedo y Valdéz's *La historia general y natural de las Indias*.[22] When not testifying, the Spaniards toured Mexico City, partaking of the delights in food, drink, and women that were available to Spaniards in the country being conquered for Spain and the Catholic Church. Esteban also ventured into the city as a new celebrity. As one of the viceroy's favored houseguests, no one would have dared offend Esteban.[23]

No record of their meeting exists, but the "Black Conquistador" Juan Garrido lived in Mexico City and probably took the opportunity to meet Esteban, a now famous fellow African. Garrido was a free black man who had fought on the side of the Spaniards for almost thirty years and would have been in his fifties when Esteban arrived. Nearly every other African in

Mexico City was a slave, along with Indian slaves from elsewhere in the New World.

Aztec commoners worked in the viceroy's mansion and other Spanish and European homes and businesses as unpaid Indian servants, a forced labor indistinguishable from slavery. The Spaniards assigned labor levies, which were filled with commoners sent by Aztec tlatoanis (lords), such as those of Texcoco, Tacuba, and other Aztec districts, who administered Mexico City in consort with Viceroy Mendoza.

Exploration North

Probably even before the four Narváez travelers reached Mexico City, Viceroy Mendoza began plans for exploring to the north. Horsemen would have reached him with the survivors' stories of hearing about rich Indian cities north of Mexico. Upon arrival, however, all three of Esteban's Spanish companions showed increasing signs that they'd endured enough fearful wandering in the desert and mountains of northern Mexico.

Mendoza could request any of the Spaniards to go north and explore for prosperous Indian cities, but their standing as heroes could make matters awkward. King Carlos I would soon become aware of them and consider them national treasures of Spanish endurance and courage. Forcing them to do something they didn't want to do might test Mendoza's authority in ways he didn't relish. But the resourceful and confident slave Esteban who'd traveled with them was not entitled to a right of refusal.

To plan and organize such an expedition, obtain the king's permission, and send anyone northward would take twenty-eight months after the four travelers returned. Castillo stayed in Mexico City for some time. By October, however, Cabeza de Vaca and Dorantes left to sail to Spain. Their initial plan was foiled by a hurricane and they returned, but they left again in the spring of 1537. So for much of more than two years from July 1536 to November 1538, Esteban was one of two Narváez survivors to be celebrated and accommodated in Mexico City.

Cabeza de Vaca kept claiming he knew something so important about rich northern Indian cities that he could only tell it to the king. To Spaniards, "important" meant gold, silver, and other riches ready to be claimed by anyone strong enough to seize them from Indians. Before Cabeza de Vaca left for Spain, rumors, half-truths, speculation, and outright lies were speeding across Mexico as fast as storytellers could gallop their horses. The talk across Mexico somehow resulted in the northern Indian towns the travelers had heard about but never seen becoming known as the Seven Cities.

Although he didn't testify, Esteban must have fascinated Mendoza with stories of what he'd seen, heard, and experienced crossing the vast distance between Florida and the Pacific Ocean. Mendoza was so impressed that he developed an admiration for the African slave that had to have surprised both of them. He reflected that admiration in the tone of his letters afterward to King Carlos I. Mendoza's challenge would be to win the king's permission for him to explore northward, but Spain's most powerful conquistadors were maneuvering to be chosen instead.

Mendoza represented King Carlos I in the Americas and was a personal friend, as well as a member of one of the wealthiest and most politically powerful families in Spain. He ruled Mexico almost like a king because an ocean separated him and his sovereign. But in the final analysis, with the king holding ultimate authority, the viceroy was a politician and administrator.

Conquistadors like Hernán Cortés were serious rivals for the king's favor because they poured immense quantities of gold, silver, and Indian tribute into the king's treasury. Cortés even held the king's appointed post of Marqués del Valle de Oaxaca. However, the Mendoza clan was so entrenched within the king's inner circle that Cortes's influential position was still secondary to Viceroy Mendoza's. Another Mendoza advantage was that the four travelers were under his roof and protection. Also, many religious leaders, including the powerful first bishop of Mexico, Franciscan Friar Juan de Zumárraga, favored the viceroy over any conquistador. Zumárraga was the bishop associated with reports of apparitions in 1531 near Mexico City of the Virgin Mary, now known as Our Lady of Guadalupe.[24]

Who should lead an expedition north? Any one of the three Spaniards would have priority. They had seen parts of the country, although not the unknown lands north of today's boundary between Mexico and the present states of Arizona and New Mexico. One by one, however, Mendoza saw each Spaniard slip away as candidates to go north.

- Cabeza de Vaca was willing to go back if he could succeed to Narváez's unfilled position of governor of Florida, which would have included all of the present southern states plus Texas. He sailed back to Spain in 1537 to try to win the king's appointment. Florida, as the Spaniards thought of mainland United States at that time, stretched more than a thousand miles from the Atlantic Ocean to the River of Palms on today's eastern Mexico coast. It would have extended northward as far as a bold governor could control, theoretically encompassing what is today the eastern and southern United States. At the farthest reach to the Canadian border, there was the potential of the northern mainland being twice the size of Mexico. But King Carlos I granted the coveted Florida governorship to Hernando de Soto instead, so Cabeza de Vaca settled for becoming governor of a large area in South America that included portions of today's Brazil, Argentina, Paraguay, and Bolivia.

- Castillo never seemed interested in going back to the north where he'd suffered so much. He set his sights on an easier life. Mendoza arranged a marriage for Castillo with a rich widow who owned a lucrative Indian labor and tribute-generating encomienda around the present city of Tehuacán, about 130 miles southeast of Mexico City. He later served as treasurer of Guatemala.
- Dorantes entered into extensive negotiations with Mendoza, who offered him the position as leader of an expedition. But Dorantes hesitated about returning north and backed out of the deal before everything was finalized. In a 1539 letter to King Carlos, Mendoza wrote: "I spoke with [Dorantes] many times because it seemed to me that it could be of much service to Your Majesty to send him with forty or fifty horse[men] to learn the secrets of those regions. When I had arranged what was necessary for his journey and had spent a great deal of money for this purpose, the [agreement] came apart, I do not know how."[25]

Disgusted with his attempts to deal with the three Spaniards, at some point Mendoza decided the perfect guide for an expedition would be the African slave who beguiled him day after day with stories about his travels across the continent.

The average price for a slave in those days was 100 to 150 pesos. Mendoza sent a silver plate heaped with 500 pesos to Andrés Dorantes to buy Esteban.[26] However, Dorantes turned down the offer, telling Mendoza he couldn't bear to part with his personal slave. Some have interpreted Dorantes's refusal to sell Esteban as indicating a sentimental attachment between master and slave. But researcher Goodwin gave a more prosaic reason. "As long as Esteban remained his property," Goodwin wrote, "Dorantes could stake his own claim to any riches his slave might discover.... There may have been a strong emotional bond between the two men after their years together in the wilderness, but Dorantes's reported refusal to sell Esteban to Mendoza was at least in part a commercial decision."[27]

But Dorantes knew Mendoza already was furious with him for refusing to lead the expedition, and it couldn't seem prudent to further antagonize the most powerful man in Mexico. Under whatever persuasion, he relinquished Esteban to Mendoza, saying his generosity was for the greater glory of the king and emperor.

In describing the transaction, Mendoza created what might have been a precedent in referring to an African slave by name to Spain's king. Mendoza wrote to the king on December 10, 1537, "I purchased from Dorantes a black named Esteban for this purpose [exploring to the north]."[28] Mendoza continually referred to Esteban by name. In another letter to the king in April 1540, for example, Mendoza made a point of mentioning "Esteban el negro."[29] The transaction is ambiguous, but Spanish records imply that Mendoza freed Esteban, appointing the African to his personal guard of forty men on horseback and on foot.[30]

Typical in vagueness about Esteban's status was a letter Coronado also wrote to the king in July 1539, in which he said he recruited Indians from the provinces of Petatlán and Cuchillo for the expedition. "I charged them to take inland Fray Marcos with every security," Coronado wrote, "and ... a Negro, whom the viceroy bought for this purpose from one of those who escaped from Florida whose name is Estéban."[31] Did Esteban remain a slave lent by Dorantes, or a slave now owned by Mendoza, or did the viceroy grant his freedom? It isn't certain. A hint is in the viceroy's letters and in Marcos's account, in which neither ever refers to the African by his slave nickname again, instead calling him Esteban de Dorantes, or simply Esteban.[32]

Whether still a slave or a free man, Esteban the African became an indispensable man because Mendoza now had a guide who knew much of the country and who also was well regarded by Indians along the northward route's Mexico portion. Any Indians who hadn't met Esteban when he was with Cabeza de Vaca would have heard about him from Indians who had.

The choice of a Franciscan friar to lead the Seven Cities expedition, which ordinarily would have been reserved for conquistadors, resulted from Bishop Zumárraga's insistence in letters and personal meetings urging Mendoza to send a peaceful delegation of Franciscan friars north. Zumárraga explained his naïve reasoning in a letter to the viceroy, saying, "If a few friars whom I know here in New Spain were to go with these Narváez survivors to those lands [in the north] . . . they would show that war is unnecessary." Zumárraga recommended to Mendoza that his friend Friar Marcos de Niza should lead that exploration.[33] Thus, when Mendoza won the king's approval to explore northward, he made one of the most unusual decisions in the conquest's history. He picked two Franciscan religious men to go forward peacefully and try to find the rumored rich Indian cities. The Franciscans were Friar Marcos and lay brother Onorato.[34] Mendoza described Marcos and Onorato as "persons of virtuous life and good conscience" who "have been in this part of the world a long while."[35] Once Friar Marcos was selected, Mendoza wrote instructions to the Franciscan, saying:

> If, with the help of God, Our Lord, and the grace of the Holy Spirit, you find a route by which to travel on and penetrate the interior, you will take with you as guide Esteban de Dorantes, whom I ordered to obey you completely, as me myself, in whatever you might order him.[36]

With that, the viceroy put Esteban on notice of penalties that befall those who do not obey. For any African, slave or not, those would be painful and could be fatal. The fact that Esteban was ordered to obey Marcos, an order that would have been understood and unnecessary for a slave, is further indication that Mendoza might have given Esteban his freedom. As Hsain Ilahiane points out, "Estevan's free acts and resistance [toward Marcos] . . . suggest that he held the status of [the viceroy's] employee."[37]

Racial Tensions

Regardless, Esteban would realize a more compelling reason to get out of Mexico City and go anywhere else. On September 24, 1537, an informant told Mendoza that the city's African slaves were planning a revolt, and the viceroy launched a swift offensive. "I was advised that the blacks had chosen a king and had reached an agreement to kill all Spaniards and seize the land, and that the Indians were also involved," Mendoza wrote to the king. Because Indians and African slaves outnumbered Europeans in and around Mexico City, Mendoza worried that "the blacks might overwhelm us."[38]

Mendoza ordered four African men and one woman arrested and tortured to make them confess to a plot. Then Mendoza turned the Africans over to his young protégé, Francisco Vázquez de Coronado, who had his Indians execute the five, very likely gruesomely. In line with the Castilian idiom that "dead dogs don't bite," Coronado also had several Africans drawn and quartered whom he suspected of planning a rebellion at the nearby mines of Amatepeque.[39] Mendoza would reward Coronado's assistance in capturing and executing suspected plotters by having the king appoint Coronado at the age of twenty-eight to Guzmán's old governorship of Nueva Galicia on April 18, 1539.[40]

Meanwhile, Spanish paranoia increased. Every enslaved or free African in or around Mexico City was eyed suspiciously as Mendoza continued investigations and more interrogations. Esteban would have realized that one mistake, one misidentification, one accusation, could cost him his life in Mexico City. The most promising chance to leave before it might be too late was to stay under the viceroy's protection and join the expedition to find the Seven Cities.

That 1537 event was the first of many African slave revolts in Mexico. Spaniards became so panicked that Mendoza asked the king to temporarily suspend shipments of African slaves to Mexico to keep down their numbers. He also mobilized about a thousand conquistadors, in effect calling up a sixteenth-century National Guard.[41]

With new incentive after the 1537 executions of Africans, Esteban assured Mendoza that he could smooth the way for uncontested passage through Indian country. He'd already been as far north as the Village of the Hearts, in the Ópata country of central Sonora, where the unknown lands to the north began.[42] And the Indians also knew and liked him throughout Sinaloa, where he'd traveled before he and the others were taken to Mexico City after being found. Mendoza decided the African could guide the Spaniards through the area safely, especially since he'd guaranteed Indians would not be enslaved if they cooperated. Mendoza concluded he didn't need to send a military force. By the fall of 1538 Coronado would escort Esteban and Marcos west to Nueva Galacia. Esteban had to be relieved to escape Mexico City's racial antagonisms.

Cortés, Guzmán, and other conquistadors had heard rumors about rich Indian cities to the north, but they'd failed to find them. It didn't take much for Cabeza de Vaca's stories about rich Indian cities far to the north to stir imaginations into thinking about the fabled Seven Cities of Antilia. That was a centuries-old Spanish legend accepted as fact by most in those days that said Portuguese bishops established seven rich cities somewhere across the Atlantic Ocean.

At this time the Spaniards still believed in Columbus's Indies and thought the riches of India and China were tantalizingly close if they went in the correct direction.[43] It was still believed at the time that North America would reveal a land route to China and India, which held the world's four most precious goods: silk, spices, dyes, and porcelain. Blocked by the Ottoman Turks from traveling across Eurasia, Spaniards hoped in the 1500s that North America could provide a back door. Sixteenth-century Europeans would believe anything if possible wealth were involved.

Although disguised as an exploration and mission to convert the Indians, Mendoza brimmed with bigger plans. Woodbury Lowery describes Mendoza's real agenda, noting that "the expedition, ostensibly undertaken for the glory of God . . . received direct authority [from Mendoza] to take possession" of discovered new country in the name of Holy Roman Emperor Carlos V, who also ruled Spain as King Carlos I.[44]

Bishop Zumárraga wrote in a 1539 letter, "The viceroy takes [the new lands] for the emperor and desires to send friars ahead without arms and wishes the conquest to be a Christian and apostolic one and not butchery."[45] As guide, Esteban would deliver on his promise to protect and guide the friar. He would smooth the way for Marcos, arranging for Indians to greet the friar warmly on the entire route north, ensuring that the friar was provided with food and necessary provisions at all times.[46]

When Marcos returned months later with tales of having seen a rich Indian city he called Cíbola, Zumárraga campaigned against allowing Cortés to go there. Zumárraga argued that right of discovery belonged to Mendoza because the viceroy had sent Esteban and Marcos, and therefore Mendoza should be the one deciding what to do. Mendoza appointed Coronado to lead an expedition north to follow up on Marcos's reports. In late February 1540, Coronado took about 375 European men-at-arms, most of them from Castile, as well as up to 2,000 Mexican Indian warriors, including Aztecs and Tarascans.[47]

Zumárraga and Mendoza

Routine pious Spanish rhetoric might explain why most writers on the period ignore the fact that Bishop Zumárraga and Viceroy Mendoza also could be butchers. The same month that Esteban and Marcos were sent north, Zumárraga arrested an Aztec noble named Don Carlos Chichimecatecuhtli, also known as Ometochtzin, which is "Two Rabbit" in the Aztecs' Nahuatl language. Zumárraga headed the Inquisition in Mexico, which found the Aztec leader guilty of religious heresy. Under Zumárraga's order, the Aztec was burned at the stake on November 30, 1539.[48]

King Carlos I became so concerned that executions of Aztec nobles could result in Indian rebellion that he removed Zumárraga as apostolic inquisitor. The king also exempted Indians from future Inquisition trials. However, ways were found to get around the king's prohibition and continue to persecute Indians who defied Catholic teachings.[49]

Zumárraga was a religious fanatic known as a millenarian, as were most Franciscans of the early to mid-1500s.[50] He believed that conversion of Indians to Catholicism would result in a thousand-year terrestrial paradise ruled by Jesus Christ before the end of the world, which is how Franciscans interpreted the Bible's Book of Revelation.[51] Millenarianism spurred Franciscans into a frantic and often violent effort to convert native peoples of the Americas as quickly as possible into Catholics, embracing a fervor that mandated destroying native religions and cultures. This convert-or-die evangelism predicted that the sooner Indians could be converted, the sooner Christ would return.

As a millenarian, Zumárraga was kind to Indians who converted to Catholicism or might be converted, establishing Indian schools and hospitals. However, he persecuted Indians if they held or reverted to native beliefs, which he considered Satanism and heresy. In such categories the bishop also included Jews, Lutherans, Muslims, blasphemers, idolaters, and anyone else outside the Catholic Church.[52]

Other orders such as Dominicans didn't believe in millenarianism, so their friars, such as Friar Bartolomé de las Casas, devoted themselves to the care of Indians, converts or not. They opposed Franciscans who emphasized conversion no matter how many natives died in the process. Even the Franciscans drifted away from the millenarian belief over the last third of the sixteenth century. The shocking deaths of millions of Indians from European disease and warfare shattered Franciscan acceptance of millenarianism. The Catholic Church came to consider millenarianism as an errant doctrine.[53]

Like Zumárraga, Viceroy Mendoza would also be merciless toward opposing Indians when he led Spanish forces in the Mixtón War of 1541–1542 in northwestern Mexico, although his motivation was secular instead of religious. Mendoza recruited thousands of Aztec and Tarascan warriors to help quash the rebellion by Caxcan and other northern tribes against Spanish rule. Mendoza ordered the slaughter of war prisoners, including women and children. In Spain, the Council of the Indies conducted a secret investigation of Mendoza's violence against Indian prisoners and civilians. In addition to hangings, the council's investigators said, "Many of the Indians seized in the conquest were slain in his [Mendoza's] presence and by his orders. Some were placed in a row and blown to pieces by cannon fire; others were torn apart by dogs."[54] The investigation into his Mixtón War tactics worried Mendoza, but nothing came of the inquiry.

The Mixtón War was still more than a year away when Friar Marcos wrote in his journal: "I, Friar Marcos de Niza, a professed friar of the Order of San Francisco . . . departed from the villa of San Miguel in the province of Culiacán on Friday the seventh day of March in the year 1539.[55] . . . I also took with me Esteban de Dorantes, a Negro."[56]

CHAPTER 15

An African in Arizona and New Mexico

AFTER HIS CROSS-CONTINENT survival, the next challenge for Esteban was finding his way north across the Sierra Madre Mountains after several conquistadors had tried and failed. Hernán Cortés, Nuño Beltrán de Guzmán, Pedro de Alvarado, and Francisco Vázquez de Coronado were among those who had assumed after Mexico and Peru that there must be fortunes to be won to the north, but they'd failed to find a way through mountains and hostile tribes.

When Cabeza de Vaca returned with tales of rich Indian cities, Cortés traveled to Spain to seek the king's permission to let him search to the north some more, but the king endorsed Viceroy Mendoza's decision to send an unarmed expedition guided by Esteban and led by "humble friars." Esteban, without the help of any European, found the unknown way, led by his contingent of Mexican Indian guides.

The importance of Esteban's selection to guide Friar Marcos de Niza forward in 1539 is made clear by Viceroy Mendoza's report to the monarch in a letter, which said: "Among the things that had been readied [for the expedition to Cíbola], a black who came with Dorantes remained with me . . . I sent [him] with Friar Marcos de Niza. . . . When the groundwork for the entrada had thus been laid and Friar Marcos and his companion [Onorato] had spent ten or twelve days with the black and other slaves and Indians whom I had given them, they departed."[1]

Coronado took Esteban, Friar Marcos, and Brother Onorato with him from Mexico City to present-day Tepic in western Mexico, where Compostela was located at the time. Coronado was going to Compostela anyway to assume governorship of New Galicia. Once there, he would provide safe escort for Esteban and the two Franciscans three hundred more miles north to Culiacán.

Accompanied by a hundred or more Indians promised freedom from war and slavery, Esteban and the Franciscans departed Culiacán in March 1539. Esteban's presence inspired hundreds of additional Indians to join along the way because they remembered him, and his fame had spread for more than three years among them, growing in importance as such hearsay testimonials do. Onorato would soon be sent back with illness.

Those who write about Esteban and Marcos's journey like to glamorize it as a search for "cities of gold," but that expression was not used in the 1500s. American writers concocted the term in the 1800s, excited by gold rushes in California and Alaska.[2] Nevertheless, it's often seen in books about Esteban's journey northward. The term used in Esteban's time was just "the Seven Cities," and later "the Seven Cities of Cíbola." The incentive to go northward in the 1500s was to look for riches other than just gold, although precious metals remained an indicator of wealthy societies.[3] Another hope for northern exploration was to find Asia and its wealth.

From the time of Mendoza's decision to send the African and the Franciscans in late 1538, until the return of Marcos in late summer the following year, communications between the highest-ranking Spaniards in Mexico continually mentioned the Seven Cities expedition. Esteban's role as guide was emphasized. Mendoza had ordered Marcos to keep him informed by sending back runners with dispatches, and Marcos's over-optimistic reports fueled excitement across New Spain.

Rodrigo de Albornoz, the king's former secretary in Spain and the king's accountant in Mexico's New Spain, wrote in 1539: "The lord viceroy dispatched a friar and a black who had come from La Florida.... According to the information the black had obtained, these [individuals with Marcos] were going to travel until they reached an exceedingly rich land."[4]

John Bakeless, in his book *America as Seen by Its First Explorers*, describes Esteban's importance:

In the wilderness he was an important and independent person—well known to the Indians, among whom he had traveled with Cabeza de Vaca ... known to have effected remarkable cures. Probably he was especially admired because of his color, for when Lewis and Clark took the latter's Negro slave, York, on their expedition, the black man was a far greater sensation among the Indians than the white men.[5]

Indians turned out in crowds to welcome Esteban when he returned to Sinaloa and Sonora. He spoke to them in their own language and by universally accepted sign language, and they volunteered to accompany him northward. There had to have been some tension from the beginning between Esteban and Friar Marcos. The stern Franciscan priest might have felt that Esteban's popularity with Indians threatened his authority. Esteban's perceived shamanism also might have been a scandalous affront to the friar's Catholic perspective, not to mention the African's Muslim heritage. It also had to annoy Marcos to realize that the Indians relegated him—a priest and the expedition's leader—to a secondary role.[6]

After a month of travel, at an unverifiable Indian village in southern Sonora that the friar called Vacapa, Marcos told Esteban to go forward. Marcos wrote in his report that he sent Esteban on ahead with a large group of Mexican Indians on Passion Sunday, April 2, 1539.[7] Vacapa probably was near the Río Mayo because linguists believe it's an approximation of a Yaqui/Mayo word, *vaka'apo*.[8] It would have been close to today's Navojoa, Mexico.

The viceroy had instructed Marcos to obtain reliable information about the coast to the west, claim land and inhabitants for Spain as he traveled northward, and send back frequent reports. Marcos said he stayed at Vacapa for messengers returning from the coast while sending Esteban ahead toward the north.

Marcos knew that success or failure depended on him finding some way to work with the African. If he sent Esteban back, there would be no guide through the unknown country ahead, because Esteban was the only person the Indians would show how to reach the Seven Cities. The African also was the only one who could persuade Indians to provide food, shelter, and a pleasant reception for Marcos in every village. Marcos settled on the strategy of sending Esteban to scout ahead by 130 to 160 miles. Esteban set forth with hundreds of Mexican Indian guides as well as two greyhound dogs from Castile.

Forward, Alone

Esteban was instructed to send runners back with news of his progress. A written message would have been so difficult as to be impossible, whether Esteban was literate or not. It would involve carrying paper and ink, specially prepared quills, the right sand to prevent smudging, a suitable writing surface, and a means to protect all of that from the elements.[9] That would have been difficult enough for just the friar to manage, and historians think Esteban probably was illiterate. So instead, Marcos told Esteban to send runners back with crosses, making the crosses bigger as news got better.

It's not clear why Esteban couldn't just tell the runners, who spoke some Spanish, and they could then tell Marcos, because Marcos did report receiving Esteban's verbal messages from messengers about other points. Perhaps Marcos didn't trust the Indians, although he often swallowed anything else they told him. It's likely the friar felt news about the Seven Cities would have more religious significance if crosses were involved.

Meanwhile, Marcos made himself comfortable at Vacapa, preaching to the Indians and resting. Besides conducting Mass and preaching, he also had sixteenth-century priest duties to fulfill, explaining that he did what Esteban and the three Spaniards had done on their trek across the continent. "They brought their sick to me that I might heal them, and they tried to touch my garments," Marcos reported. "I recited the gospel over them."[10]

Many of the Mexican Indians traveling with Esteban had been to Zuni territory where the Seven Cities were thought to be. The Indians probably kept telling Esteban with mutually understood words and sign language how to proceed. So Esteban traveled fast for three days, arriving in Yaqui territory, probably near today's Vícam, Mexico, where he sent a runner back with a cross the size of a man and advised the friar to start out as soon as possible.

When the runner arrived back at Vacapa on the fourth day, Indians with Marcos claimed it was thirty days' travel from where Esteban had sent the cross to the first of the Seven Cities. In fact, by the route traveled, it was about six hundred miles to Hawikku—a reasonable distance in thirty days for

Indians, but not for a friar traveling with a large group of Indians, considering Marcos had covered only about 230 miles in the first month.

Marcos did not leave Vacapa for more than two weeks after Esteban, departing one day after Easter on April 17, 1539.[11] After leaving Vacapa, Marcos reported "always finding settlements, good lodging, excellent reception, and many turquoises [arranged for him by Esteban].... The inhabitants all spoke to me of [the Seven Cities of] Cíbola.... They told me that Esteban was ahead."[12] In return for such kindnesses, as the viceroy had instructed him, Marcos took possession of each village for Spain and declared the inhabitants to be subject to the Catholic Church and to Spanish laws.

Marcos wrote that he thought Esteban would wait for him at the place from which he sent the cross. However, he'd written a few paragraphs earlier in his account that he and Esteban had agreed the African could return in person or send back runners with a cross. There was no mention then that Esteban couldn't continue after sending back a cross, and so Esteban kept moving forward, not yet having gone the agreed-upon advance of 130 to 160 miles.

Esteban soon sent a second cross as large as the first, his runners telling Marcos that Esteban wanted him to follow quickly because the land they were seeking was "the best and greatest that had ever been heard of."[13] It's hard to believe Sonoran Indians would describe the arid and mountainous lands of New Mexico that way, so Esteban might have exaggerated to keep the friar moving forward. Or Marcos might have embellished his account for the viceroy.

Indians of the 1500s offered effusive praise for what they considered the wonders of the Seven Cities, Marcos reporting that Indians claimed Cíbola was "the most wonderful thing in the world."[14] But an Indian concept of what was wonderful differed dramatically from the European concept. It would be a cultural misunderstanding that would result in the Coronado expedition the following year, and which has been elaborated upon by writers' imaginations ever since.

At the place where Esteban had sent the first cross, the Indians told Marcos that they often went to Cíbola to work as hired agricultural workers and were paid with turquoises and hides of large animals, to be known later as bison or buffalo, that roamed a sprawling grassland far to the east.[15] They said the first of the Seven Cities was called Cíbola, which would turn out to be the Zuni village of Hawikku.

Esteban arranged for Indians to provide Marcos with food, lodging, and welcome all along the route, as he'd promised the viceroy. It's doubtful anyone else could have managed to do that. It was testimony to how much the Mexican Indians of several tribes liked and respected Esteban to agree to such efforts. J. A. Rogers discusses the Mexican Indians who knew Esteban from three years earlier:

> The journey proved a veritable triumph for Estevanico. Everywhere he was received with honor, thanks to his size and strength, his dark skin, his daring, bravery, and bluff, as well as his good nature and ready wit, his reputation as a medicine man, and his knowledge of Indian life and lore.[16]

A day's travel farther, Marcos wrote, "Here I found a large cross that Esteban had left for me," and Marcos wrote that Esteban had left word that he would wait for the friar at the far edge of the first *despoblado*, a Spanish word for deserted country. Many days later in one town "in green irrigated land," perhaps in Ópata country, Marcos was impressed when the chief and two brothers approached him dressed in cotton clothes and wearing turquoise necklaces. "They brought me much game, consisting of deer, rabbits, and quail, and maize and [piñon nuts]," Marcos wrote.[17] He was pleased to find that Esteban's Indians provided food and built huts for him at each stop of the four days the friar traveled across a later deserted landscape. When Marcos entered that unpopulated region, he wrote that "at the place where I was to eat, I found huts and plenty of food near an arroyo. At night I found houses and also food, and this continued during the four days which I spent in the [unpopulated region]."[18]

Along the journey, Marcos expressed gratitude for how Esteban had arranged for Indians to welcome him, take care of him, and tell him about the wonders and riches of Cíbola. Did the Indians really tell Marcos about an animal at Cíbola larger than a cow with one horn that was curved toward its breast and then turned outward, or did Marcos misunderstand, or perhaps make up the story? Marcos's excitement grew as he traveled farther, always many days and even weeks behind his African advance scout. "[The Indians] told me that more than three hundred men from here had accompanied the Negro Esteban, carrying food for him, and that many also wanted to go with me."¹⁹ However, every time Marcos moved ahead to where Esteban had sent his latest report, the African had moved on again.

About twenty years later, Pedro de Castañeda, an expeditionary with Coronado, accused Esteban of seeking glory or wealth by going on to Cíbola without the friar. But Esteban could not have been seeking wealth and glory. He would have known that any wealth he found would not be his to keep, and any glory of discovery would be credited instead to the friar, as indeed many writers have tried to do since. Neither Castañeda nor anyone else could know what Esteban was thinking because no European ever saw him again. Everything reported about him after Vacapa, including many of the most repeated stories, true or not, consists of hearsay and imagination.

Henry O. Flipper, the first black graduate of West Point, thought Castañeda damaged Esteban's reputation by uncritically accepting Indian and Spanish rumors.²⁰ In the 1896 article "Did a Negro Discover New Mexico and Arizona?," Flipper was the first to challenge the negative assumptions about Esteban that had already become integral to what people thought about him.²¹

Being so far from the friar's control, Esteban must have given a lot of thought about what to do. To go back to Mexico City, he might have feared he'd be a slave again to either Dorantes or Viceroy Mendoza. Esteban had to have asked himself, what would the Spaniards do to him, an African, possibly still a slave, if he accomplished the mission and returned? Cover him with glory? Not likely. Decide he'd used up his usefulness? Very possible. Blame him if anything went wrong? Absolutely. Robert Goodwin suggests the solution would have been obvious to Esteban:

> Esteban had also seen how treacherous the Spaniards were and how brutally they treated slaves, Indians, and even each other. The massacre of Africans in Mexico City was still a vivid memory.²²

Esteban might have decided the best hope for the rest of his life was to escape into the wilderness. A runaway slave.

He persuaded the Indians at every village to treat the friar like a visiting dignitary, feed him, and listen to his preaching. Another part of his plan was to keep enticing Marcos to follow him but never allowing him to catch up. With each cross he sent back, Esteban lured Marcos farther up the trail but stayed "tantalizingly out of reach," as Goodwin put it.

In late April or early May 1539, Esteban crossed into what is now Arizona southwest of Bisbee. If he climbed into the nearby Huachuca Mountains, he would have left a desert environment and entered one up to 7,800 feet in elevation with pine trees, thin air, and vistas of the surrounding land.[23] It would have been a side trip hard to resist if he wanted a view of the country his Indian guides were leading him into. Esteban the African slave thus became the first person from the Old World to enter into what is now Arizona.

Unheralded

A part of this mountainous landscape has been set aside as a memorial. But not to Esteban. The area is the Coronado National Memorial, named for the Spaniard who did not arrive until a year later. As of early 2016, Esteban was not mentioned in any of the memorial's exhibits.

There is another monument, this one dedicated to Friar Marcos near Lochiel, Arizona, which is about twenty-nine miles west of where Esteban and later the friar would have entered Arizona. That monument does not mention Esteban either. The Marcos memorial, erected in the 1920s, credits the friar for being "the first European west of the Rockies." Some historians doubt the Franciscan ever made it into Arizona on that trip. If he did, the marker inaccurately claims Marcos arrived in Arizona on April 12, 1539, which is weeks before he could have gotten that far. Nowhere is there a monument to Esteban, who was the first non-Indian in Arizona, and soon afterward the first to enter New Mexico. Although it's certain Esteban went all the way to Cíbola/Hawikku, a major myth that Friar Marcos made it that far is not true.

Castañeda, who traveled with Marcos and Coronado the following year, and who might have talked with Marcos on that expedition, said the friar was sixty leagues behind Esteban by the time the African arrived at Cíbola, the Zuni village of Hawikku.[24] Sixty leagues would place Marcos about 160 to 180 miles to the south.[25] The sixty leagues in Castañeda's statement is the approximate distance the Gila River passes south of Hawikku on both the Arizona and New Mexico sides of the state line. Many historians believe the Gila River is the farthest point Marcos could have reached.[26]

But Marcos didn't walk that far. He didn't leave Vacapa until April 7, and he wouldn't have reached the village from which Esteban sent the first cross until at least April 10. Marcos reported that he reached the final stretch of unsettled land on May 9.[27] Esteban would have already arrived at Cíbola/Hawikku in late April or early May.[28]

Marcos reported to the viceroy that he walked twelve more days—until May 21—when an Indian who had been with Esteban told him that the Zunis had killed the African. Marcos wrote that he continued walking to "one day's journey from Cíbola." He doesn't give a date, but it would have been about May 23 at the earliest when he wrote that two more Indians from Esteban's group met him and said Esteban had been killed the previous day, which would have been on about May 22—but if so, that would have been more than two weeks after Esteban actually arrived, not the single day in the Indians' story.

On May 9 the friar would have been 197 to 225 miles from Cíbola. Due to the discrepancy between the times of the different Indians' reports about Esteban's fate and the vagueness of Marcos's account after May 9, some historians believe he turned back at about that time or soon afterward.[29] That 197 to 225 miles is close to the distance from today's Mexico border to Cíbola/Hawikku.

While the first historical writers wanted to believe a priest's word that he'd traveled all the way to Hawikku, few researchers still believe that. In addition to the mileage discrepancy, Marcos's description of Hawikku as being at the base of a hill instead of on top of it, the Indian pueblo being larger than Mexico City, what was a desert prairie around it being the "greatest and best" land ever discovered, and other exaggerated aspects of the area, indicates he was reporting back to the viceroy what his Indians told him. Or, as many speculate, what Marcos knew the viceroy wanted to be told.

Because Esteban did make it all the way to Cíbola/Hawikku but Marcos didn't, one writer suggests that books should rename the journey attributed to Marcos to instead be the Expedition of Esteban.[30]

Entry into Today's United States

Esteban is believed to have entered Arizona along the San Pedro River, which is one of the few north-flowing rivers in what is now the United States. The

San Pedro is born in Mexico's rugged Sierra Madre. It flows north into Arizona and then northwest until it joins the Gila River about eighty miles southeast of Phoenix. Esteban, as well as Marcos and Coronado the following year, traveled twenty to fifty-five miles north along the San Pedro River after entering Arizona, depending on which scholar's estimate is used. They then turned away from the river and headed northeast. In all scenarios, everyone needed to thread their way through passes between mountain ranges and canyons. The route for Esteban and eventually Coronado could not have been too different because some Mexican Indians who'd accompanied the African also traveled with Coronado.[31]

One of the more inaccurate maps for Coronado's route is the first one ever published, which was in the Fanny Bandelier translation of the *Relación* in 1905. Adolph Bandelier's guesswork map for that book shows a route for the four Narváez survivors that resulted in much misunderstanding for more than a century.[32] Adolph Bandelier's book *The Gilded Man* even suggests that remnants of "a slender and small" wooden cross that Marcos claimed he erected near Hawikku might still be there 366 years later.[33]

Herbert E. Bolton compounded Bandelier's mistaken route with his book about Coronado in 1949, still in print despite its errors.[34] Borrowing from Bandelier's guesswork, Bolton also decided that Esteban and later Coronado traveled north on the Arizona side of the state line with New Mexico, although his route is east of what Bandelier proposed.[35] Almost every scholar since then has accepted Bolton's theory. However, the route Bolton reported for Coronado, and presumably also for Esteban, was based not on physical evidence but instead on the bravado of Bolton's insistence. Both the Bandelier and Bolton routes go through areas of Arizona that would have been too rugged for Coronado's expedition with its thousands of livestock. Their routes prove how misleading it can be to project a course through mountainous areas by driving on modern roads. In addition, later research details were unknown to Bolton and even less so to Bandelier.[36]

Nevertheless, for more than a century, Bandelier and then Bolton's Arizona routes became folklore by being reprinted in books and on the Internet. Bolton often was prone to disseminating personal opinions as fact, even though he admitted that "folklore is not always good history."[37] The latest research supported by archaeological discoveries indicates both Bandelier and Bolton were wrong, revealing instead that Coronado, and presumably

Esteban a year earlier, traveled north to the Zuni town of Hawikku by going mostly on New Mexico's side. Bandelier and Bolton's mistakes about where Coronado traveled are why Coronado's name can be found all over Arizona. Eastern Arizona has eleven separate portions of the national forest named for Coronado, with one overlapping into New Mexico, and also numerous places named for Coronado all across the Grand Canyon State.

Esteban's precise route is unknowable because he never returned to Spanish society, so what route did Marcos have Coronado take to Cíbola? Coronado believed he followed the trail that the African discovered. Maybe he did, but all that can be known for sure is that he followed the trail that Marcos *thought* Esteban had walked on but at some point had not traveled over himself. Esteban seemed to have walked unerringly toward the Zuni towns. Ópata, Sobaipuri, and Pimans from northern Sonora led Esteban forward on Indian trade routes, as did other Mexican Indians who joined along the way.

Marcos's guidance had been adequate most of the way, but he appeared disoriented after entering Arizona with Coronado the next year, giving incorrect information about Esteban's route that often jeopardized Coronado's expedition and cost some men their lives from starvation and thirst.

The Updated Route

The first challenge to the Bandelier and Bolton routes came with the publication in 2011 of Nugent Brasher's on-the-ground research.[38] The Bandelier, Bolton, and Brasher routes start out and end in the same places. All believe Esteban and Coronado entered the present United States a few miles southwest of Bisbee, Arizona, along the San Pedro River. The routes then split up to eighty miles apart going north on opposite sides of the Arizona/New Mexico state line until they reunite near St. Johns, Arizona, and go up the Zuni River to Hawikku.

US Highway 191 in Arizona is an unintended bad compromise. Designated as the Coronado Trail National Scenic Byway, it's a north-south highway about midway between Bolton's hypothetical route and Brasher's on-the-ground researched route. Most Internet maps claiming to show Coronado's route to Hawikku follow Highway 191. It's an Arizona myth that Coronado traveled that route, however, because Highway 191 would have been impassable through the rugged White Mountains for the livestock on Coronado's expedition in 1540. Nevertheless, Coronado's name is scattered along Highway 191, including a restored Coronado Railway steam locomotive displayed in Clifton that served the strip-mining copper district. A car ride on the highway found no mention of Esteban, even though he traveled a year earlier on whatever route Bolton believed that Coronado and presumably Esteban would have taken.

Bolton had laid out his Arizona route in 1949 with such declarations of certainty that it went unquestioned by other scholars for more than sixty years, although Bolton was making assumptions based on vague Spanish chronicles. Brasher, however, is a geologist who devoted his own money and survey expertise to exploring possible Coronado routes with excavations, interviews, and hired crews. His excavations produced sixteenth-century Spanish artifacts of metal attributed to Coronado that were on New Mexico's side of the state line, and he found verified Spanish campsites.

Brasher also consulted with modern ranchers on the feasibility of livestock travel along the New Mexico route for the expedition's thousands of horses, cattle, and sheep. He concludes that Coronado's expedition left the San Pedro River and turned northeast on an Indian trade route near Lewis Springs, Arizona. Presumably, Esteban also did so a year earlier. Bolton had theorized that everyone traveled about 36 miles farther along the San Pedro River before turning northeast, and Bandelier believed they traveled about 105 miles beside the San Pedro to its junction with the Salt River before shifting northeast. On Brasher's examined route, Coronado went through Apache Pass in Arizona and entered New Mexico near where Interstate 10 crosses the state line, traveling north toward Cíbola on the New Mexico side of the state line. He shifted northwest back into Arizona to present-day St. Johns, after which he followed the Zuni River to Hawikku.

Coronado's expeditionaries said Marcos was not familiar with the route from at least the Gila River and perhaps sooner.[39] Neither the trail nor the landscape the expeditionaries encountered resembled what Marcos had reported to the viceroy. Most expeditionaries had invested everything they had to go with Coronado, and they feared they faced financial ruin because of what seemed to be the friar's lies. They became infuriated with Marcos. Rebellion was building upon arrival at an old Indian ruin known as Chichilticale in southeast Arizona, because they had "found nothing of worth."

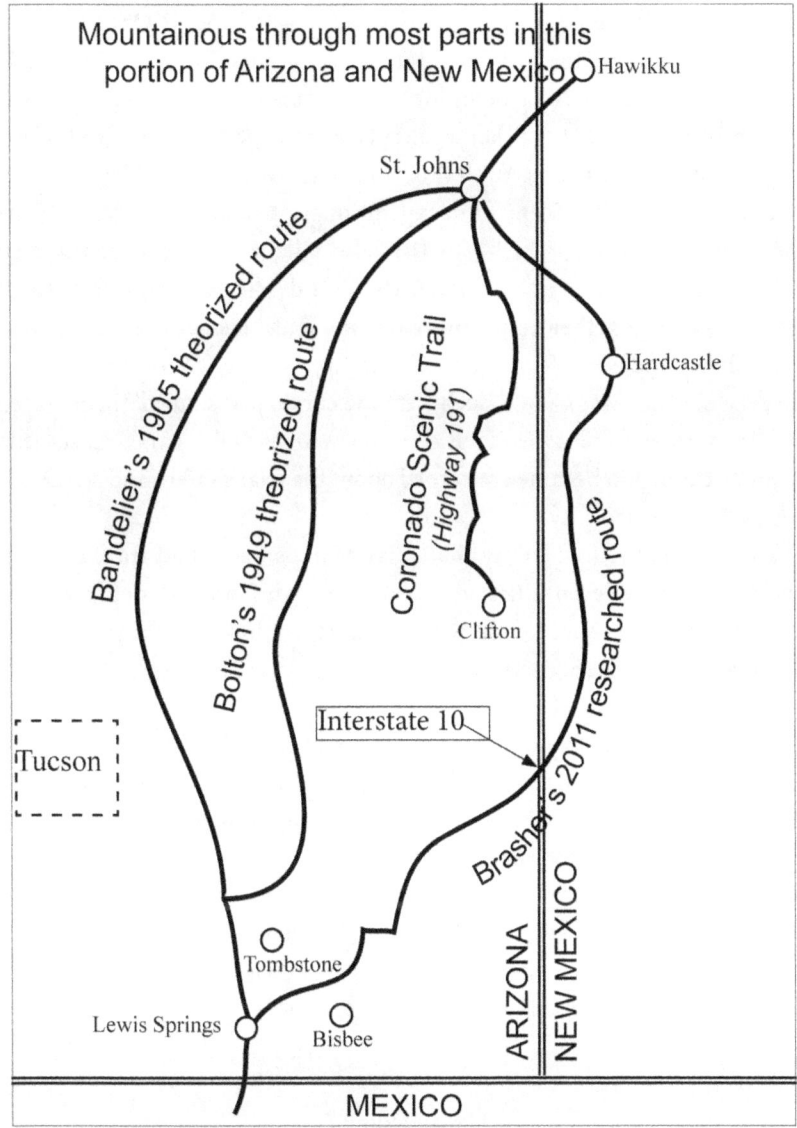

Figure 13. This map shows approximate routes that have been published for Coronado. The Bandelier route, which he believed was identical to Coronado's later route, is from *Journey of Alvar Nuñez Cabeza de Vaca*, in 1905. Bolton's route is from 1949's *Coronado: Knight of Pueblos and Plains*, while most Internet maps for Coronado's route follow US Highway 191. Only that portion designated as the Coronado National Scenic Byway is depicted. The Nugent Brasher route is adapted from *The Latest Word from 1540* (2011). This map's route for the Brasher portion from Hardcastle to St. Johns is speculative. Composite map by Dennis Herrick.

Where were all the riches that Marcos had boasted about? Or at least the wealth claimed in the rumors that spread across Mexico? Castañeda reported: "Marcos de Niza, being aware that some were upset, dispelled that danger by vowing that . . . [he] would place the expedition in a land where they could fill their hands. With this, [the anger] was quelled."[40]

Several days later, Coronado's expeditionaries came within sight of the long-heralded Cíbola, which was the Zuni village of Hawikku. The men became enraged again at the friar. Castañeda described Cíbola as a "small town crowded together and spilling down a cliff." He declared there were Spanish haciendas in Mexico with a better appearance. "When they saw the first town, which was Cíbola, such were the curses that some of them hurled at Friar Marcos that may God not allow them to reach [his ears]," Castañeda wrote.[41] Coronado became concerned about the friar's safety and sent Marcos back to Mexico City.

Cortés was the first to say that Friar Marcos never had traveled close enough to see the Seven Cities on his earlier expedition with Esteban. Cortés ridiculed Marcos's subsequent report in a deposition to the royal court in Spain on June 25, 1540, declaring:

> I deny that [Friar Marcos] had seen or discovered [the Seven Cities], instead, what the friar says he has seen he has stated and states solely through the account which I have given him of the news which I had from the Indians of the country of Santa Cruz . . . because everything the friar says is the same as those Indians told me. The putting forward of himself in this matter, manufacturing and stating what he had neither seen nor saw, is nothing new, because many other times he has done this and it is a custom of his, as is well known.[42]

Lies and Rumors

Coronado had taken Marcos as a guide because he thought the friar had been to Cíbola and knew the way. He concluded in a letter to the viceroy that "what had been so highly praised and about which the father had told so much, should turn out to be so very different. . . . Everything which the friar had reported turned out to be quite the opposite."[43]

Marcos brought back stories, but his report's sole mention of gold was a tall tale Indians told him about a valley in Mexico. Nevertheless, any mention of gold was enough to inspire rumors, which expanded in the retelling to indicate that gold could be found at Cíbola. An Italian translation of Marcos's report in 1554 contained numerous exaggerations that reflect the types of rumors about wealth cascading through Mexico after Marcos returned, leaving Esteban behind. The rumors built into a get-rich excitement among Mexico's colonists and officials that resulted in the Coronado expedition months later.

The Italian version stated the following fantasy as though it were fact about the people who would become known as the Zunis: "[Cíbola] exceeds twenty thousand households. The people are nearly white. They go about clothed and sleep in beds. They possess many emeralds and other jewels, though they do not prize them, but rather only turquoise. With this they decorate the walls at the doors to their houses, their clothing, and their drinking cups. It is spent like money in all that country. They dress in cotton and [bison] hides. [Cotton] is more valued and desirable to wear. They use drinking cups made of gold and silver, since they have no other metal. They employ [gold and silver] more often and in greater quantity than in Peru. They buy from the province of the tattooed people with turquoise."[44]

If that is an indication of the kind of talk going around, no wonder Coronado found it so easy to recruit adventurers and attract investors for Spain's largest and most expensive expedition into what is now the United States.

Even without exaggerations, Marcos is believed to have been influenced by a need to tell Mendoza what the viceroy wanted to hear so more expeditions to the north could be launched. Historian Carl O. Sauer concludes that Marcos's report was "a strange tissue of hearsay, fantasy, fact, and fraud."[45] Others have characterized Cabeza de Vaca's account in much the same way.

As for Esteban's route north through Mexico before reaching the border, a good approximation can be seen on Google Earth or a map. Routes passable in historic times often become highways in the modern era, so Esteban, and Coronado after him, probably traveled close to the route of Mexico 15 out of Culiacán, passing through San Rafael near where the returning travelers had met Alcaraz, following the coast but inland to Navojoa, up through Cócorit before turning closer to the coast, on to Hermosillo (near Krieger's Village of the Hearts with Ures also not far away), and then turning eastward near Imuris along today's route of Mexico Highway 2 through mountain passes, until encountering the San Pedro River and following it to the international boundary.

The Mexico portion of that route alone would cover more than 1,250 miles from Mexico City to Arizona, with 300 more miles still to go to reach Cíbola/Hawikku. Esteban walked the entire way, more than 1,500 miles.

CHAPTER 16

A Mysterious Fate

IMAGINE THE SCENE where the first person from the Old World makes contact with the Zuni people of the New World. The Zunis watch as a man with dark skin approaches Hawikku. They have never seen a black man before. It is early to mid-May 1539.[1]

One depiction of how he might have looked while scouting ahead of Friar Marcos de Niza is by the well-known artist José Cisneros.[2] Viceroy Antonio de Mendoza sent Esteban forth as his emissary to Cíbola, and it's known that Esteban carried four green dinner plates and had two greyhound dogs. It's logical that Viceroy Mendoza also would have outfitted Esteban similar to a Spanish hidalgo, with changes of shirts and trousers, with boots, a hat, and perhaps even a sword as a status symbol, like the Cisneros artwork depicts him. No longer barefoot and naked as he would have been on his cross-country journey, Esteban was sent forth in style to impress the natives.

The African carries a gourd rattle to Hawikku that Mexican Indians had given him and which he'd used before in the belief it granted him healing powers. He wears "[small copper] bells and [exotic tropical bird] feathers on his ankles and arms" to dress more in a manner familiar to Indians, and he decorates the gourd in the same way.[3]

Esteban is on a diplomatic mission, intended by Viceroy Mendoza and Bishop Juan de Zumárraga to open relationships with Indians north of Mexico on a peaceful basis. The Mexican Indians accompanying Esteban carry bows and arrows for hunting. Everyone proceeds to Cíbola, which turns out to be the southwesternmost Zuni village called Hawikku.

He passes a river in that early May 1539 with fields being readied for planting with maize, beans, and squash. Walking with him are a reported three hundred Indian men and women who joined his trek north through Mexico.[4] Because they go every year to Cíbola, many of the Mexican Indians with Esteban and the Cíbolans understand words in each other's languages, which encourages Esteban to learn some words as well.

The Zunis are familiar with the Mexican Indians walking with Esteban because of trade and fieldwork. Elders and warriors gather at Hawikku's entrance at the sight of up to three hundred men and women from the Pima family of tribes such as the Sobaipuri coming toward them with the black stranger. Some from other tribes were also in the group, such as Yaquis, Ópatas, and Mayos.

A few men rush to Hawikku's underground kivas to don the painted cylindrical head covers and regalia of katsinas, believing that by doing so they become the ancestor spirits that protect and guide them.[5] When the katsinas reappear in their ceremonial finery, all the Zunis move out onto the long flat plain toward the approaching alien crowd.[6]

Esteban's arrival is not a surprise. He delivered notice a day in advance that he would visit, sending some of his entourage ahead with his medicine gourd rattle. He and the Indians with him had also been watched for days, with runners racing back and forth to Hawikku with the news.[7]

No one can doubt Esteban's confidence and courage. Marcos was told through hearsay that Esteban's messengers had returned and informed Esteban he was not welcome at Hawikku because the Zunis considered the gourd rattle he'd sent as belonging to enemies. He decides to go anyway. In a third-hand paraphrase of what Esteban might have said, Marcos wrote that Esteban had told those Indians that their initial rejection was of no importance because those who showed anger received him better.[8]

Esteban has made friends with every tribe he has met, able to bond with even those who appear hostile at first. Unlike the Spaniards with their superiority complex, Esteban's life as a slave has always helped him identify with Indians on a mutually respected level. He feels he can also impress and win over Cíbola's natives.

As he walks across a desert prairie, he sees ahead a permanent Indian town—a multistory apartment complex in a dry-grass desert. Adobe houses climb up the sides of a hill to its top. He marvels at the sight. He has never seen such a substantial Indian town. It has walls three and four stories high built of adobe plaster over sandstone slabs.[9] The walls look six stories high at a glance, until Esteban realizes the buildings on top of the hill are towering over the buildings on the slopes below them, and the result seems to combine their heights.

Scores of Zuni men come forth. Esteban's guides have told him that the people refer to themselves as A:Shiwi.[10] Esteban is surprised at the sight of men wearing head covers that he considers grotesque. They are like nothing he has ever seen among tribes in his travel across the continent, completed just three years earlier, although their head covers are somewhat similar to what he'd seen in Mexico.[11] Coming toward him are men wearing painted cylinders of leather covering the person's entire head instead of just face masks. Katsina head covers of the Pueblo tribes have surreal and exaggerated features, such as large or no ears, bulging eyes, beaks, long tongues hanging out between serrated teeth, protruding lips, horns, feathers, wings on the head, and other nonhuman qualities.[12]

Esteban assumed these Indians north of Mexico would have different customs and a different religion, but he isn't sure what to make of the stunning, decorated head covers in the forefront. The most fearsome is Masaû Katsina, with its skull-like head cover and blood-splattered clothes.[13] Esteban also is surprised to see elders in the front ranks. Elders had not been respected in many other tribes he'd encountered, but here the oldest men seem to be the leaders. The Zuni men are fully dressed and draped with painted blankets or buffalo robes, and the leader wears a long cotton shirt and narrow belt plus several colorful blankets.[14] Esteban doesn't see any women. The Zunis greet Esteban's companions from tribes they recognize. But they are wary of Esteban and curious about his dark skin color.

What remains of a language barrier is overcome by arms-and-hands sign language and many words in the trade network language, which is spoken by Indians far to the south in the Land of Everlasting Summer. Some Mexican Indians with Esteban help with Zuni words they've learned. Although subject to confusion, the two groups communicate with each other.

Friar Marcos would later write that Esteban's Mexican Indian companions reported that the Zunis were friendly at first. It's the nature of the Pueblo tribes to be hospitable and to share food. Still today, visitors invited into Puebloan homes at feast day celebrations are surprised by Puebloans' generosity in sharing food with scores of guests, both native and non-native, invitees or drop-ins, friends or strangers.[15] But the longer Esteban talks, the more the Zunis start thinking that this dark-skinned visitor might have dangerous reasons for coming.

If Esteban boasted about his influence among other tribes, as traditionalist writers assume he did, the Zunis would not be impressed. To them, the wandering vagabond tribes of the Southwest and the more settled tribes of northern Mexico are nothing more than traders and people who help in their fields. Some are enemies.

Alarming News

Then Esteban reportedly makes a mistake. He tells the Zunis they must defer to him because he is the vanguard of light-skinned, bearded men who conquer every tribe they encounter. Just as he found Hawikku, these strangers also will arrive soon.[16]

That scenario comes from Arizona Indians, acting on hearsay. They would tell Hernando de Alarcón, the Spanish ship captain in a straight-line distance of four hundred miles west on the Colorado River, that the Zunis killed Esteban because "the chieftain of Cíbola asked the Negro if he had any brothers, and he answered that he had an infinite number, that they had numerous arms, and that they were not very far from there."[17]

If Esteban really said that, he was referring to Spaniards hundreds of miles away in Mexico, because there are only Indian guides and Friar Marcos several days behind him. And if that's what he did say, the Zunis are alarmed because they possess more information about the Spaniards than the Spaniards know about them.

For almost twenty cycles of seasons, traders from the south have told them how bearded men conquered the powerful warriors of the Mexica nation. Even though they are hundreds of miles away, the Zunis know the Spaniards have been occupying the Mexica capital of Tenochtitlan and rebuilding it as Mexico City.[18] They also have heard how these same light-skinned men have waged pitiless war against other tribes throughout Mexico. They know about Spanish raids for slaves to the south, where natives have been led away tied at the necks to dig in the mountains for rocks.[19] They have heard the name of "Bloody Guzmán"—Nuño Beltrán de Guzmán—whose men rode on beasts as large as elk, killing and enslaving Indians in Mexico until recently.[20] They realize that these invaders known as Castilians and Christians have been approaching ever nearer to them.[21]

The Zuni leader and elders step back to talk. Warriors and katsinas block Esteban from moving forward. Soon the elders return and then, according to Marcos, who wasn't there, tell Esteban to go to a nearby building outside the village. They tell him to stay there while they discuss what he has said. His Indians can camp in the prairie around the house, but no one is allowed to enter the village.

The Friar's Story

Friar Marcos wrote in his account that an Indian who was the son of a chief and who had run back from the village met him about three days' distance from Cíbola/Hawikku. Marcos said the man's face and body were covered with sweat from running.

Marcos wrote that the Indian told him that he'd gone in the morning to a nearby river for a drink when Zunis attacked. Marcos reported that the Indian told him that from the river he "saw Esteban fleeing and people from the city pursuing him, and they killed some of those who came with him."[22]

Marcos reported that he insisted on continuing toward Cíbola, and he said that a day's distance from the village two more Indians appeared. Unlike the first Indian, who was sweaty and exhausted, the friar wrote that the next two Indians "were bloodstained and had many wounds."[23] Those two Indians told Marcos an even more frightening story than the first man. Marcos wrote that the pair told him:

> During this whole night they did not give us to eat or drink. The next day the sun was one lance [high] Esteban left the building, and some of the [leaders] with him. Immediately many people came from the city. When [Esteban] saw them, he started to flee, and we too. Right away they gave us these arrow wounds and injuries. We fell down and other dead people fell on top of us. We stayed that way until night without daring to stir. We heard great shouts in the city and saw many men and women who

were on the lookout from the roofs. We saw no more of Esteban. Rather we believe they shot him with arrows as they did the rest of us who were traveling with him.[24]

Those two Indians claimed "more than three hundred men were dead," which would have been about everyone who had gone with Esteban.[25] "They said that they would no longer dare to go to Cíbola as they used to," Marcos wrote, in what has been described as his "wildly exaggerated report."[26]

They *assumed* the Zunis shot Esteban. But is that what really happened? None of the three Mexican Indians stated outright that Esteban was killed. Instead they recited assumptions that Zunis killed him. Friar Marcos then concluded that the Zunis killed Esteban, as did Spaniards of the time and most writers since. However, Zuni warriors would not have massacred a peaceful Mexican Indian delegation without an extreme reason. Zunis traded with the powerful and numerous tribes of Mexico's Sonora. And there was no devastating vengeance taken by the much more numerous Sonoran tribes. Thus, the encounter could not have happened the way Marcos said those Indians described it.

If Zunis did kill Esteban, a plausible explanation is written on an exhibit wall in Albuquerque's Indian Pueblo Cultural Center. It reads: "The Zuni people have said that Estevan came into their pueblo impersonating a medicine man. He demanded women as well as riches. Since the things Estevan demanded were immoral and improper for medicine men to request, the Zunis killed him."[27]

Similarly, Coronado's de facto chronicler Castañeda wrote that he'd heard the Zunis killed Esteban because "he asked them for turquoises and women."[28] Coronado described Esteban's actions as more than just requests, writing that Esteban was killed because "he was touching their women. . . . Therefore, they decided to kill him."[29]

Were the Pueblo center's accounts of Esteban demanding women and riches accurate oral history, or did Coronado and Castañeda's later unproven accusations influence the exhibit's narrative centuries later?

CHAPTER 17

Death? Or Freedom?

THE LATE ZUNI historian Edmund J. Ladd believed his ancestors did kill Esteban. He was silent about the fate of Mexican Indians with the African, perhaps because he assumed the idea of Zunis attacking people from tribes as powerful as those from Sonora was too obviously foolhardy to mention. Recounting Zuni oral history, he wrote in 1997 that Esteban "was killed not because he was black, not because of his demands, but because of his statement that he was leading white men more powerful than himself."[1]

Ladd envisioned a meeting in a kiva like what Zunis and other Puebloans still use as ceremonial chambers for religious purposes. In the kiva, men also discuss issues facing their pueblo. In such a meeting, the men would have descended into the kiva by ladder through a roof opening and been seated around its walls. An elder would rise, light a branch of juniper from the small fire at one end of the chamber, and then waft the sweet purification smoke with a fan of eagle feathers in the six directions: east, south, west, north, the heavenward zenith, and the nadir of the inner world. Stillness would envelop the room like dusk. No one would speak as the sun set, the moon climbed higher in the sky, and the interior darkened with only a flickering fire lighting the kiva's dark recess. Each elder would contemplate silently, striving to understand the will of the Zuni community. The elders were advisers to the sun priest, who would make any final decision.[2] Perhaps Esteban was ordered into the kiva meeting, where he could have been condemned—or he could have made a deal. No one can be certain what the decision was because, if Esteban had been summoned, he would have gone alone.

Juan Francisco Maura, a professor of Spanish at the University of Vermont, in 2002 challenged today's prevailing impression that Zunis killed Esteban for one of the reasons conjured by serious historians and fabulists alike. Maura offers what he calls "new interpretations" after studying the sixteenth-century chronicles. A published authority on conquistador chronicles, Maura raises the possibility that Zunis faked Esteban's death to fool the African's Spanish masters.[3] However, because his books and publications are in Spanish, many writers in English are not aware of his research.

If there was deception by Esteban and the Indians, it was so successful that what Maura labels "the supposed death" of Esteban is reported as certain in most books today, and it even became part of one Zuni oral history, but not the one discussed in the next chapter that said the Zunis "kicked" Esteban back to Mexico.

Maura notes that "all testimonials or references to the death of Esteban are spurious and second-hand. . . . Esteban's death is merely a hypothetical assumption by the Indian messengers [who reported back to Friar Marcos]."[4] Maura offers the possibility that Esteban and the Zunis plotted together to fake his death so he could live as a free man among Indians. Maura notes that others "have not hesitated a moment" in declaring that Zunis killed Esteban based on unverified assumptions and perhaps lies.[5]

Two Muslim scholars, Lhoussain Simour of the Moroccan Cultural Studies Centre and anthropologist Hsain Ilahiane of the University of Kentucky, are also among those who leave open the possibility of Esteban's survival. Simour writes that Esteban's death "remains a matter of controversy" and that "he had to invent his own death and disappear from sight forever."[6] Ilahiane says that the question of whether Zunis killed Esteban is not settled, and he believes it's possible the Zunis hid and protected Esteban, citing a Zuni oral history that they did not kill the African.[7]

Maura, Simour, and Ilahiane make up a minority of scholars who believe that Esteban was not killed. Almost all other writers, from sixteenth-century Spanish writers to early and present American historians as well as fiction and nonfiction writers, maintain that the Zunis killed Esteban. Advocates of each viewpoint are stuck with unprovable positions. Neither side has physical proof, and each is skeptical of the other's position. Those who believe Zunis did not kill Esteban rely on informed speculation and arguments of logic. Those who've decided that Zunis did kill Esteban cite assumptions by Indians and Marcos, and it is their conclusion that has become the conventional wisdom. Those who believe Zunis killed Esteban have stated their conclusive viewpoint in several books, but usually not their reasons. The following are some reasons most scholars think Zunis killed the African.

Esteban was a threat scouting ahead for Spaniards that Zunis knew to be dangerous, so they might have considered him to be an enemy spy. The Zunis reluctantly provided the Coronado expedition the next year with an interpreter—a Mexican Indian from Petatlán named Bartolomé, who had accompanied Esteban, so Vázquez de Coronado had an eyewitness source of Esteban's arrival. Spaniards readily used torture to acquire information, and they could have tortured Bartolomé, although the chronicles don't report such action.[8] Even if Bartolomé hated Spaniards, as well he might have, would he have gone along with any Zuni deception about Esteban's death?

Some Sonoran natives who traveled with Esteban to Hawikku might also have joined Coronado's advance guard the next spring. They admitted to Marcos they hadn't seen Esteban killed, but perhaps they shared other never-reported details with Coronado that would have confirmed his death. Coronado's expeditionaries felt they had strong reasons to believe the Zunis killed Esteban. Perhaps the Zuni elder telling them Esteban was killed was convincing enough. There also were many months of opportunity to hear about what happened to Esteban from other Zunis or people from other pueblos who might have known whether a Zuni story about Esteban's death was false.

A Life Spared?

But there remains the other, seldom-considered possibility. This biography is not asserting whether Zunis killed Esteban or spared his life. Instead, it examines both possibilities because a biography should consider alternatives for an aspect of Esteban's life as important as his final fate.

In presenting the most detailed examination in writing to date about the alternate possibility that Zunis did not execute Esteban, the following points should be considered.

Instead of thinking of Esteban as an enemy, Zuni leaders might have regarded Esteban as a valuable source of information about the pale, bearded invaders approaching ever nearer. For years, traders had been warning them about men with horses, armor, and metal weapons, and that these invaders were fighting tribes all across Mexico and heading their way. It's logical that Zunis might have valued Esteban as an intelligence asset. It's also logical, with death as an alternative, that Esteban might have tried to persuade them that they should.

The Indian messengers' reports from the previous chapter make it clear that they did not see Esteban shot and killed by arrows. They only assumed it. Even that traditional story seems to have changed over the centuries. A researcher a few years ago said his Zuni guide to the Hawikku site told him that Esteban had been tortured and then hanged in a Zuni plaza. The guide handwrote statements that he said he obtained from several Zuni elders who also declared Esteban was hanged.[9] If true, a hanging is very contrary to the centuries-old story of Esteban being shot with arrows while attempting to escape. No European witnessed either outcome.

Marcos was careful not to declare that the Zunis killed Esteban. Instead, he reported that some Mexican Indians told him they thought the Zunis killed him even though they didn't see it happen. All three Indians said they saw Esteban running away.

The chief's son claimed to have gone to a "nearby river," from where he'd seen Zunis killing escort members and Esteban fleeing, but the nearest river to Hawikku is two and a half miles away, too far for him to have seen details. He lied without fear of being found out because Marcos didn't know the distance.[10] The Zuni River is also about 150 feet lower than the plain in front of Hawikku.

There must be a suspension of belief when Marcos implied in his account that he was three days from Cíbola when the son of a chief arrived to tell him that Esteban's group had been attacked. If Marcos is to be believed, the final two Indian messengers met him one day's travel from Cíbola, which couldn't have been earlier than May 24.[11] The two messengers talked about a massacre that happened a day earlier, but Marcos would have arrived two weeks or more after Esteban's arrival.

Esteban proved over the years that he could establish excellent rapport with one tribe after another. It seems peculiar how so many books insist that the only natives Esteban couldn't win over were the Zunis.

The Mexican Indians accompanying Esteban revered him. If he told them—as he assuredly did—that upon his return to Mexico he feared he might be enslaved again, they might very well have agreed to deceive Friar Marcos so Esteban could live as a free man among Indian tribes.

After Coronado defeated the Zunis at Hawikku Pueblo in 1540, he reported that a Zuni elder told him that they had killed Esteban the previous year and showed him Esteban's clothes. The clothes indicated Esteban had arrived, but they were no proof he was dead. On the basis of just seeing Esteban's clothes, Coronado wrote to the viceroy that Esteban's death "is a certainty, because many of the things he was carrying have been found here."[12]

Coronado never was able to reach the top of the Dowa Yalanne refuge mesa, where the Zuni people fled. Anyone, including Esteban, could have been up there.

Coronado did not believe Marcos's account that Esteban's delegation was massacred. Coronado wrote the next year to the viceroy that the Zunis "did not kill any of those who came with [Esteban]."[13] Coronado's version makes more sense than Marcos's report that all were killed. The Ópatas, Sobaipuris, and Piman tribes from Sonora would have launched an annihilating attack of revenge if Zunis had killed their people on a peaceful mission. But they never did, which proves the falsity of the Indian messengers' report to Marcos.

Hernando de Alarcón was captain of Spanish ships on the Colorado River about four hundred miles to the west carrying never-delivered supplies for Coronado's expedition. His report of Esteban's fate consisted of a hearsay account by an Arizona Indian, who told Alarcón that the Zunis decided to kill the black man so he could not reveal their location to Spaniards still in Mexico.[14] However, as Coronado pointed out, the Indians accompanying Esteban were allowed to leave even though they also knew Hawikku's location.

Friar Marcos said the Indians who reported back to him convinced the friar that they were now afraid of the Zunis, but they suggested their fear could be relieved if Marcos would hand over all his trade items and supplies to them, which Marcos did.

The usual Indian reason given for why Zunis allegedly killed Esteban is different from the Spanish version.[15] Ladd says his ancestors feared Esteban was ahead of white invaders, which is what Alarcón's Arizona Indian also told him.[16] However, the Spanish version repeated by most Eurocentric writers is that Esteban molested Zuni women, a claim first made by Coronado a year later. Esteban might have asked for Zuni women, as the Pueblo Cultural Center's exhibit says, but his Mexican Indian companions insisted he didn't enter Hawikku, so he never would have seen Zuni women up close, let alone touched them. The accusation that Esteban abused Zuni women might be nothing more than sixteenth-century racist stereotyping of Africans and camp gossip of the time that continues to be repeated.

Robert Goodwin is puzzled why Zuni people dependent on peaceful relations with Mexican Indians would turn on those with Esteban or kill Esteban while under their protection. "Zunis tend to show incomprehension and a sense of disbelief when faced with Spanish accounts of how their ancestors murdered Esteban," Goodwin wrote.[17] He recalls meeting a Zuni elder who seemed to be "struggling to find a motive for an act that was completely out of character for his culture."[18]

If Esteban was not slain immediately, as the Spanish chronicles claim, perhaps he was accepted at first and then Zunis killed him later. A possibility could be that Zuni men took offense because he became too familiar with Zuni women after a period of time.[19] No one knows.

Some points of interest have been ignored by most writing about Esteban's encounter at Hawikku. Even if Zunis did attack Mexican Indians with Esteban, it's unrealistic to think the Zunis could kill three hundred Sonoran warriors in a running battle, especially because the Mexican Indians with Esteban outnumbered Hawikku's Zuni warriors. Many historians are convinced Marcos lied when he wrote that he reached Hawikku and saw it from a distance, thereupon retreating back to Culiacán with "more fright than food," covering the distance in an unreasonably short time. Coronado's assertion that Zunis did not kill any Mexican Indians throws Marcos's report into further dispute. And it's known that at least one Mexican Indian named Bartolomé traveled with Esteban and was living at Hawikku when Coronado arrived the following year.[20] Coronado wrote about Bartolomé, saying, "He is acting as interpreter.... he understands [Zuni and Spanish] well."[21]

A unique theory is that Zunis couldn't have killed Esteban because he never made it to Hawikku. Researchers Adorno and Pautz declare in their 1999 three-volume biography of Cabeza de Vaca, "We can surmise that Estevanico met his death in northern Sonora sometime in April 1539."[22] If so, that would mean Mexican Indians killed him, not Zunis. All other researchers believe that Esteban did make it to Zuni Hawikku.

These major counterarguments to the usual postulated development of events raise reasonable doubts about what's been written by early Spaniards and later writers, none of whom witnessed the events they wrote about. There are also conflicting versions about how Zunis killed Esteban, if they did, through ideas put forth by traditionalist writers who created their own myths. Some will be described later.

Like Maura, Simour, and Ilahiane, who believe Zunis might have faked Esteban's death, Robert Goodwin also is not convinced that Zunis killed Esteban. "Perhaps," Goodwin speculates, "Esteban warned his hosts at Zuni what to expect from the Spaniards. Did he then move on farther north, away from the relentless advance of the Spanish frontier? Or did he stay at Zuni?"[23] In any case, Esteban would need to reach an agreement with the Zunis if he wanted them to release or protect him in exchange for information about the pending invaders. He possessed more information than anyone they'd ever met about the formidable alien invaders. That's a major reason why Esteban might have persuaded the Zunis to let him stay with them in safety or release him. Esteban would have realized that obvious desertion was not feasible. If he deserted Marcos, the Spaniards would have searched for him so he could be punished. If they thought he was dead, however. . . .

No one will ever be able to prove Zunis killed Esteban. That was just an assumption in the first place that Marcos's Indians made, although it's expressed as a certainty in most history books. It also cannot be proved whether he gained his freedom among the native peoples he'd found so easy to know amid mutual respect.

Loss of Independence

Esteban experienced what it was like to be an independent person on his earlier travel across North America and Mexico. The three Spaniards with him depended on his ability to make friends and communicate with the tribes they encountered. Upon returning to Mexico City, however, his enslavement had been reaffirmed while the three Spaniards were treated as returning heroes.

Three years later, traveling weeks ahead of Friar Marcos, Esteban was reminded what it was like to be a free man instead of someone's property. The experience must have been exhilarating. Would he want to return and risk enslavement if the Pueblo world of acceptance, freedom, and equality lay open before him? He could see he had a second chance to escape Spanish slavery. He felt loyal to his fellow survivors, Dorantes, Cabeza de Vaca, and Castillo, but he felt no such connection with Friar Marcos or Viceroy Mendoza, who both used him as a tool to achieve their goals.

No one can know with certainty. But some novelists have used literary license to present what Esteban must have thought, knowing his freedom might be at risk after the Marcos mission was accomplished. "Surely Esteban was thinking about his future survival," novelist Elizabeth Shepherd writes. She points out that Esteban had lived around Spaniards long enough to fear the viceroy might keep or make him a slave again. Esteban's best chance for freedom, Shepherd theorizes, was to never return to Mexico.[24]

In a novel about Tenamaztle, the Indian leader of the Mixtón War, novelist Gary Jennings's Tenamaztle advises Esteban to lead Friar Marcos north in search of the Seven Cities but then to desert so the Spaniards could not return him to slavery in Mexico.[25] Even though that book is fiction, the advice is plausible and might have been offered by someone.

Disappearance

Northwest Mexican tribes had known about Esteban for three years. Indians left their villages in the Mexican states of Sonora and Sinaloa so they could walk with him to Cíbola. He met tribes all across the continent, identifying with them as an outsider. Fearful of the invaders, who'd killed and enslaved so many of them, the Mexican Indians looked upon Esteban as a fellow victim of pitiless sixteenth-century European aggression. So it's possible that Esteban and Mexican Indians accompanying him—and perhaps even with aid of the Zunis—could have pulled off a great hoax, resulting, as Maura puts it, in Esteban's "mysterious disappearance and freedom."[26]

Some ignore the possibilities that statements by early historians could be in error, contain a false concept, be ignorant of the facts, be hearsay, or be fabricated. Most writers disregard the fact that just as Zunis have an oral history saying their ancestors killed Esteban, there is also Zuni oral history saying they did not kill him. That alternate oral history says that Zunis held

Esteban prisoner for three days, not one night, as Indians reported to Friar Marcos. Then, Esteban "was given a powerful kick that sent him through the air back to the south from which he came."[27] A 1911 historian reports that members of the Zuni Ka-Ka Clan "took Esteban out of the pueblo during the night" and banished him southward.[28] A few early writers recount the same story, but most fiction and nonfiction writers since then dismiss it or are not aware of it.

Because oral histories, and often folklore, are memories of an actual event romanticized by the retelling, perhaps the powerful kick story is referring to a documented version that exists of Esteban's final days—spent not at the Zuni village of Hawikku, but far to the south. An undated report found in Mexico's government records recounts that Esteban retreated to southern Sonora, Mexico, a few miles from the Gulf of California. The document states: "Esteban arrived at the Río Mayo, was struck by the beauty and handsomeness of the Mayos, hid himself there and stayed. Later he married four or five women, according to the customs of the land, had offspring, and in the year 1622 his son Aboray was living there, a tall, withered Mulatto . . . a captain or chief of a section of Tesia village."[29]

That report came from a man named Ruiz, presumably a Spanish priest, eight years after the first missionaries arrived in the area in 1614. Tesia still exists as a small village near Navojoa, Mexico, on the Mayo River. About a fourth of its population still consists of Mayos.[30] It's about five hundred miles south of Hawikku. The Mexican Indians who accompanied Esteban north to Hawikku very likely included Mayo Indians, who spoke a mutually intelligible language with Yaquis. Both tribes lived on the route that Esteban led Friar Marcos on, which Esteban had traveled three years earlier with Cabeza de Vaca.

It's conceivable the Mexican Indians sent back one volunteer to Friar Marcos with a story that the Zunis killed Esteban so the friar would be afraid to go farther. When Marcos insisted on going forward, perhaps they sent two more messengers, but this time with self-inflicted wounds and bloodstained clothes. If so, the ploy worked. Then it's easy to envision them taking Esteban back to Mexico with them, wounded or not, to an out-of-the-way area of the Sonora River valley where Spanish missionaries would not arrive for another seventy-five years.

Maybe that's why one Zuni oral history says they killed him, thereby discouraging any major effort to look for him, while another oral history says they kicked Esteban to the south. Then the Zunis could have made up tales about Esteban and women and other demands that would convince contemporary Spaniards and many writers since that Esteban's death at Hawikku was an absolute fact rather than the deception it might have been.

Esteban's origins in Africa remain uncertain and are likely never to be documented. Knowledge about the man himself is vague, and the only aspects of the Hawikku incident were told in dubious accounts and rumors written by Spaniards through the lens of their sixteenth-century worldview of slavery and racial prejudice. It seems fitting that Esteban's fate should also be an enigma.

CHAPTER 18

The Durability of Myth

MOST OF TODAY's books cite as a certainty the hearsay that Esteban was killed at Hawikku. Was he killed, as so many books insist? Or did he escape to Mexico, as a historical document found in Mexico asserts? The answer might be in the way many writers reinforced racist stereotypes, repeating and enlarging upon speculation that the Zunis killed Esteban for touching Zuni women, despite Mexican Indians with Esteban saying there were no Zuni women at his arrival.

The only three eyewitnesses to write about Esteban's activities were Cabeza de Vaca, Dorantes, and Friar Marcos. None ever mentioned anything derogatory about Esteban in their writings. Viceroy Mendoza also knew Esteban and wrote to the king saying Esteban was a "persona de razón," an intelligent person, which was unusual praise by a Spaniard about a slave. In 1610 the poet-conquistador Gaspar Pérez de Villagrá referred to "El grande negro Esteban valeroso"—the big black, courageous Esteban.[1]

Not much good about him has been written since.

Certainly no one should depict Esteban as a celibate saint. But the people who knew him never described him as a man who molested women. All such reports that he did are secondhand gossip or writers' assumptions. Marcos's only comment involving women was that "three hundred men, besides many women" traveled in Esteban's entourage.[2] The friar's meager reference has motivated many writers to insinuate that the women were along because of Esteban, an accusation implied in almost all books mentioning the African.

The presence of women was not unusual, however, because many Mexican Indian warriors would refuse to go on long expeditions without their wives or female companions.[3]

An obsession about Esteban and women started the year after the African's disappearance when Coronado wrote to the viceroy in 1540. Slaveowner Coronado reported that Zunis killed Esteban "because he was touching their women," which Coronado never witnessed and the Indians with Esteban never said he did.[4] Perhaps that's what Zunis told Coronado to help conceal Esteban. In any case, Coronado's next claim to the viceroy was a whopper: "Christians did not kill anyone's women, but he [Esteban] did kill them."[5] Coronado wrote that self-serving propaganda a few weeks after he'd ordered the executions of Indian women at Chiametla, Mexico.[6] And Spaniards and other Europeans had been killing thousands of women and children for decades in the Caribbean and Americas. Coronado's letter is a good example of how conquistadors would lie even to one another if they knew their words would end up in official records.

An unnamed person writing in a prestigious historical journal in 1928 declared that Esteban "assaulted and killed women," parroting Coronado's accusation.[7] Another writer said Esteban killed a woman at Chichilticale. Such an incident is nowhere in contemporary records, although Coronado wrote a letter saying that Chichilticale Indians told the Zunis they did not like Esteban and also that Esteban "did not like the Christians."[8]

One writer says the Zunis killed Esteban because of "demands for food and women."[9] Another claims Esteban demanded "turquoise, gold, and women."[10] Many others list different demands he supposedly made.[11] These comments are despite the Mexican Indians, who reported to Marcos about Esteban's encounter with the Zunis, never mentioning any demands.

Esteban's detractors have been giving life to what they want to believe rather than what they can prove to be true. The demands they accuse him of do not exist in Spanish records of the time.

How Myths Grow

Some mistakes that live on are due to carelessness. For example, some accounts report that Esteban crossed the Rio Grande or went close to it to find Hawikku.[12] The Rio Grande is 135 miles east of Hawikku at its nearest point, but Esteban approached from the southwest by going through Arizona and western New Mexico. Honest mistakes such as these are the least problematic.[13] Much more troubling are deliberate falsehoods because a historical distortion needs to appear only once in a book for it to be picked up and repeated and often enlarged upon by subsequent writers. Usually these unsubstantiated statements attack Esteban's character or assert that Zunis killed him and deal with differing versions of how or why.

Coronado's unfounded accusation about Esteban and women led to author Ralph E. Twitchell writing in 1911 that Esteban "met with a deserved death."[14] Warren E. Rollins wrote in a historical magazine in 1919 that Esteban deserved to be killed.[15] As late as 1961, historian Frank D. Reeve wrote that "[Esteban] did not receive a friendly welcome at Zuñi, nor was he entitled to one."[16] It's doubtful these men and others who have written variations of the same theme would have felt death an appropriate punishment if Esteban had been a Caucasian.

American writers still tend to describe Esteban in escalating negative terms without any proof to confirm their opinions, such as in 1979 when a historian wrote, "The black had come north again swaggering. He had made demands on the Zuñis, and they had killed him."[17] In 1991, Nancy Lemke described Esteban as eccentric, demanding, and flamboyant.[18] A 2013 book that is promoted as *nonfiction* described Esteban as rude, presumptuous, a con man, and "appalling."[19] No person who knew Esteban ever described him in these negative terms. No evidence is ever offered for such descriptions of the African, because there is none.

Such negative characterizations of Esteban became standardized in 1893, when archaeologist Adolph Bandelier published derogatory opinions about Esteban that he represented as fact. Without any evidence, Bandelier charges on successive pages that the African was greedy, lustful, rude, unwise, reckless, abusive, and "incurred mortal hatred."[20] If true, such flaws beg the question: why did tribe after tribe like, admire, and assist Esteban?

Character assassinations continue in today's books. Coronado and Bandelier's negative tones became even more exaggerated by later writers respected in their day, such as Twitchell, Cleve Hallenbeck, Herbert Bolton, and Morris Bishop.[21] F. Ross Holland Jr. wrote a government pamphlet in 1969 accusing Esteban of being a womanizer. He went on to write that

Marcos was "shocked by his behavior" and therefore ordered Esteban to go forward without him because "Esteban's conduct became more than the priest could bear."[22] However, Marcos never wrote anything that would justify such statements, which Holland simply made up.

In the 1500s many and perhaps most men of any nationality or race could have been characterized in such a negative way because women, especially outside of marriage, held low social position. But most writers about Esteban have singled him out as especially notorious in his treatment of women.

Coronado's charge against Esteban was reinforced twenty years later by the chronicler Castañeda who, typical of his time, had a racist attitude toward Africans. Most telling is the fact that Coronado and Castañeda both established that stereotype of Esteban based on camp gossip, neither having witnessed any abuse of women by Esteban. Castañeda, who never met Esteban, wrote in his later account as if he'd known Esteban well. He expanded on what he'd read in Friar Marcos's account with details never found there, and turned rumors into *facts* accepted by writers ever since on his word alone. For example, not knowing Esteban or having been present didn't stop Castañeda from accusing Esteban of going on ahead of Marcos so he could receive credit for finding Cíbola. Castañeda also wrote without documentary evidence that Esteban arrived at Cíbola with "numerous turquoises and some beautiful women." Later writers picked up on that, building on Castañeda's quote to claim that Zunis killed Esteban because he demanded riches and Zuni women. Some traditionalist histories have insisted Esteban demanded gold or silver, even though Zunis did not know what gold and silver were.

Even that *bible* of Indian research, Smithsonian's twenty-volume *Handbook of North American Indians*, lapsed into hedged speculation by saying Esteban was "killed by the Zunis, probably because of his demands or threats."[23] Most stories are based on the generally accepted theory that Zunis killed him. The Indians with him said they assumed he was shot with arrows, and that is the usual fate that most subsequent writers have put forth as fact.

There are other versions of dubious provenance. A well-known Southwest historian came up with a unique scenario in his 2006 book, claiming the Zunis gave Esteban a "divinity test" and that when he failed they threw him off a mesa.[24] One problem with that theory is that there is no mesa at Hawikku. Another author, claiming information from unspecified Zuni oral history, says the Zunis considered Esteban holy and cut off both his lower legs to prevent any escape, adding, "Esteban lives in this way many years."[25] However, modern surgeons believe chances of survival would be very unlikely from a double amputation of legs inside an Indian village in 1539 because of shock, hemorrhage, and infection.[26]

Although never mentioned in Spanish chronicles, imaginative details appear often. A popular school textbook states Esteban was killed because "Estevan, who was black and wore feathers and rattles, may have looked like a wizard to the Zuni."[27] Pure speculation. Another book incorrectly identifies Esteban as an Arab and picks up Castañeda's wording to accuse Esteban of demanding "turquoises and beautiful women" at every Indian village along the way. There's no record of him doing that other than Castañeda's hearsay, and besides, Europeans did not put much value at that time on turquoise stones.[28] A 2009 book claims an "arrogant" Esteban rode into Hawikku on a horse—an animal not present on the Marcos journey.[29] Similarly, a Time-Life Book declares that Esteban "swaggered north like some fantastic potentate," justifying that characterization by describing Esteban's "long, bright-colored robes" and other "regal attire"—although no such clothing is described in any record of the time.[30] A 2014 book claims Friar Marcos objected to Esteban because the African "descended into paganism and lechery to further his ambition and carnal desires."[31] There is no record of the friar ever saying that or anything similar.

Many stories differ so much from the Sonoran Indians' eyewitness accounts that they must be fabricated. Morris Bishop in 1933 dramatizes Esteban's confrontation with the Zunis by writing, "Esteban stood forth in the manner of Joshua and called on the city to surrender. He was answered with a shower of arrows."[32] A 1973 book reports that Zunis killed Esteban while he was bathing in an eroded dirt arroyo.[33] In a 1976 book, imagination takes over: "[Esteban] dashed from the house.... In ten yards he was brought down by a hail of arrows, pierced, it has been written, by twelve of them."[34] Really? Shot down in exactly ten yards? Struck by exactly twelve arrows? None of that appears in any Spanish record. Another author specifies that Zunis executed Esteban by firing squad with exactly forty-four arrows.[35] Still another writer states that an arrow wounded Esteban in the thigh, but he still managed to flee to a river and hide for a while before they found him, tied him up, and killed him with lances.[36] The author doesn't explain how he could know that. The nearest river is two and a half miles away—a long way to run across open ground wounded and with Indians in close pursuit shooting arrows.

Putting forth scenarios that no European or Mexican Indian could have witnessed is a favorite tactic of many writers considered to be "historians" in the past, with their imagined events often reprinted in other books and passed on as fact.[37] One of the most imaginative writers about the past was Mabel A. Farnum. She marketed her 1943 book *The Seven Golden Cities* as history, but her books were what is known as costume-drama fictionalized history. She could make up quotations for dramatic effect, rearrange facts, insert her own interpretations and prejudices, revile Esteban as disgusting and unprincipled, invent events, ignore or distort facts inconvenient to her story line, and emphasize Indians as "unholy ones" while she lionized the European Christians.[38]

Statements of false beliefs become entrenched. Each retelling becomes more exaggerated and includes the detail so many love because falsehoods can seem credible if they're detailed enough. David J. Weber discusses such writers' fictions, noting the "tendency to write pietistic history.... All peoples seem to engage in the making of myths and passing them off as fact ... historians have perpetuated many a previously demolished argument and hoary myth."[39]

James W. Loewin in *Lies My Teacher Told Me* explains that "cultural imperialism" is a deliberate process in which even scholars can get caught up, replacing historical facts with myths favoring the dominant culture.[40] The result, historians David Chipman and Robert Weddle observed in 2013, "is that myths and falsehoods [seem] to rise ... like fog above a swamp."[41]

Bobby Lee Patton, who traced and walked Esteban's route as closely as possible in 1984, summarized African Americans' frustration about the way American writers have presented Esteban's story. Referring to the negativity, Patton said: "A lot of things the earlier writers said were unfair. There is no conclusive evidence that allows us to make such a summation about Estevan. ... These historical accounts should have been as unbiased as possible."[42]

Moroccan scholar Lhoussain Simour points out that in colonial narratives the nonwhite cannot be a hero. "The 'Other' as hero is to be declined, fragmented, and put into total oblivion because [of] his racial attributes," Simour writes. "Heroism is attributed to the conquistadors whereas the 'Black Moor' becomes an excluded actor of history."[43]

Hsain Ilahiane puts it another way. "Because they silenced the marginal persons or minimized their roles in the colonization of the New World," he writes, Spaniards denied a meaningful role for Esteban and made him a footnote of history.[44] He believes conquistadors suppressed Esteban's voice and role so the benefits and booty of discoveries would go to the Spaniards.[45]

Who Was First?

Chroniclers from the sixteenth century to the present often are quick to assign the worst traits to black historical figures and the best traits to whites. Accomplishments by blacks, such as Esteban being the first non-Indian to enter Arizona and New Mexico, were ignored or belittled. Debate remained focused instead on who was the first *white European* to arrive.

Historian Lansing B. Bloom exemplified such chauvinism in 1940. In asking the question "Who discovered New Mexico?," he never considers Esteban a candidate, dismissing him as merely a slave. Instead, he debates right of discovery between Friar Marcos and Coronado.[46] It's an absurd choice. Most historians are convinced Marcos never reached Hawikku.[47] As for Coronado, he did not arrive in New Mexico until a year after Esteban. Some books never mention Esteban and just credit Friar Marcos as the first non-Indian to see Hawikku/Cíbola.[48]

A few do give Esteban credit for his role in history. For example, a 1970 article emphasizes, "It was Estevanico alone who probed first and farthest in the northward search for the fabled cities of Cibola."[49] One researcher points out, "Historians have known and recognized that Esteban reached the Seven Cities first, but they nevertheless have made the priest the hero of the expedition."[50] William Loren Katz writes, "That an African slave should first search the New World for a mythical land of wealth [and be ignored] is symbolic of the black experience in America."[51] Former US Secretary of the Interior Stewart L. Udall, who grew up in St. Johns, Arizona, just across the state line from the Zuni pueblos in New Mexico, became fascinated with Esteban's story. "Esteban's skin color and religion are not the critical facts," Udall states. "What is vital is that we accord this man the recognition he has long been denied."[52]

In Pensacola, the Florida Black Chamber of Commerce annually awards the Estevanico Cultural Heritage Award, with the following wording: "Estevanico is truly an unsung hero.... His life serves as an inspiration for those who serve without recognition, forgotten because of their unselfish service for the benefit of others."[53]

Moroccan authors treat Esteban as the expedition's heroic figure, both in their fiction and in academic writings. A Moroccan historian writes in French in his 2006 book: "[Esteban] knew all sorts of situations: simple servant, soldier, sailor, explorer, slave, healer and shaman, defender of the oppressed Indians and idolized by the natives.... He had learned Indian languages. He knew the indigenous soul and was steeped in the culture of the different tribes with which he had stayed."[54]

Myths, assumptions, mistakes, and fabrications have combined to tell iconic stories. But are the stories repeatedly told about Esteban true or false? Can Esteban's character ever be determined after almost five hundred years? Probably not. But that's what people who write about Esteban should report, instead of creating different profiles that are nothing more than their personally favored hypotheticals—unless they admit they're writing entertainment fiction, not history.

As for writing about his fate, everyone should consider whether only the one possibility that Zunis killed Esteban should continue to be stated with categorical insistence while the alternative possibility that they didn't, at least not right away, is dismissed without mention. It's unlikely there will be any proof after almost five centuries, but the common practice of making up facts just to make history more dramatic or to fit preconceived notions or biases dishonors the memory of Esteban as a real person with both virtues and faults. That practice recalls the chapter 1 quote by Voltaire from the seventeenth century, in which he states, "All the old histories, as one of our great minds used to say, are only fables agreed upon."[55]

CHAPTER 19

Inhumane Bondage and Historical Context

ESTEBAN'S SLAVERY WAS a common fate shared by millions. National powers that enslave others have been at the heart of wars, economies, and religions throughout Eurasia for millennia. It also was a tradition among African tribes and natives throughout the Americas.

The perennial victims have been women and children taken as prisoners of war over the centuries—defeated males were usually massacred—plus criminals, foreigners, and people of races, religion, and attributes unacceptable to a dominant society.

The first documents revealing the existence of slavery come from Sumeria in 2000 BCE.[1] Throughout the world, in advanced as well as primitive societies, slavery existed long before it was systemized and addressed by laws, such as the Hammurabi Code of the second millennium BCE.[2] It owed its origin to pre-mechanized societies' need for manual labor. David Brion Davis, a leading authority on slavery and abolition, believes that slavery might also have been modeled on the domestication of animals.[3]

England took pride in not enslaving its own citizens despite its global slave trafficking of Africans into the 1800s. But England did have its slave past, with up to 30 percent of its population estimated to be slaves by the twelfth century.[4] Afterward, slavery crept back into British society for several thousand Africans and other foreigners until court decisions and legislation ended it by 1833 in England, although not in some other parts of the British Empire.

Slavery scholar Orlando Patterson points out that a slave had no worth other than being the property of another. "Slavery is the permanent, violent domination of natally alienated and generally dishonored persons," he wrote in his 1982 book, *Slavery and Social Death*.[5] "The power of the master over both black and white servants was near total," he wrote. "Both could be whipped and sold."[6]

Spaniards have received the most blame for mistreatment, enslavement, and killing of native inhabitants of the Americas, due to anti-Spanish propagandizing by their European enemies. The irony is that in 1542 Spain became the first nation to make Indian slavery illegal. Colonists and clergy found ways to get around the law and keep Indians in various conditions of forced labor for far longer, but no other European nation even made an attempt to declare Indian slavery illegal as soon as Spain did.

There was certainly great Spanish cruelty in the Americas, but the British, French, Dutch, Germans, Russians, Portuguese, Americans, and others also committed atrocities.

European enslavement of Indians was a widespread strategy for reducing large native populations. In North America, the French enslaved Indians in Canada and Louisiana, but nowhere near to the extent of the British or, in South America, the Portuguese. Mexico's government, considering Yaqui Indians an "obstacle to civilization," captured and sold thousands as slaves in the first decades of the 1900s to tobacco, henequen, and sugarcane plantations, where most died within a year from overwork and starvation.[7] *Indian Slavery in Colonial America*, edited by Alan Gallay, reports how British and other European colonists enslaved and sold an uncountable number of Indians from New England and along the Atlantic coast and into the interior during the 1600s and 1700s as a deliberate policy to reduce the Indian population in what is now the United States.[8] British colonists enslaved Indians, especially women and children, and many if not most were sold as slaves to the Caribbean or other distant places so there'd be no hope of return.

All colonial powers have used violence and cruelty to exploit, dispossess, and kill indigenous people to secure mineral riches or other wealth, land, slaves, and hegemony. An American warfare and relocation policy against its indigenous population continues to cause bitterness today, as does the long history of enslavement of Africans and Indians.

Even the most privileged slave, as Esteban seems to have been, remained always subject to an owner's whim for severe punishment, sale to another master, and even death. All slaves experienced Patterson's "social death" in that they had no purpose in life except to fill their owner's wishes.

Slavery has long been justified by religious beliefs. An example is the 1633 sermon by Portuguese Jesuit Antonio Vieira. Preaching to a congregation of masters and slaves, Vieira said slaves should never revolt against their owners no matter how cruelly they are treated, saying their obedience in this life would ensure their freedom in heaven—a religious hell-and-then-paradise argument for slave passivity and even martyrdom.[9] Vieira's priestly endorsement of slavery despite its inherent contradictions put into words the rationalization used to enslave others throughout human existence.

Repeatedly, even when laws were passed to eliminate slavery, many societies carried on as before. An example is Spain, which in 1542 outlawed the enslavement of Indians in the Americas but continued the encomienda system that certainly felt like slavery to Indians. "Not only did the Spaniards continue to enslave some Indians," Davis says, "but encomenderos made large fortunes by exploiting Indian workers as if they were worthless slaves who could not be sold or purchased."[10]

Another example is Brazil, which was the last place in the Americas to abolish slavery. It was not ended until May 1888 by the Portuguese imperial family, although de facto forced labor known as "debt peonage" continues on large estates called *fazendas*. Caucasians were enslaved in Europe over the centuries by each other and in wars between Christians and the Muslim Moors and Ottoman Turks, where all three sides took tens of thousands of captives as slaves. In 1514, twenty-two years after hostilities between Christians and Moors supposedly ceased, a Spanish force invaded North Africa and freed fifteen thousand Christian slaves.[11] Most captives enslaved in Europe's wars were never seen again, no matter who captured them. Both Christians and Muslims of the time justified enslavement, killings, and torture as showing devotion to God.[12] Davis points out that American slavery became focused on people classified as Negroes, even though many African Americans had large percentages of European ancestry.

Portuguese ships sent African slaves to the North American continent throughout the 1500s, followed by the French sending captive Africans to the Caribbean and South America and eventually to the United States.[13] The first Africans for plantation work in today's United States arrived in 1619, when a British pirate ship that had overwhelmed a Portuguese slave ship sold twenty Africans to work for British colonists in Virginia's earliest tobacco fields.[14]

Native Americans also were captured and sold as slaves for about two hundred years in many parts of the United States, especially French and Spanish colonies from Louisiana to California. President Andrew Johnson ordered New Mexico's slave trade suppressed and Indian captives freed in June 1865. But in rural areas, some Indians continued to be held illegally until the end of the century.[15]

Slavery Rises Rapidly

Portuguese ships began delivering Africans to the New World through the Atlantic slave trade system within a few years of Columbus's first voyage. Although slaves were sold to Spaniards, the acquiring and shipping of slaves had been Portugal's virtual monopoly since the mid-fifteenth century.[16] One estimate suggests that trafficking in slaves equaled or surpassed the gold or spice trades' profitability by the early 1500s.[17]

Nicolás de Ovando, Spanish governor on Hispaniola, was given royal permission in 1505 to import blacks as slaves. Spain's King Ferdinand then shipped 17 African slaves to Hispaniola that April and promised 100 more in November. In 1510, Ferdinand sent 250 slaves to work in two gold mines.[18] Even earlier, Ovando had taken an unknown number of black and mulatto servants and slaves in his convoy of ships, landing at Hispaniola in 1502. The first African to escape from slavery in the Americas arrived on one of those ships, an anonymous man who "escaped to the Indians" in Hispaniola's mountainous interior soon after arrival.[19]

Africans were used in every way possible, and some even fought on the side of the conquistadors or the Indians. By 1514, Africans and people of African descent surpassed the numbers of Iberian Caucasians on Hispaniola, according to historian Leslie B. Rout Jr.[20]

Prior to 1441 Europeans had exhibited no preference for black slaves, figuring any non-Christian person was enough of an *other* to enslave. Blacks became preferable when Africa's intertribal wars led to them being captured or bought in large numbers with relative ease. Raiding and capturing sub-Saharan blacks raised moral questions, however, that had to be rationalized. Taking captives in war, such as the Muslims who dominated the Iberian Peninsula for centuries, had been justified by cherry-picking the Bible's Old Testament passages, with its many rules on acquiring and treating war captive slaves. But sub-Saharan Africans were not at war with Iberians, so how to justify enslaving them?

Rout says that understanding how enslaving black Africans was rationalized gives a "sobering comprehension as to why a basically inhumane institution resisted all efforts to destroy it for hundreds of years" in Christian societies.[21] Millennia-old slavery practices were called upon for justification, and the Bible was used again. In addition to the Bible's passages on the enslavement of war captives, eventually Genesis 9:25–27 was cited. In that passage, Ham is described as the son of Noah, and he commits some unspecified offense that led Noah in the book of Genesis to illogically curse not Ham but the descendants of Ham's son, Canaan, condemning them to be slaves to all other races.[22]

Because Christians had come to believe that Canaan's descendants settled in Africa and somehow became a separate black race, they associated Africans with the biblical curse. Pseudoscientific theories were then spread about blacks "in an attempt to find an unassailable argument. . . . why one part of the human race should live in perpetual indebtedness to another."[23] By citing the Bible, and using the reinforcement of two fifteenth-century papal bulls that justified enslavement of pagans so they could be Christianized, Christian slaveowners persuaded themselves that they were following God's law by buying and using black slaves.

This attitude carried over into government, where laws conspired to treat blacks as inferiors based on the color of their skin. Slavery had to be rationalized because it had become such a socioeconomic foundation for the young United States and the conquest of the Americas. People who profited could not imagine how they could retain their wealth and manage their plantations without slaves.

As one example, Thomas Jefferson owned hundreds of slaves, but in his rhetoric he expressed doubts about the morality of the system that made him rich. At one point, Jefferson characterized slavery as "the most unremitting despotism on the one part, and degrading submission on the other."[24] Another of his quotations is on the third panel of the Jefferson Memorial: "Commerce between master and slave is despotism. Nothing is more certainly written in the book of fate than that these people are to be free."[25] The hypocrisy of his rhetoric is evident in his will, in which he freed only five relatives of his mistress Sally Hemings and ordered about two hundred other slaves to the auction block to profit his estate.[26]

European and American traffic in "black gold" lasted for more than four hundred years. UCLA political scientist Anthony Pagden characterizes it as "the largest forced migration in human history." In his analysis and history of slavery in a magazine article in 1997, Pagden points out that five times more Africans than Europeans went to the Americas between 1492 and 1820.[27] Pier M. Larson, a professor specializing in slavery studies at Johns Hopkins University, estimates that 11.3 million Africans such as Esteban were sold into slavery between 1400 and 1900 through the Atlantic trade, the overwhelming majority of them enslaved across the Americas in the 1700s and 1800s.[28]

European and American enslavement also extended to Indians, especially in the first years of the United States. Indian slavery is less well known than African slavery, but enslavement of millions of natives over four centuries throughout the Americas is detailed in the 2016 book *The Other Slavery: The Uncovered Story of Indian Enslavement in America*. Author Andrés Reséndez notes: "Colonial Americans in places such as New England, Virginia, and the Carolinas had Indian slaves.... But the institution was subsequently eclipsed by African slavery. By the middle of the nineteenth century, the memory of these earlier Indian slaves had been so sufficiently erased that many Easterners experienced the phenomenon of Indian slavery in the West as a novelty."[29]

Slavery Today

Forms of slavery still exist today with war captives, undocumented immigrants intimidated into forced labor, children abducted or sold to become soldiers or indentured servants, sweatshop laborers, the involuntary sex trade, and lifelong debt bondage trapping generations of families. The global human rights organization Walk Free Foundation reported in 2014 that the adult and children slave populations totaled 14.3 million in India, 3.2 million in China, and 2.1 million in Pakistan, with a total of almost 30 million people in involuntary servitude worldwide.[30]

But it doesn't stop there. Unpaid or low-pay labor by prisoners also continues today, and it's legal because the United States' Thirteenth Amendment's abolition of slavery did not apply to prisoners. That led to prison road gangs and prisoners working for token wages today for major corporations, although many companies end the practice when it's brought to public attention. Several for-profit corporations make goods, from weapon systems to household appliances, with prison labor paid pennies on the dollar.[31]

Indians Enslaving Indians

Reséndez describes how Indians of the Americas, like almost every other culture in the world, also indulged in slavery: "Native Americans had enslaved each other for millennia, but with the arrival of Europeans, practices of captivity originally embedded in specific cultural contexts became commodified, expanded in unexpected ways, and came to resemble the kinds of human trafficking that are recognizable to us today."[32]

The Inca had a public service requirement where males fifteen to fifty worked for free several months every year for the emperor and government in the *mit'a* system, which enabled the Inca to build great public works such as paved roads, temples, monuments, bridges, and to work in the mines for gold. It was forced labor for the common good, with mit'a workers also assigned to fields for the emperor and also for the disabled, elderly, sick, and for absent warriors in wartime. People provided tribute to the government in the form of labor instead of taxes.

The Aztecs had slavery, although still different from European concepts of forced servitude. Aztec slaves were known as *tlacotin*, but it was not hereditary. A tlacotin's children were free, possessions were allowed, and a tlacotin could buy his or her freedom and even own other slaves. Tlacotin were distinct from war captives, who were sacrificed to the Aztec deities. However, upon being sold three times for incorrigibility, a tlacotin also could be purchased for sacrifice. Criminals and anyone who did not pay their debts could be enslaved, and people also could sell themselves into slavery.

Maya society consisted of four classes: royalty, priests, commoners, and slaves known as *Pencat'ob'*, which made up a major part of the Mayan population. Before the Spaniards arrived, the Maya of the Yucatán Peninsula are believed to have relied less on agriculture than upon their famous production of honey, salt, cotton cloth, and slaves, who were commoners taken in war. Opposing nobles and war leaders were sacrificed to Mayan gods.[33]

During his 1540s governorship in South America, Cabeza de Vaca reported numerous incidents of Indians enslaving other Indians. In what is now the United States, the best-known example of Indians enslaving other Indians, because of its unusual nature, is the Iroquois League's "mourning wars," waged against neighboring tribes to replace deceased Iroquois members. Some captives were adopted into families to replace lost ones. They would in time become acculturated Iroquois. Although not slaves in the usual sense, they were forcibly removed from loved ones, prevented from escaping, and forced to live in alien Iroquois families.[34] War captives not considered suitable for adopting were killed or forced into slavery.[35]

A more recognizable practice is how many US tribes raided one another for war captives long before European contact across all of North America, especially women and children for slavery or adoption, and men and women for torture and sacrifices.[36] Intertribal raiding and selling of Indian slaves grew to be a major part of the economy throughout North America, and it persisted in the American Southwest into at least the late 1800s. By taking on other guises, such as debt peonage under which people are forced to work off debts, and even vagrancy laws, forced labor continued in the Southwest and West long after the United States banned slavery.

As desire increased for European trade goods such as muskets and powder, northeastern tribes used captive slaves as a form of currency in trading with or selling to each other and to settlers.[37] James F. Brooks writes, "Horses, sheep, guns, and buffalo hides spring immediately to mind as customary exchange items, but women and children proved even more valuable."[38]

Enslavement of Africans started in the American South very early among Americans, and some Indian tribes also adopted the practice of African slavery, especially in the South. By 1860 African slaves made up 10 to 18 percent of the populations of the Creek, Choctaw, Cherokee, and Chickasaw populations. American southerners often objected to Indians not disciplining their slaves as harshly as white-owned plantations. "A slave among wild Indians is almost as free as his owner," one complained.[39] Frederick Douglass observed in 1850, "The slave finds more of the milk of human kindness in the bosom of the savage Indian than in the heart of his Christian master."[40] Nevertheless, a slave was still property and could not leave except rarely through manumission, escape, or death.

Indian tribes farther from the slave-holding culture of whites often tended to welcome Africans into their societies.[41] The tradition of Indians enslaving other Indians and selling them as slaves was concentrated in the West in the eighteenth and nineteenth centuries with the growing market for slaves among European, American, and Hispanic buyers. Utes, Comanches, Kiowa, Apaches, and Navajos were active in kidnapping and selling captives into slavery, intermarriage, or adoption, whether other Indians, Hispanics, or Caucasians. Raid-and-trade networks extended deep into Mexico and eastward to the Mississippi River, and Indian-held captives of many races could end up anywhere from New England to Mexico City.[42]

CHAPTER 20

What Isn't Known about Esteban

THE VAGUENESS AND ambiguity of the few Spanish documents mentioning Esteban have left a fragmentary image of the man behind a haze of centuries.

Records of his time speculate but never state with certainty when he was born, whether at Azemmour or elsewhere in Africa, whether he was enslaved first by an Arab master, or if he grew up free and volunteered to be a slave on the Iberian Peninsula to survive Morocco's drought. There are no direct quotations from him because nothing except paraphrases of what he said were ever recorded. There's no clue whether he had brothers or sisters, or what his childhood or Islamic parents were like, or much else of what you'd expect to see in a biography such as this.[1]

Modern writers often provide detailed descriptions of Esteban's appearance, but physical details in the documentary record say nothing except he was tall, a relative term for the 1500s, and that he was a "black man who wore a beard."[2]

He must have had a likeable personality or he never would have become so popular with Indians and accepted by Spaniards. His demonstrated hardiness indicated the stature and physique of an athlete. There is so little recorded about his appearance that not much else can be inferred. He was a slave, so Spaniards did not pay much attention to him as a man.

It's not known if he was branded, as most slaves were then, and if so, if a brand had been burned onto his face, a shoulder, or elsewhere. It's not known if his back was striped with scars from a whip. Many slaves were whipped when first acquired or for the slightest infraction to prove that their master was boss. As social scientist Orlando Patterson notes, "There is no known slaveholding society where the whip was not considered an indispensable instrument."[3] The life of any field slave, from ancient times through the 1800s, was brutal and exhausting. Personal slaves such as Esteban, often euphemistically referred to as "servants" but slaves nevertheless, had an easier life, but they still were subject to whippings, beatings, and arbitrary sale to worse masters.

The process of turning a free and independent person into a slave was always marked with violence and the constant threat of being sold or killed. Slavery was, in effect, a substitute for death. Patterson explains, "The condition of slavery did not absolve or erase the prospect of death. Slavery was not a pardon; it was, peculiarly, a conditional commutation. The execution was suspended only as long as the slave acquiesced in his powerlessness."[4]

In rare and very defined circumstances, a slave could one day be freed, albeit to a life still marred with discrimination. Most could only pray and dream for such an end. The vast majority of slaves and generations of their descendants were trapped for their lifetimes, although there have been some areas in South America where manumission was common, resulting in a society with a mix of free and enslaved blacks.

Spanish chronicles are silent on how Dorantes treated Esteban. However, there is a documented example about treatment of a favored personal slave for a man named York, whose experience parallels Esteban's in many ways. As the African American slave of William Clark of the Lewis and Clark expedition, York enjoyed the kind of faux freedom on the 1804–1806 expedition that Esteban experienced crossing the continent more than two and a half centuries earlier. York risked his life to save Clark at least once, smoothed the way for good relations with Indian tribes, and voted on expedition issues. York was allowed to carry weapons but also often assigned to manual labor.

Like Esteban after his crossing of the continent, upon completion of the Lewis and Clark expedition York reverted to being simply his master's slave. Once back in Missouri, Clark sold York's wife to a slaveowner in Louisville, Kentucky. When York asked to be set free or at least sold to his wife's new owner, Clark threatened to sell York to "some severe master." He then had York given "a severe trouncing," which in the parlance of the times could mean a torturous whipping.[5] Clark did not free York until about ten years after returning from the expedition.

York's treatment gives insight into Esteban's situation—or at least into what Esteban might have imagined his future could be if he returned to Mexico from Hawikku. Although it would be illegal to re-enslave him if the viceroy had indeed freed him, it's not certain whether the viceroy sent him north as a free man or a slave. Even if he had been freed, would Esteban be willing to risk the chance of being re-enslaved by someone other than the viceroy?

As with Esteban, original journals never once mentioned York in terms of sexual activities. In 1814, however, an editor of another narrative distorted the record with imaginary tales of York and Indian women. A PBS website notes, "This has resulted in a lasting impression of York's assumed sexual powers, perpetrated by writers of fiction and nonfiction alike, who have greatly magnified the importance of the creative 1814 version."[6] Such a portrayal of York is similar to later writers' treatment of Esteban.

In fact, there's a curious omission of sex by the entire Cabeza de Vaca group over the eight years of their travel across the continent. While enslaved, that's understandable, but in the last year and a half while they were on friendly terms with Indian women often naked or nearly naked, it seems less credible. This is mentioned because writers have made major and escalating accusations against Esteban about having sexual liaisons with native women, stating their opinions as fact despite no evidence. Yet they write not a word about the three Spaniards, who would seem to have led lives of devout celibacy—at least according to all history books. However, upon arrival with the Avavares in Texas and afterward there are hints that perhaps the Spaniards were not as chaste as history books indicate. Dorantes might have left a clue when he said the Avavares let the travelers "live in liberty and do anything they pleased" for the six or seven months they spent with the tribe.[7] Nevertheless, it is only Esteban's morality that later writers questioned.

York's story is always told through the words and perspectives of others, just as Esteban's story is. Both were slaves, so members of the dominant societies writing about them often referred to each in a condescending way. An Oregon Public Broadcasting documentary points out that written accounts about York presented the "preponderance of inaccuracy, prejudice, and stereotype reflecting the attitudes of the times in which they were written."[8] That's also true of accounts written about Esteban. Similarly, both Esteban and York might have found refuge among Native Americans.

After the eight-year ordeal with Cabeza de Vaca and the other two Spaniards, Esteban was turned over to the viceroy to guide Marcos northward. Zunis then either killed Esteban, which is the conventional belief, or Esteban attained his freedom. As for York, upon gaining his freedom, he also disappeared from history. Or perhaps not. Mountain man Zenas Leonard reported he met an African American man living in a Crow Indian village in north-central Wyoming in 1834. In his autobiography, Leonard wrote: "In this village we found a Negro man, who informed us that he first came to this country with Lewis & Clark—with whom he also returned to the State of Missouri, and in a few years returned again with a Mr. Mackinney, a trader on the Missouri river, and has remained here ever since, which is about ten or twelve years. He has acquired a correct knowledge of their manner of living, and speaks their language fluently. He . . . assumes all the dignities of a chief."[9] The man Leonard met might have been York, who would have been in his sixties in 1834.[10] It's logical York might have returned close to the route he traveled on the expedition, where Indians had treated him with respect.

Did Esteban experience final days like that? No one can prove anything one way or the other. At least, neither Dorantes nor Clark had their personal slaves Esteban and York killed. That was always an option for a slaveowner handling any defiant man or woman resisting enslavement. Killing a slave was always a possibility because it was a rare slaveholding society that imposed a significant penalty for murdering a slave. Throughout history, masters could murder slaves and face only a fine or excommunication from the church for a few years. Often there was no penalty at all.[11] If a person killed someone else's slave, the usual penalty was to reimburse the owner for the slave's cash value.

The disregard for a slave's life or death accounts for the historical neglect of Esteban for almost five hundred years. This surprised Tony Horwitz, who writes: "Nowhere in the half dozen Spanish accounts of Estevanico's journey is there any expression of regret over his death, or appreciation of his service."[12]

Whether we blame it on racial prejudice, refusal to give a slave or even former slave any credit, or the lies Europeans told one another to claim history for themselves, Coronado and Castañeda set a negative tone about Esteban that continues today and becomes ever more negative in many books.

Facts about Esteban are that no Mexicans Indians or Europeans saw him killed, but almost everyone thinks he was, and that a priest and conquistadors who traveled with him never mentioned anything about Esteban abusing women, but almost everyone thinks he did.

This biography of Esteban has wrestled with Eurocentric perspectives, misunderstandings, prejudices, assumptions, falsehoods, and myths. They form the foundation of so much of what Americans think they know about Esteban. However, Esteban's place in history should not be judged on hearsay and fictions that have dominated analysis of his life and achievements. Against the odds, this African slave earned a prominent role in the slaveholding Spanish society of the early 1500s.

Esteban's fellow Moroccans hope to restore Esteban's reputation. Referring to Esteban by the North African name of Mostafa al-Azemmour, Moroccan scholar Lhoussain Simour states in the *European Review of History* that Esteban "turns into a real hero" despite Cabeza de Vaca's attempt to keep him in the background. "Yet why is it that [his] name and achievements have remained in obscurity so long? He is still one of the most important adventurers and explorers of America's Southwest, who transformed the cultural and historical landscape of the New World."[13]

APPENDIX

An American Sculptor's Tribute

One of the "blue men of the Sahara," as they're known, wearing the blue-dyed robe and turban of an ancient Berber tribe of Morocco, rode his camel past John Sherrill Houser. The American sculptor realized he'd found the model he'd been seeking for a statue of Esteban. The camel rider was a young man named Lachel Eldassi. He'd never modeled before, but he agreed to pose for Houser to create a clay bust that would be cast in bronze.[1]

Houser recalled in an interview his excitement upon seeing the camel rider, who was about the same age that Esteban had been while traveling with the three Spaniards south of today's El Paso, Texas, in 1535.[2] Houser had gone to Morocco in hopes of finding the best ethnic model for his bust of Esteban and believed he'd found one. Eldassi even had an ancient Portuguese trade bead strung around his neck. Enhancing Houser's discovery was that Eldassi modeled for him in Azemmour, Esteban's presumed birthplace or at least childhood home.[3]

For the modeling session, Eldassi took off his turban and flowing robe, both dyed blue from the ink of sea urchins from the Mediterranean. In place of those, Houser sculpted a buffalo robe and a feather in the hair for the bust. Eldassi's trade bead hangs around his neck in the sculpture.

Houser planned to have his depiction of Esteban as part of a larger sculpture intended for El Paso's "XII Travelers Memorial of the Southwest." Houser mentioned that funding problems prevented him from completing that sculpture, "although at one time there was even interest in installing a duplicate [of the bust of Esteban]" in Azemmour.[4] When funding is finalized, he said, the finished sculpture might combine "Estebanico the Black" with a figure of Cabeza de Vaca, commemorating their passage near El Paso.

Other than Houser's effort, there is little in the way of public recognition of Esteban. The only sculptural display of Esteban's likeness is Houser's bronze bust, which is exhibited in a predominately black neighborhood of El Paso inside the McCall Neighborhood Center and in a museum at St. Petersburg, Florida. It's the sculpture seen on this book's cover. The late Alex Haley, famous for his book *Roots: The Saga of an American Family*, about his African heritage, was among those who expressed support for Houser's plans to erect a statue honoring Esteban.[5] The late author James Michener also wrote a letter to Houser supporting a sculptural tribute to Esteban.[6]

The first public space named for Esteban is a small park near downtown Tucson, Arizona. Estevan Park, using the Anglicized spelling with the letter *v*, is in a neighborhood first settled by African American Buffalo Soldiers and their families in the 1800s. A school built in 1918 next to the park was named in honor of a son of former slaves, the black poet and novelist Paul Laurence Dunbar. The neighborhood with its park and school was a center of African American community life for generations. A USO for African American soldiers was established near Estevan Park during World War II to be a welcoming place for black troops stationed at Arizona's Fort Huachuca.[7]

Perhaps the only other public space named in Esteban's honor is Esteban Park in Phoenix, spelled with the letter *b*. Nearby are housing and apartments also by that name as well as the Phoenix Business Park.

Other public recognitions of Esteban are rare. He is briefly mentioned in the exhibits room of the visitor center at the Cabrillo National Monument in San Diego. A paragraph there talks about Cabeza de Vaca and Esteban but omits the names of Dorantes and Castillo, thus elevating the African to being one of the two most important of the cross-continent travelers. It reads, "Álvar Núñez Cabeza de Vaca and three companions including the enslaved African, Estebánico, were the sole survivors of Narváez's ill-fated expedition." The Cabrillo monument's tribute is inaccurate in some ways, including lack of mention that Juan Ortiz and Lope de Oviedo also survived as captives of different tribes. The paragraph at the monument committed more historical errors when it added: "The four spent the next eight years traveling 6,000 miles through Texas, New Mexico, Arizona, and northern Mexico." Few believe anymore that the four

Figure 14. Estevan Park near downtown Tucson, Arizona, is the first of only two public spaces named for the African explorer in the United States. It is in a neighborhood where many African-American Buffalo Soldiers made their homes in the 1800s. "Estevan" is an Anglicized spelling for the Spanish name of "Esteban." Photo by Dennis Herrick.

traveled through Arizona or New Mexico, although Esteban did enter both states three years later. Also, the Cabrillo monument's stated distance is about double what they actually walked.[8]

Esteban's role in history also earned him a place in a mural painted inside the Arizona state capitol building in Phoenix. Esteban is credited as the first known Muslim to arrive in the United States by America's Islamic Heritage Museum and Cultural Center in Washington, DC.

Because he was found in North Africa, Esteban also is often identified as a Moor. Throughout Europe there are numerous statues of North African blacks, all categorized as Moors, and they also are in paintings and remembered through Moorish architecture. But if Houser's sculpture of Esteban is completed, it will be the first nonreligious statue in the United States of a man many people have come to categorize as a Moor.[9]

Although he might have thought of himself more as a Berber than as a Moor, that general classification for anyone from North Africa seems bound to stick. Regardless of how he's labeled, Houser could help bring more recognition in the United States of Esteban, the African explorer of America.

John Sherrill Houser, sculptor and painter, died in January 2018 at the age of eighty-two.

Notes

Notes for the Modern Reader

1. The John Upton Terrell quote at the front of the book comes from his *Estevanico the Black* (109). The Joe S. Sando quote comes from his *Pueblo Nations* (50). The Richard Holmes quotation in the preface is from his 2004 *Tommy* (xxi–xxii).
2. Aztecs were known in Coronado's time as the Mexica (pronounced meh-SHEEH-kah). Aztec is a reference not coined until the 1800s by naturalist Alexander Von Humboldt. (Mann, *1491*, 124). He derived the word from the Nahuatl word "Aztecah," meaning "people from Atzlan," which was their mythological place of origin.

Chapter 1

1. Hallenbeck, *Álvar Núñez Cabeza de Vaca*: "Zunians who never fought except defensively." See also Ladd, "Zuni on the Day," 190.
2. George P. Hammond and Agapito Rey, "Letter of Coronado to Mendoza, August 3, 1540," in *Narratives*, 177.
3. Ladd, "Zuni on the Day," 189.
4. Ibid., 190.
5. Flint, *No Settlement, No Conquest*, 32.
6. Richard Flint, e-mail to author, July 2, 2016. Flint is an expert in sixteenth-century Castilian and he translated old records written in Castilian and wrote several books on the Coronado expedition of 1540–1542.

7. "The use of nicknames [in Spain] are common, not only to slaves and servants, but to everyone. Many kings, sportsmen, bullfighters, politicians, etc. have their own. Even today, if you are looking for someone in a little town you better know his/her nickname to find this person." E-mail to author from Juan Francisco Maura, July 21, 2016.
8. Any book referring to the centuries-old Pueblo religion of kivas and katsinas as a "cult" is propagandizing a Eurocentric, Christian viewpoint antagonistic to Puebloan beliefs. A form of the traditional religion is still practiced today. Calling Puebloan religion a cult instead of an ancient religion just because it's not Christian is an offensive categorization often used by scholars who should know better.
9. McDonald, "Intimacy and Empire," 26. See also Flint and Flint, "Esteban the Moor."
10. A Puebloan term for Mexico and points south. Green, *Zuñi*, 174.
11. Ladd, "Zuni on the Day," 188–89.
12. Ibid., 189.
13. Ibid., 173–74.
14. Ladd's knowledge of Zuni history led him to believe that Esteban went to Hawikku, not Kyaki:ma. Ladd, "Zuni on the Day," 188. Researcher Debra McDonald refers to Cushing's lecture but lists the village not as Kyaki:ma, but as O'aquima, which she identifies as Hawikku. McDonald, "Intimacy and Empire," 26. She borrowed the name of O'aquima from Bandelier's 1893 book, where he said the Zuni name for Hawikku was O'aquima. A. Bandelier, *Gilded Man*, 160.
15. There are other ways to be "black" outside the terms of race. Some Indian warriors across the Americas painted their faces and/or bodies black when at war, for example. Men with full black beards could be referred to that way by natives not used to seeing beards, and black clothing could also influence the ways Indians referred to people, to mention a few other possibilities.
16. In his telling of the story, Cushing seems to strain to conform Zuni estimates of a time in the past to the American concept of a generation being about thirty years so that "eleven men's ages" will approximate more than three hundred years.
17. Puebloans generally prefer the spelling of katsina to the Anglicized version of kachina, according to N. Y. Davis, *Zuni Enigma*, 171. Other spellings include caczina, katchina, k'ats'ana, k'ats'ina, lhatsina, and catzina, while the Zuni often call them Kokko.
18. Ibid., 171.
19. Coze, "Kachinas," 219. Also see Fisher, "Kivas of the Living Pueblos," 91: "The masks are considered to be the corporeal substance of the katcina [sic]. In putting on the mask, the wearer through a miraculous transformation becomes a katcina."

20. Dockstader, *Kachina and the White Man*, 10. Dockstader's research was originally published in May 1954 as Bulletin 35 of the Cranbrook Institute of Science.
21. Stewart, "Power of the Kachina Tradition," 19.
22. Dockstader, *Kachina and the White Man*, 11. Because of commercialization by Puebloan and non-Puebloan artists since the late 1800s, the katsina figurines or "dolls" have long since passed from the sacred realm to secular collectors' items and art, just like carvings and paintings in Christianity and other religions. Schaafsma, *Kachinas in the Pueblo World*, 5. An exception still today is when the miniature figure is made as a ceremonial object for a young girl. Edmund J. Ladd, "The Zuni Ceremonial System: The Kiva," in Schaafsma, *Kachinas in the Pueblo World*, 21.
23. Hopi guide Gary Tsa provided the phonetically spelled Hopi word to Brian and Carolyn Gilmore, friends of the author. Polly Schaafsma gives the spelling as "Tsakwaina" for warrior katsinas in "The Prehistoric Kachina Cult and Its Origins as Suggested by Southwestern Rock Art," in *Kachinas in the Pueblo World*, 71.
24. For discussions of "the black katsina," see Calloway, *One Vast Winter Count*, 133, and Sando, *Pueblo Indians*, 45–46.
25. James E. MacDougald, e-mail to author, April 2, 2017.
26. McDonald, "Intimacy and Empire," 26–27.
27. Colton, *Hopi Kachina Dolls*, 160. An image identified as the Chákwaina katsina is depicted as painted black with a black goatee in Dockstader, *Kachina and the White Man*, 14A.
28. B. Wright, *Kachinas*, 99. Painted black with a long, black goatee, the Chákwaina katsina depicted there has the crescent moon and a star on its cheeks.
29. B. Wright, *Hopi Kachinas*, 34.
30. Goodwin, *Crossing the Continent*, 368.
31. Sando, *Pueblo Nations*, 52.
32. Ilahiane, "Estevan de Dorantes," 11.
33. Parsons, "Humpbacked Flute Player," 337.
34. Tedlock, "Stories of Kachinas," 162. Signs still today will announce closures of pueblos to the public when religious ceremonies featuring katsinas are held.
35. For an artifact theft investigator's look at the sacred art world of modern Puebloans, see L. D. Schroeder, *Plunder of the Ancients*.
36. Trimble, *People*, 41.
37. Weber, *Spanish Frontier*, 46. Cíbola is usually spelled now without the Spanish accent mark.
38. "Esteban: Negro or Dark Arab?," A11.
39. Ibid.
40. Cox, "Estebanico, Black Explorer," 142.
41. Weber, "Esteban," 24.

42. Goodwin, *Crossing the Continent*, 6.
43. The term "Europeans" was not coined until the seventeenth century, but I use it in this biography to point out that many nationalities moved to the Caribbean, not just Spaniards.
44. Lavender, *DeSoto, Coronado, Cabrillo*, 56.
45. Terrell, *Estevanico the Black*, 12–13.
46. Nugent Brasher, "The Coronado Exploration Program," in Flint and Flint, *Latest Word from 1540*, 229–69.
47. Thanks to author Forrest Fenn, former owner of Santa Fe galleries renowned for collections of Spanish colonial and Native American artifacts of the Southwest, for reminding me of Voltaire's quote. The full quote is from Voltaire's 1674 moral tale: "All the old histories, as one of our great minds used to say, are only fables agreed upon."
48. Born and raised in Morocco, Lalami became professor of creative writing at University of California-Riverside.
49. Herrick, "Tiguex War," 428.
50. Hudson, "Historical Significance," 289.
51. Seymour, "Evaluating Eyewitness Accounts," 405.
52. Abdul-Jabbar and Steinberg, *Black Profiles in Courage*, 1–2.

Chapter 2

1. Morocco native Laila Lalami in reply to the author's question, September 22, 2014.
2. Craig Carter interview, February 4, 2015, about his trip to Morocco.
3. Simour, "(De)Slaving History," 5.
4. Angelo R. Cervantes, director of the Iberian Peninsula DNA Institute, Albuquerque.
5. The final five words in Cabeza de Vaca, *Naufragios*. See also Cabeza de Vaca, *Relacion*.
6. Comparisons from eight leading researchers, all translating the phrase differently, are presented and each dismissed as inaccurate in Adorno and Pautz, *Álvar Núñez Cabeza de Vaca*, 1:416–17. In discussing the grammar, they make a convincing case for "Arabic-speaking Negro."
7. Richard Flint, manuscript commentary, October 26, 2016.
8. T. B. Smith, *Full Text*, 195.
9. Redfield, interview with Hallenbeck.
10. Bandelier, "Discovery of New Mexico," 4:30.
11. Bolton, *The Spanish Borderlands*, 36, 45.
12. Hallenbeck, *Álvar Núñez Cabeza de Vaca*, 101. Another edition without Cisneros artwork appeared in 1939.

13. In discussions about this book, I repeatedly encountered people who thought Esteban was an Arab.
14. Covey, *Cabeza de Vaca's Adventures*, 43. Also Fernández, *Alvar Nuñez Cabeza de Vaca*, 119. See also Frye, *Chronicle of the Narváez Expedition*, 90.
15. Logan, "Estevanico," 305–14.
16. Ibid., 311.
17. Ibid.
18. Mirsky, *Gentle Conquistadors*. Mirsky was referring to racial stereotyping of blacks in the United States.
19. Both quotes are from Weber, "Esteban," in Glasrud, *African-American History*, 24. Also see Mutuku, "Estevanico," 217–33; and Nodal, "Estebanillo," 45–55.
20. Goodwin, *Crossing the Continent*, 98. Esteban was depicted as being from sub-Sahara Africa in a highly imaginative children's book written in the first person, ostensibly by Esteban in a fictional letter to the king, as well as by Friar Marcos in a fictional recounting. See Parish, *Estebanico*.
21. Portugal treated that city's residents as vassals from 1486 to 1541.
22. "Azemmour," 216; my translation from the French.
23. Ottmani, *Fils du soleil*, 10; my translation.
24. Ibid., 9; my translation. In the original French, Ottmani wrote: "D'aucuns prétendent que son vrai nom était Mustapha, devenu par analogie Estevan, au moment du transfert forcé du jeune homme en pays chrétien. L'analogie est certes séduisante, mais à notre connaissance, aucune preuve ne vient confirmer cette affirmation. Quoi qu'il en soit, pour la suite de notre récit, l'homme sera désigné par le nom que lui a attribué l'histoire a savoir Estevanico ou . . . Estevanico de Azemor en lieu et place de superbe patronyme que lui ont donné affectueusement ses admirateurs marocains, à savoir: Mustapha El Azemmouri."
25. Wa'rab, "Rencontre."
26. Lalami, *Moor's Account*, 3.
27. Halifi, "Mostapha el Azemmouri/Estebanico."
28. Ibid.
29. Simour, "(De)slaving History," 15.
30. Ottmani, *Fils du soleil*, 19.
31. Goodwin, *Crossing the Continent*, 86–89.
32. Ottmani, *Fils du soleil*, 9; my translation.
33. Simour, "(De)slaving History," 15. Throughout his article, Simour uses Esteban's Arab name, Mostafa al-Azemmour.
34. Hnyen, "Remp'Arts Honore."
35. The appendix describes an effort to create an American sculpture honoring Esteban.
36. Goodwin, *Crossing the Continent*, 99. The Spanish name of the city is Sevilla, but the Anglicized version of Seville is used here because it would be more familiar to English language readers.

37. Morse, "Esteban of Azemmour," 2–9.
38. Simour, "(De)slaving History," 8.
39. MacNutt, *Bartholomew de Las Casas*, 103. See also Mann, *1493*, 293–94; and Goodwin, *Crossing the Continent*, 102.
40. Pike, *Aristocrats and Traders*, 177–80.
41. Richard Flint, manuscript commentary, October 26, 2016.
42. Horwitz, *Voyage Long and Strange*, 130. See also Pike, *Aristocrats and Traders*, 175.
43. Schmidt-Nowara, *Slavery, Freedom, and Abolition*, 50.

Chapter 3

1. Christopher Columbus was a man of several names. He was baptized as Cristoforo Colombo in Italy, changed his name to Cristovao Colombo when he moved to Portugal, and called himself Cristóbal Colón when he moved to Spain. During his lifetime, no one knew him by the Anglicized name of Columbus.
2. Condemnation of Spanish genocide against Caribbean natives began with a sermon by Friar Antonio de Montesinos in 1511 on Hispaniola. King Fernando II was horrified by a report by Montesinos, saying he'd not known the conditions. He issued the Laws of Burgos in 1512 and 1513 in an attempt to stop abuses. There was open and virulent dispute raging in Spain concerning treatment of natives of the Americas from that time until at least the mid-1540s. Richard Flint, manuscript commentary, October 26, 2016.
3. The flood of treasure from the New World to Europe intensified exponentially with the discovery of silver at Zacatecas and Potosi in the 1540s.
4. Castanha, "Adventures in Caribbean Indigeneity."
5. Rouse, *Tainos*, 142.
6. Jameson, "Journal of the First Voyage of Columbus," in *Northmen, Columbus and Cabot*, 198.
7. Renowned ship archaeologist Barry Clifford believes he found the wreckage of the *Santa Maria*, which foundered off the northern coast of Haiti on Christmas day, 1492. Chappell, "Christopher Columbus Ship."
8. Columbus, *Journal*, 41. See also Columbus, *Log of First Voyage*, 99, in which the entry is translated as Columbus being "certain that with these people I have with me, I could subjugate all of the Indians."
9. Jameson, "Journal of the First Voyage of Columbus," in *Northmen, Columbus and Cabot*, 182.
10. Rouse, *Tainos*, 17.
11. Diamond, *Guns, Germs and Steel*, 241–42.
12. The atlatl predated the bow and arrow. The back end of a dart would be placed into a stick, and the extra leverage provided by the stick enabled the long dart

to fly farther and with more power than if simply thrown by the arm, as with a spear.
13. MacNutt, translation of "The Brevissima Relación," in *Bartholomew de Las Casas*, 319.
14. Friar Las Casas wrote: "Among these gentle sheep [Taínos] the Spaniards entered as soon as they knew them, like wolves, tigers, and lions . . . and since forty years they have done nothing else." MacNutt, "Brevissima Relación," 315. Although "Europe" was not a term used for another century, it is used in this biography to indicate that people from across the continent and not just Spaniards went to the Caribbean.
15. When Columbus took possession of the island in 1492, he named it the Latin "Insula Hispana," meaning "Spanish Island," and in Spanish "La Isla Española." Dominican Friar Bartolomé de las Casas shortened the Spanish name to "Española." And when Pietro Martire d'Anghiera detailed his account of the island in Latin, he translated the name as "Hispaniola." Because Las Casas and Anghiera's literary works were translated into English afterward, the name "Hispaniola" became the most frequently used term for the island in English-speaking countries' literary and cartographic works.
16. Morison and Obregón, *Caribbean as Columbus Saw It*, 34.
17. Sauer, *Sixteenth Century North America*, 184. The closest to the Caribbean "barkless dog" might be the African Basenji, although even it makes noises. Aztecs called the barkless dog an *itzcuintli*.
18. The papal bull *Sublimis Deus* in its original Latin as well as MacNutt's English translation are in MacNutt, *Bartholomew de Las Casas*, 426–31. Other translators' versions of the full text of the bull are online, including at http://papalencyclicals.net/Pau103/p3subli.htm as well as http://historyscoop.com/2012/08/16/papal-bull-sublimis-deus-and-the-humanity-of-native-americans.
19. Schmidt-Nowara, *Slavery, Freedom, and Abolition*, 17. Conquistadors and colonists were basically the same people, depending on what role they played at a given time.
20. Vickery, *Bartolomé de las Casas*, 50.
21. Las Casas was also referred to as the "Defender of the Indians."
22. Gustavo Gutíerrez, "Foreword," in Sanderlin, *Witness*, xx.
23. A Dominican refused to hear the confession of Bartolomé de las Casas, who was at that time a priest but also an encomienda owner during his early years in the Americas. MacNutt, *Bartholomew de Las Casas*, 60.
24. Montesinos enraged his congregation on Hispaniola with his sermon: "In order to make your sins against the Indians known to you, I have come up on this pulpit. . . . Tell me by what right or justice do you keep these Indians in such a cruel and horrible servitude? On what authority have you waged a detestable war against these people, who dwelt quietly and peacefully in their own land? . . . Why do you keep them so oppressed and weary, not giving them enough to

eat nor taking care of them in their illness? For with the excessive work you demand of them they fall ill and die, or rather you kill them with your desire to extract and acquire gold every day. . . . Are these not men? Have they not rational souls? . . . Be certain that, in such a state as this, you can no more be saved than the Moors or Turks." Hanke, *Spanish Struggle for Justice*, 17.

25. Simpson, *Encomienda in New Spain*, para. 8.
26. Ibid., para. 101.
27. Reséndez, *Other Slavery*, 3.
28. Simpson, *Encomienda in New Spain*, para. 155.
29. King Carlos I also ruled as Holy Roman Emperor Carlos V. The sovereign's name is almost always Anglicized as Charles in English-language books.
30. Schmidt-Nowara, *Slavery, Freedom, and Abolition*, 17.
31. Hanke, *Spanish Struggle for Justice*, 60, 125.
32. Williams, *Documents of West Indian History*, 119. See also Paiewonsky, *Conquest of Eden*, 169.
33. Melzer, "Exiled from Isleta," 3.
34. Yardley and Neuman, "In Bolivia," A4.
35. The pope told his mostly Mayan Indian crowd, "Some have considered your values, culture, and traditions to be inferior. Others, intoxicated by power, money, and market trends, have stolen your lands or contaminated them." Associated Press, "Pope Celebrates Mass," A8.
36. More than four hundred years after his death, Dominican friars voted in 1985 to seek sainthood for Las Casas, and the Catholic Church began the lengthy process toward beatification in 2000. Dart, "Friars Seek Sainthood."
37. "Resolution on Racial Reconciliation."
38. The title in Spanish is *Brevíssima relación de la destrucción de las Indias*. It can be found in its entirety in Spanish at http://ciudadseva.com/textos/otros/brevisi.htm.
39. Sanderlin, *Witness*, 52. The original quote is from Las Casas, *Historia de las Indias*, 536. In the book's sixteenth-century Castilian Spanish, Narváez asks, "Qué parece a vuestra merced destos nuestros españoles, qué han hecho?" and Las Casas replies, "Que os ofrezo a vos y ellos al diablo!"
40. Hanke, *Spanish Struggle for Justice*, 7.
41. Ibid., 71. Hanke gives the original citation from Gómara, *Historia General de las Indias*, 297.
42. The hidalgo mindset is examined in Duncan, *Hernando de Soto*, 13–14.
43. Flint and Flint, "Hearing on Depopulation Charges, February 26, 1540," in *Documents of the Coronado Expedtion*, 177–178.
44. Terrell, *Estevanico the Black*, 18.
45. Ibid., 20.
46. MacNutt, *Bartholomew de Las Casas*, 320. See also Griffin, *Short Account*, 115.
47. Karunanithy, *Dogs of War*, 183.

48. Ponce's Spanish-speaking Indian must have been a Caribbean island refugee.
49. Terrell, *Journey into Darkness*, 5.
50. His date of birth is in dispute. As for the manchineel tree, its fruit looks like a small apple. The Spanish word is *manzanilla de la muerte*, "little apple of death." It grows in Florida, Mexico, several Caribbean islands, and in Central and South America.
51. MacNutt, *Bartholomew de Las Casas*, 172.
52. I recently learned that scientist Jared Diamond made a similar point in *Guns, Germs, and Steel*, 397. He questioned whether Europeans could have established themselves at the Cape in southern Africa if, instead of scattered Khoisan herdsmen, they had instead first encountered the densely populated, well-armed, and fierce Xhosa warriors.
53. Flint, "Without Them," 65. Many historians have acknowledged this.

Chapter 4

1. Europeans blamed many slave insurrections on the Wolof people, who came from present-day Senegal, the Gambia, and Mauritania. Many Wolof men had been horse-mounted warriors in Africa before being captured and sold as slaves.
2. Rout, *African Experience in Spanish America*, 104–25, presents a history and analysis of numerous slave revolts from 1522 to 1804 in the Americas.
3. Terrell, *Journey into Darkness*, 7.
4. Simpson, *Encomienda in New Spain*, para. 28.
5. Terrell, *Journey into Darkness*, 9.
6. Stuller, "Cleanliness," 126.
7. Paiewonsky, *Conquest of Eden*, 76. The life expectancy figure was reported by Friar Bartolomé de las Casas.
8. Many sources, including Chipman, "Alonso Alvarez de Pineda," 370. See also MacNutt, *Bartholomew de Las Casas*, 31; and Varnum, *Álvar Núñez Cabeza de Vaca*, 33–34.
9. Associated Press, "Large Gold Nugget," A8.
10. The formal *carrera de indias* fleets didn't begin until the 1560s, but the transatlantic sailings occurred frequently in the early years, with such serious losses that single-ship trips were officially forbidden after 1525. Richard Flint, manuscript commentary, October 26, 2016.
11. Rouse, *Taínos*, 157.
12. There are many sources on the mass suicides of Indians, which Las Casas says resulted in the deaths of thousands of Taínos. Griffin, *Short Account*, 29–30. See also Hazard, *Santo Domingo*, 39; and Bengston, "Images of the New World."
13. Paiewonsky, *Conquest of Eden*, 112.

14. Las Casas, *Historia de las Indias*, 2:206.
15. Many sources, with details in Rouse, *Tainos*, 158. See also Hazard, *Santo Domingo*, 45.
16. A royal ordinance on September 3, 1500, permitted the governor of Hispaniola to import African slaves. MacNutt, *Bartholomew de Las Casas*, 102.
17. Varnum, *Álvar Núñez Cabeza de Vaca*, 29.
18. Paiewonsky, *Conquest of Eden*, 112.
19. Varnum, *Álvar Núñez Cabeza de Vaca*, 29. See also Altman, "Revolt of Enriquillo," 597.
20. Known as Bernal Díaz, his full name was Bernal Díaz del Castillo, but the last portion of his name is usually dropped. Several Spanish accounts report that the name of the African smallpox victim was Francisco Eguía or a similar spelling.
21. Guitar, "Documenting the Myth."
22. Las Casas, *Historia de las Indias*, 2:445, translated and cited in Vickery, *Bartolomé de las Casas*, 50.
23. Sanderlin, *Witness*, 2.
24. Terrell, *Journey into Darkness*, 25.
25. MacNutt, *Bartholomew de Las Casas*, 414.

Chapter 5

1. The Taínos had wiped out the few settlers Columbus left behind at La Navidad on the northern coast of Hispaniola when he returned to Spain in late 1492, but in that case the Spaniards were isolated and vastly outnumbered. After that, the Spaniards had little trouble conquering Taíno opposition.
2. Morison and Obregón, *Caribbean as Columbus Saw It*, 197.
3. Major, "Third Voyage," in *Christopher Columbus*, 211.
4. Major, "An Account," in *Christopher Columbus*, 212.
5. The arquebus musket is often spelled in English as "harquebus." The Spanish word is *arcabuz*.
6. Tunon, "Indian Warrior's Ornament."
7. Major, *Christopher Columbus*, 183.
8. Altman, "Revolt of Enriquillo," 587–614.
9. Olivo, "Rebelión del Bahoruc."
10. Sullivan, *Indian Freedom*, 192.
11. Altman, "Revolt of Enriquillo," 601.
12. Galván, *Cross and the Sword*, 328, 336, 340, 348. See Altman, "Revolt of Enriquillo," 598.
13. MacNutt, *Bartholomew de Las Casas*, 179. See Altman, "Revolt of Enriquillo," 599.

14. Altman, "Revolt of Enriquillo," 604–7.
15. Ibid., 608. See Helps, *Spanish Conquest in America*, 108.

Chapter 6

1. Vickery, *Bartolomé de las Casas*, 23.
2. MacNutt, *Bartholomew de Las Casas*, 56.
3. The ordeals of the seldom-mentioned other two will be told in chapter 11.
4. Terrell, *Journey into Darkness*, 36.
5. Bandelier and Bandelier, *Journey*, 1. The port now is spelled "Sanlúcar de Barrameda." Like Seville (Sevilla), it is on the Guadalquivir River, but about fifty miles downstream at the river's mouth to the Atlantic Ocean. June 27 and all subsequent dates quoted from Spanish chronicles are according to the Julian calendar. For an equivalent date in the Gregorian calendar, which was adopted in 1582, ten days should be added. That would make the date for departure in the modern calendar July 7, 1527.
6. Terrell, *Journey into Darkness*, 37–38.
7. Ibid., 38.
8. Schneider, *Brutal Journey*, 43–44.
9. Terrell, *Journey into Darkness*, 39.
10. Known as Francisco Chicorana in some sources. The translation by Francis Augustus MacNutt is online at Daniels, "Testimony of Francisco de Chicora." The testimony was published in 1530.
11. Drake, *Indian Tribes*, 11, 33. The Indians and their town were known as Cofitachequi by the time Hernando de Soto's expedition encountered them, and a woman ruled the chiefdom.
12. Maura, *Gran Burlador de América*, 283–84.
13. Goodwin, *Crossing the Continent*, 192. A discussion of the settlement is at "San Miguel de Gualdape."
14. Hudson, *Knights of Spain*, 36.
15. David J. Weber believes San Miguel de Gualdape was built on Sapelo Sound in present-day Georgia. Weber, *Spanish Frontier in North America*, 31.
16. "African American History Timeline."
17. Theisen, "Expedition of Pánfilo de Narváez," 1.
18. Ibid., 95–96.
19. Thomas R. Hester's introduction to Krieger and Krieger, *We Came Naked and Barefoot*, 5.
20. The Joint Report wording is in book 35, chapters 1–6, of Oviedo's *La historia general y natural de las Indias*, which was translated by Gerald Theisen in his booklet, "The Expedition of Pánfilo de Narváez."
21. Aguirre, *Grandes conflictos sociales y económicos*.

22. Oviedo's novel was titled *Book of the Very Striving and Invincible Knight Don Claribalte*.
23. Goodwyn, "Pánfilo de Narváez," 150. The quote is from the 1875 Madrid edition of *Las Casas's Historia de las Indias*, 4:6, as translated by Goodwyn.
24. Goodwyn, "Pánfilo de Narváez," 150–51. The most popular images of Narváez depict him with a dark or red beard in artists' confusion over what had been intended to describe his complexion.
25. Goodwyn, "Pánfilo de Narváez," 153. The precise statement is in Hedrick and Riley, *Journey of the Vaca Party*, 4.
26. Bandelier and Bandelier, *Journey*, 3.
27. The league is an uncertain measure of distance, basically the distance a man could walk in an hour. The *legua legal* was about 2.6 miles. Many sources, including Varnum, *Álvar Núñez Cabeza de Vaca*, 47–48.
28. Bandelier and Bandelier, *Journey*, 5–6.
29. Terrell, *Journey into Darkness*, 43.
30. Varnum, *Álvar Núñez Cabeza de Vaca*, 49. A brigantine was half the length of a caravel and, unlike a caravel, a brigantine was broad and could navigate rivers and other shallow waters. It used one or two sails and also was fitted with benches for oarsmen.
31. Theisen, "Expedition of Pánfilo de Narváez," 1. See also Terrell, *Journey into Darkness*, 43.
32. Terrell, *Journey into Darkness*, 132. Also Adorno and Pautz, *Álvar Núñez Cabeza de Vaca*, 2:71.
33. Adorno and Pautz, *Álvar Núñez Cabeza de Vaca*, 2:77.

Chapter 7

1. Beatríz Rivera-Barnes, "Is There Such a Thing as Too Much Water?," in Frye, *Chronicle of the Narváez Expedition*, 209.
2. Frye, *Chronicle of the Narváez Expedition*, 90.
3. Florida folklore often claims Esteban was the first African to reach the present state.
4. Restall, "Black Conquistadors," 171–72.
5. "Juan Garrido, African Conquistador."
6. It's a "golden rattle" in Bandelier and Bandelier, *Journey*, 10. It's "a timbrel of gold" in Theisen, "Expedition of Pánfilo de Narváez," 2. It's a "jingle" of two small disks in Frye, *Chronicle of the Narváez Expedition*, 9.
7. Terrell, *Journey into Darkness*, 48.
8. Bandelier and Bandelier, *Journey*, 10.
9. Generations of English-speaking writers have used the false cognate "requirement," but "ultimatum" is a better translation. Richard Flint, manuscript commentary, October 26, 2016.

10. Hanke, *Spanish Struggle for Justice*, 35.
11. A complete text of *El Requerimiento* in English with its Catholic-oriented worldview is at http://users.dickinson.edu/~borges/Resources-Requerimiento.htm (accessed March 18, 2014).
12. Bandelier and Bandelier, *Journey*, 10.
13. Vega, *Florida of the Inca*, 68. This account proves Narváez took war dogs to Florida, which Cabeza de Vaca never mentioned. See also Drake, *Indian Tribes of the United States*, 17.
14. Not all Caribbean natives were as vulnerable as the Taínos. The Caribs were formidable opponents for years against the Europeans.

Chapter 8

1. That friar's name is also spelled as Xuárez and Juárez. Some accounts refer to him as the first bishop of Florida, but the Catholic Church disagrees, although there might have been an agreement to make him bishop if the expedition succeeded. Engelhardt, "Florida's First Bishop"; Varnum, *Álvar Núñez Cabeza de Vaca*, 35; Adorno and Pautz, *Álvar Núñez Cabeza de Vaca*, 2:25.
2. Bandelier and Bandelier, *Journey*, 11.
3. Ibid., 189. See also Schneider, *Brutal Journey*, 67. Oviedo doesn't indicate any mention by Dorantes of the ship's loss in the *Historia*'s Joint Report.
4. There were many varieties of maize in the Americas with solid and mixed colors as well as varied starchiness.
5. Sauer, *Sixteenth Century North America*, 211. The description of a maize field by Nicolas de Challeux is from Gaffarel, *Histoire de la Floride Française*, 462.
6. Bandelier and Bandelier, *Journey*, 12.
7. Ibid.
8. Through some historical fluke, the Appalachian Mountains were named after the Apalachee, even though they never lived there.
9. Hirrihigua's revenge will be discussed in chapter 11. "Story of Juan Ortiz."
10. Bandelier and Bandelier, *Journey*, 14.
11. His name is sometimes spelled Alaniz.
12. Bandelier and Bandelier, *Journey*, 190.
13. Ibid., 18–19.
14. In the *Historia*, Oviedo says there were 260 men on foot and forty cavalry; see Theisen, "Expedition of Pánfilo de Narváez," 8. Another translation says, "a total of 300 men . . . Those of us (horsemen) going with them numbered forty," which can be found in the 1555 translation of the *Relación*, http://alkek.library.txstate.edu/swwc/cdv/book/1.html. The 1871 T. Buckingham Smith translation says three hundred left and added, "We of the mounted men consisted of forty." T. B. Smith, "Full Text of Relation of 'Alvar Nuñez Cabeça de Vaca.'" In the slightly revised *Los Naufragios* edition of 1555, Cabeza de Vaca wrote, "La suma

de toda la gente que llevábamos era trescientos hombres; en ellos iba el comisario fray Juan Suárez, y otro fraile que se decía fray Juan de Palos, y tres clérigos y los oficiales. La gente de caballo que con estos íbamos, éramos cuarenta de caballo." That might imply the horsemen should be counted separately.

15. A footnote to Fanny Bandelier's translation provides that original text. Bandelier and Bandelier, *Journey*, 19.
16. Mann, *1493*, 305.
17. Although Esteban was among those who moved inland on May 1, it would be another year before the *Relación* ever mentioned him.
18. Ibid., 77–78. Malaria and yellow fever were not known in the New World until the arrival of people from other parts of the globe. Infected with smallpox, measles, and other diseases, millions of Indians died across the Americas from introduced diseases.
19. Bandelier and Bandelier, *Journey*, 19.
20. Terrell, *Journey into Darkness*, 67–68.
21. "Timucua" is a misnomer that, like so many early European references, inaccurately refers to an Indian tribe by a word the tribe's members never called themselves. Thornton, "Surprising Late Date."
22. Terrell, *Journey into Darkness*, 70.
23. Daniels, "Narrative of Le Moyne," 4.
24. Swanton, *Indians*, 533.
25. Bandelier and Bandelier, *Journey*, 22.
26. Schneider, *Brutal Journey*, 137–38.
27. Bandelier and Bandelier, *Journey*, 23.
28. Schneider, *Brutal Journey*, 93.
29. Bandelier and Bandelier, *Journey*, 23–24.
30. Ibid., 26.

Chapter 9

1. Schneider, *Brutal Journey*, 122.
2. Bandelier and Bandelier, *Journey*, 25.
3. Usually Anglicized as Montezuma, this spelling is more accurate for the Aztec pronunciation. There was a long tradition on the Iberian Peninsula of holding enemy leaders as hostages.
4. Bandelier and Bandelier, *Journey*, 28.
5. The Joint Report claims two or three Indians were killed in the first attack. Theisen, "Expedition of Pánfilo de Narváez," 10–11.
6. Miller, "First Contact." This paraphrased response by Acuera is from an early Spanish record. Three centuries later, James G. M. Ramsey composed what he claimed was the quotation, and his lengthy and very European-sounding

version is what's seen in most accounts and on the Internet from his 1853 book, *Annals of Tennessee*, 20. Acuera's response, in another European-sounding version, is in Vega, *Florida of the Inca*, 118.

7. Cabeza de Vaca reports twenty-five days. Oviedo's account reports twenty-six days. Theisen, "Expedition of Pánfilo de Narváez" (Oviedo's *Historia*), 11.
8. Aute might have been a cluster of villages rather than just one. Schneider, *Brutal Journey*, 159.
9. There was no mention yet of Esteban. His indispensable role was still months away.
10. Mitchem, "Archaeological and Ethnohistoric Evidence."
11. Terrell, *Journey into Darkness*, 74.
12. Bandelier and Bandelier, *Journey*, 31–32.
13. Vega, *Florida of the Inca*, 17.
14. Bandelier and Bandelier, *Journey*, 39.
15. Flint and Flint, "Muster Roll of the Expedition, Compostela, February 22, 1540," in *Documents of the Coronado Expedition*, 138.
16. Bandelier and Bandelier, *Journey*, 30–31.
17. Ibid., 32.
18. Rangel, *Narrative of De Soto's Expedition*, 80.
19. Barrientos, *Pedro Menendez de Aviles*, 106–7.
20. "Mosquito-Borne and Other Insect-borne Diseases."
21. Bandelier and Bandelier, *Journey*, 36.
22. Ibid., 35–36.
23. Ibid., 37.

Chapter 10

1. "Site of First Multi-Year."
2. Schneider, *Brutal Journey*, 22.
3. Terrell, *Journey into Darkness*, 91–92.
4. There probably were others, but the only mention in the rest of the *Relación* is of those three. If there were others, they died on the beach or on the Gulf of Mexico in the boats in which the conquistadors fled.
5. Varnum, *Álvar Núñez Cabeza de Vaca*, 83.
6. Bandelier and Bandelier, *Journey*, 39.
7. Hakluyt, *Discovery and Conquest*, 43.
8. Adorno and Pautz, *Álvar Núñez Cabeza de Vaca*, 1:xviii.
9. Bandelier and Bandelier, *Journey*, 40.
10. Esteban's boat was in the water for forty-four days, from September 22 to November 5. Cabeza de Vaca's boat took forty-five days, and it's not known how long the others were in the Gulf of Mexico.

11. As was typical of records of the day, Teodoro's African slave was never named.
12. Biedma, "Relation of the Conquest," 17. See also Terrell, *Journey into Darkness*, 102. One Soto expedition chronicler wrongly attributed the dagger to the 1526 expedition of Lucas Vázquez de Ayllón, who never landed on that part of the coast. Hakluyt, *Discovery and Conquest*, 57–58.
13. Swanton, *Indians*, 39.
14. Bandelier and Bandelier, *Journey*, 53.
15. Ibid., 54. The names and spellings of Texas coast tribes in this biography are those accepted by today's anthropologists, which sometimes differ from the sixteenth-century Spanish chronicles.
16. Krieger and Krieger, *We Came Naked and Barefoot*, 179–80.
17. Bandelier and Bandelier, *Journey*, 56.
18. Hickerson, "How Cabeza De Vaca Lived," 200.
19. Bandelier and Bandelier, *Journey*, 57.
20. Ibid., 58.
21. Theisen, "Expedition of Pánfilo de Narváez," 42.

Chapter 11

1. Bandelier and Bandelier, *Journey*, 64.
2. Taylor, "Cabeza de Vaca," 116.
3. Despite the similarity in names, the historian Oviedo and the expeditionary Oviedo were not related.
4. Theisen, "Expedition of Pánfilo de Narváez," 32.
5. Ibid., 32–33.
6. Bandelier and Bandelier, *Journey*, 64.
7. Theisen, "Expedition of Pánfilo de Narváez," 36–37.
8. Bandelier and Bandelier, *Journey*, 73.
9. Theisen, "Expedition of Pánfilo de Narváez," 36.
10. Bandelier and Bandelier, *Journey*, 113.
11. Theisen, "Expedition of Pánfilo de Narváez," 57–58.
12. Reséndez, *Land So Strange*, 147.
13. Theisen, "Expedition of Pánfilo de Narváez," 59.
14. Bandelier and Bandelier, *Journey*, 70–71, 73–74.
15. Ibid., 74.
16. Theisen, "Expedition of Pánfilo de Narváez," 33–34. See also Hedrick and Riley, *Journey of the Vaca Party*, 27.
17. Theisen, "Expedition of Pánfilo de Narváez," 35.
18. Ibid. The passage's original Spanish can be found in Hedrick and Riley, *Journey of the Vaca Party*, 111.
19. Goodwin, *Crossing the Continent*, 241.
20. Hedrick and Riley, *Journey of the Vaca Party*, 27.

21. Bandelier and Bandelier, *Journey*, 76. Despite sharing the Oviedo name, the expeditionary Lope de Oviedo was no relation to the Spanish historian Gonzalo Fernández de Oviedo y Valdez.
22. Oviedo's fate will be discussed a few pages later.
23. Bandelier and Bandelier, *Journey*, 80.
24. Hickerson, "How Cabeza de Vaca Lived," 210.
25. Bandelier and Bandelier, *Journey*, 91.
26. A pinnance was a small ship used as a tender for larger ships.
27. Vega, *Florida of the Inca*, 61.
28. Terrell, *Journey into Darkness*, 133.
29. In an indication of how open to interpretation the Spanish chronicles are, Adorno and Pautz raise the possibility that Ortiz had been a member of Cerda's crew originally. Adorno and Pautz, *Álvar Núñez Cabeza de Vaca*, 2:106.
30. A summary of Juan Ortiz's ordeal of captivity and rescue is in "The Story of Juan Ortiz."
31. Robertson, "Gentleman of Elvas Account," chapter 8. John Upton Terrell believes Elvas was Alvaro Fernández.
32. Vega, *Florida of the Inca*, 59–88.
33. Fleming, "Story of Ortiz and Uleleh," 42.
34. Oviedo y Valdéz, "Narrative of De Soto's Expedition," 57. The name's spelling in the T. B. Smith translation is "Johan." See also Bourne, *Narratives*, 57.
35. Robertson, "Gentleman of Elvas Account," chapter 8.
36. Worth, "Biedma's Original DeSoto Writings."
37. Biedma, "Relation of the Conquest," 4. Also see Worth, "Biedma's Original DeSoto Writings."
38. Vega, *Florida of the Inca*, 533. See also Swanton, *Indians*, 40. The T. B. Smith translation spells the province as Viranque.
39. His name is also given as Lupe de Oviedo. Terrell, *Journey into Darkness*, 131.
40. Krieger and Krieger, *We Came Naked and Barefoot*, 32.
41. Hakluyt, *Discovery and Conquest*, 141. The seventeenth-century English is modernized here. Hakluyt's reprint is the 1609 English translation of the account by the Gentleman of Elvas.
42. Hakluyt, *Discovery and Conquest*, 141. At that time, Hakluyt's English word "corn" referred to Indian maize.
43. Bandelier and Bandelier, *Journey*, 90.
44. Campbell and Campbell, "Historic Indian Groups," 7.
45. Chipman and Weddle, "How Historical Myths Are Born," 235.
46. Bandelier and Bandelier, *Journey*, 98.
47. Cabeza de Vaca kept time by the moons. In his account, he wrote that the date was September 1, but the new moon closest to the end of summer was September 8 according to the Julian calendar (September 18 by the modern Gregorian calendar). Frye and Stavans, *Chronicle of the Navárez Expedition*, 46n.
48. Bandelier and Bandelier, *Journey*, 98–99.

49. To the average person, learning a language without being raised as a child in it or taking formal lessons seems impossible. However, for a very few people it is not difficult. Jim Belshaw, who was stationed in Thailand during the Vietnam War, tells how he was amazed by another soldier who, after a short period listening to the Thai people, was able to talk to them in the Thai language.
50. Hickerson, "How Cabeza de Vaca Lived," 214.
51. Theisen, "Expedition of Pánfilo de Narváez," 68.
52. Terrell, *Journey into Darkness*, 163.

Chapter 12

1. "Again and again, what purports to be a record of the native viewpoint is actually what European writers thought the natives were thinking.... Spanish accounts have the inevitable bias of writers from one culture looking through the barriers of language and cultural difference at the members of another.... For the most part, there is no history of the Indians, only the history of the Spaniards in their contacts with the Indians." Spicer, *Cycles of Conquest*, 21–22.
2. Goodwin, *Crossing the Continent*, 245.
3. Bandelier and Bandelier, *Journey*, 68.
4. Ibid., 70.
5. Ibid., 100.
6. Pupo-Walker and López-Morillas, *Castaways*, 150.
7. The Spanish phrase Cabeza de Vaca often used was *niños del cielo*, which is literally "children from the sky" but is often translated as meaning the Christian concept of heaven.
8. Schneider, *Brutal Journey*, 271.
9. Vance, "Mind over Matter," 48.
10. Ibid., 49–55.
11. Krieger and Krieger, *We Came Naked and Barefoot*, 61.
12. Bandelier and Bandelier, *Journey*, 145. These were probably today's Rio Grande and Río Conchos.
13. For an analysis of many of the leading or most prominent theories on Cabeza de Vaca's route, see Krieger and Krieger, *We Came Naked and Barefoot*, 7–20; and Thomas R. Hester in the same book's afterword (150–53). See also Adorno and Pautz, *Álvar Núñez Cabeza de Vaca*, 2:xvii–xxii.
14. Theisen, "Expedition of Pánfilo de Narváez," 78.
15. Krieger translation in *We Came Naked and Barefoot*, 63. See also Bandelier and Bandelier, *Journey*, 135.
16. Alonso de León, *Historia de la Provincia de Nuevo León*, cited by Krieger and Krieger in *We Came Naked and Barefoot*, 65.

17. Flint and Flint, "Juan Jaramillo's Narrative, 1560s," in *Documents of the Coronado Expedition*, 515.
18. Ibid., 409.
19. Mecham, "Second Spanish Expedition," 271.
20. Bolton, *Spanish Exploration in the Southwest*, 173. Virtually the same translation is in Terrell, *Estevanico the Black*, 52.
21. Ibid., 173. See also Hammond and Rey, *Rediscovery of New Mexico*, 217. See also Diego Pérez de Luxán, *Expedition into New Mexico Made by Antonio de Espejo*, cited in Terrell, *Estevanico the Black*, 52, and other sources.
22. Bandelier and Bandelier, *Journey*, 146.
23. Ibid., 150. The Spanish words "Estevanico el negro" would translate into English as "Little Esteban the Black."
24. Bandelier and Bandelier, *Journey*, 150.
25. Ibid., 150–51.
26. Theisen, "Expedition of Pánfilo de Narváez," 77.
27. Bandelier and Bandelier, *Journey*, 149.
28. Varnum, *Álvar Núñez Cabeza de Vaca*, 160.
29. Bandelier and Bandelier, *Journey*, 152.
30. Ibid., 159–60.
31. Ibid., 104.
32. Ibid., 105.
33. Ibid., 106.
34. Ibid., 108.
35. Ibid.
36. Weber, *Spanish Frontier in North America*, 44.
37. Spaniards considered anyone dressed in the skimpiest clothing, for example a breechcloth, to be "naked" in their sense of the clothing that a "civilized" person should wear. It's possible the travelers were naked, and it's also possible they wore some clothing that Europeans would consider inadequate, such as a breechcloth and moccasins. If any clothing was worn, it was minimal because Cabeza de Vaca said upon his return in 1536 that the feel of clothing on his skin was almost unbearable at first because he had gone so many years without clothes.
38. The length of the stone point indicates it probably came from a spear, not an arrow.
39. Bandelier and Bandelier, *Journey*, 141, and other sources.
40. Terrell, *Journey into Darkness*, 175.
41. Weber, *Spanish Frontier in North America*, 46.
42. Morrow, *South American Expeditions*, 159.
43. Bandelier and Bandelier, *Journey*, 154.
44. Ibid., 158.
45. Ibid.

46. Shamsie, "Reconstructing the Story," 197.
47. Adorno and Pautz, *Álvar Núñez Cabeza de Vaca*, 1:154–55.
48. Krieger and Krieger, *We Came Naked and Barefoot*, 145. See also Adorno and Pautz, *Álvar Núñez Cabeza de Vaca*, 2:xxiv; Varnum, *Álvar Núñez Cabeza de Vaca*, 4; Schneider, *Brutal Journey*, frontispiece map; and Goodwin, *Crossing the Continent*, 271–86.

Chapter 13

1. Mann, *1493*, 305.
2. Bandelier and Bandelier, *Journey*, 139. However, it's described as brass in Theisen, "Expedition of Pánfilo de Narváez," 80, and it's called a large copper bell by Adorno and Pautz, *Álvar Núñez Cabeza de Vaca*, 1:207.
3. Wright, "Negro Companions," 228.
4. Theisen, "Expedition of Pánfilo de Narváez," 80. This would have occurred in late 1535 or early 1536.
5. Indian presentations of more gifts to "Dorantes" will be examined later in this chapter.
6. Moriarty, "Discovery and Early Explorations."
7. Bandelier and Bandelier, *Journey*, 142.
8. Ibid., 144.
9. Bonvillian, Ingram, and McCleary, "Observations," 155.
10. Bandelier and Bandelier, *Journey*, 172.
11. Ibid., 172.
12. John Upton Terrell, without calling it Primahaitu, describes the "immense Piman linguistic family," which many tribes developed dialects for and spoke all through northern Mexico and the southwestern United States. Terrell, *Journey into Darkness*, 230.
13. T. Buckingham Smith used a missionary's Pima dictionary, deducing that if Cabeza de Vaca meant "Pimahaitu," without the *r*, the word in the Pima language means literally "nothing," because he said Pima means "no" and Haitu means "thing." He didn't know how including the *r* might change the word. T. B. Smith, "Falling-Out with Our Countrymen."
14. T. B. Smith, "Grammatical Sketch." See also Spicer, *Cycles of Conquest*, 86. Fanny Bandelier's 1905 translation of the *Relación* describes Primahaitu as "a language they have among them, and by which we understood each other." Bonvillian, Ingram, and McCleary point out: "Primahaitu was the only such [trade routes communication] system based on speech that Cabeza de Vaca and his three companions reported running across during their lengthy journey" ("Observations," 155). However, the 1993 translation about Primahaitu in Pupo-Walker's *Castaways* reads, "A language that was common to them, which we

did not understand" (114), which seems an opposite interpretation of how Fanny Bandelier and others translated Cabeza de Vaca's passage.
15. It's not known why Cabeza de Vaca strung the words "Pima" and "Haitu" together to refer to the various Sonoran Desert tribes of northern Mexico. Perhaps addition of the *r* in some way modified the phrase to be an eponym for related tribes. Of course, maybe Cabeza de Vaca misspelled the word. Also, he undoubtedly knew less about the language than Esteban. The Pimas referred to themselves as the O'odham, which is the name they prefer today, although both names are common.
16. Pupo-Walker, *Castaways*, 114. The 1555 edition, often referred to as *Naufragios*, is online at https://www.scribd.com/doc/241406102/Alvar-Nunez-Cabeza-de-Vaca-Naufragios (accessed January 30, 2017). The wording in Spanish is on page 103 of the online version.
17. Terrell, *Estevanico the Black*, 41–42.
18. Goodwin, *Crossing the Continent*, 292.
19. Krieger and Krieger, *We Came Naked and Barefoot*, 213.
20. Theisen, "Expedition of Pánfilo de Narváez," 93.
21. Bandelier and Bandelier, *Journey*, 157.
22. Perhaps the Ópata men were naked. Or perhaps they wore a breechcloth or some other clothing so minimal that Europeans still considered them naked. See "Narrative of Alarón's Voyage," in Flint and Flint, *Documents of the Coronado Expedition*, where men wearing breechcloths and women covering their genitals with feathers were nevertheless referred to as "naked" (191 and 645n42).
23. Theisen, "Expedition of Pánfilo de Narváez," 96–97.
24. Bandelier and Bandelier, *Journey*, 156.
25. Ibid., 156–57.
26. Theisen, "Expedition of Pánfilo de Narváez," 96.
27. Bandelier and Bandelier, *Journey*, 160.
28. Theisen, "Expedition of Pánfilo de Narváez," 96.
29. From what the Indians told him, Dorantes decided that the coast was twelve to fifteen leagues away, which could have been up to forty-five miles. By the closest straight-line route, Hermosillo is about sixty miles from the coast and by heading due west it's about seventy miles.
30. William K. Hartmann and Gayle Harrison Hartmann, "Locating the Lost Coronado Garrisons of San Gerónimo I, II, and III," in Flint and Flint, *Latest Word from 1540*, 125; Krieger and Krieger, *We Came Naked and Barefoot*, 118 and 122; Adorno and Pautz, *Álvar Núñez Cabeza de Vaca*, 2:75–77.
31. Krieger and Krieger, *We Came Naked and Barefoot*, 118, 122.
32. Bandelier and Bandelier, *Journey*, 160. Coronado's first Los Corazones is assumed to be Cabeza de Vaca's original site.
33. Flint and Flint, "Vázquez de Coronado's Letter to the Viceroy, August 3, 1540," in *Documents of the Coronado Expedition*, 255 and 653n35. Coronado's

figure is likely more accurate than Dorantes's estimate of only forty miles, which he'd only estimated from what he understood coastal Indians had told him.
34. These are straight-line distances due west to the coast. Heading southwest to the coast would be ten to twenty miles shorter. Some scholars have hypothesized other locations for Los Corazones.
35. Richard Flint, manuscript commentary, October 26, 2016.
36. Nuño Beltrán de Guzmán, in one of his rare defeats, was repelled in an invasion of Yaqui territory in 1532 and forced to retreat to Culiacán. T. B. Smith, *Relation*, 182n6.
37. Krieger and Krieger, *We Came Naked and Barefoot*, 124.
38. Bandelier and Bandelier, *Journey*, 161–62. This description is a first-contact perspective by Indians who had never seen Europeans before.
39. Ibid., 163.
40. Ibid.
41. A. Bandelier, *Gilded Man*, 125.
42. Ibid., 165.
43. Ibid., 167–68.
44. Schneider, *Brutal Journey*, 304.
45. Bandelier and Bandelier, *Journey*, 169. At least, that's the closest location that can be theorized from Cabeza de Vaca's vague description. He estimated they were thirty leagues from Culiacán.
46. Bandelier and Bandelier, *Journey*, 168.
47. Covey, *Cabeza de Vaca's Adventures*, 115. Covey's translation gives a quotation rather than the paraphrase that occurs in other translations.
48. Hartmann and Hartmann, "Locating the Lost Coronado Garrisons," 139. Francisco de Ibarra led the expedition in 1565 that was told this.
49. In translations of the 1542 edition, Covey (*Cabeza de Vaca's Adventures*, 129) and Bandelier (*Journey*, 169) report twenty-eight and thirty leagues, respectively. The López-Morillas translation of the 1555 edition (Pupo-Walker, *Castaways*, 115) says the distance was twenty-eight leagues "more or less." Theisen's translation of the Joint Report ("Expedition of Pánfilo de Narváez," 106) gives the distance as thirty-five leagues or more.
50. San Rafael is a straight-line distance of seventy-four miles north of Culiacán (about 28.5 leagues), and Ocoroni is one hundred miles from Culiacán (about 38.5 leagues).
51. Bandelier and Bandelier, *Journey*, 168–69.
52. Ibid., 169.
53. Ibid.
54. Theisen, "Expedition of Pánfilo de Narváez," 103.
55. Bandelier and Bandelier, *Journey*, 171.

56. Ibid., 171–72. This speech by the Indians also appears in the 1555 revision that Cabeza de Vaca and his secretary prepared in *Castaways*, 114, but it does not appear in Oviedo's Joint Report.
57. Wood, *Conquistadors*, 260.
58. Bandelier and Bandelier, *Journey*, 170–72.
59. Ibid., 170–71.
60. A. Bandelier, *Gilded Man*, 129. Other sources agree on this point.
61. Bandelier and Bandelier, *Journey*, 164.
62. Morrow, *South American Expeditions*, xiv.
63. Bandelier and Bandelier, *Journey*, 174.
64. Theisen, "Expedition of Pánfilo de Narváez," 107.
65. Bandelier and Bandelier, *Journey*, 175.
66. Pupo-Walker, *Castaways*, 115.
67. The Audiencia in Mexico City had made Indian slave raiding illegal in 1530, but Guzmán restarted the raids out of greed.
68. Bishop, *Odyssey of Cabeza de Vaca*, 149.
69. Theisen, "Expedition of Pánfilo de Narváez," 108–9.
70. Spicer, *Cycles of Conquest*, 87.
71. At that time, Compostela was at present-day Tepic, Mexico. Compostela was moved about seventeen miles south to a more defensive position after Indian attacks in 1540. Frye and Stavans, *Chronicle of the Narváez Expedition*, 45n8.
72. Reséndez, *Land So Strange*, 148.
73. Goodwin, *Crossing the Continent*, 38.

Chapter 14

1. S. Schroeder, Tavárez, Cruz, and Roa-de-la-Carrera, *Chimalpahin's Conquest*, 204.
2. Richard Flint, commentary, October 26, 2016.
3. S. Schroeder, *Chimalpahin's Conquest*, 202.
4. The Constantinople of the 1500s is today's Istanbul, Turkey.
5. Ayer, *Memorial*, 270n80.
6. Castillo and Garcia, *Discovery and Conquest*, 190–91.
7. Mell, "Spanish Caballeros." See also Schneider, *Brutal Journey*, 45.
8. Mundy, *Death of Aztec Tenochtitlan*.
9. For an idea of what Tenochtitlan might have looked like before contact, do an Internet search for Tenochtitlan and click on Bing images, which include the Grand Temple and a bird's-eye view of the precontact city.
10. Only the 1535 illustration of Mexico City is in this book because the 1524 and 1535 bird's-eye maps look so similar.

11. S. Schroeder, *Chimalpahin's Conquest*, 362–63.
12. Juan Comas, "Historical Reality and the Detractors of Father Las Casas," in Friede and Keen, *Bartolomé de las Casas in History*, 492.
13. S. Schroeder, *Chimalpahin's Conquest*, 211. See also León-Portilla, *Broken Spears*, xxxix. Although Chimalpahin and León-Portilla are the most likely to be correct, some sources say the temple's other main Aztec god besides Huitzilopochtli was Tlaloc, the god of water. Gardner, *Mysteries of the Ancient Americas*, 286.
14. Goodwin, *Crossing the Continent*, 75. Starting in the 1400s, Spain established *audiencias* in the Americas as courts to administer the royal laws, and they became one of the most powerful colonial institutions.
15. Although the name of the Aztec monarch is usually Anglicized as Montezuma, that's an incorrect phonetic spelling from the original Nahuatl language. Closer spellings to Nahuatl phonics besides Moctezuma include Moteksoma or Mote:cuhzo:ma. Depending on pronunciation, the name translates to "a frowning, grave man." S. Schroeder, *Chimalpahin's Conquest*, 187. Another translation is "he is severe like a lord." Mursell, "Moctezuma, Montezuma, Motecuhzoma?"
16. Coyolxauqui was sister of, and rival to, Huitzilopochtli. According to Mexica histories, when Huitzilopochtli was born, he warred against his sister and decapitated her. The headless stone at the foot of the Great Temple commemorated this ancient story.
17. For example, a church honoring the Virgin Mary of Guadalupe was built on the same hill near Mexico City where Aztecs once had a temple for the Aztec earth goddess Tonāntzin, which Franciscan priests had destroyed. A nearby basilica houses a cloak containing the image of the Virgin Mary.
18. Krieger and Krieger, *We Came Naked and Barefoot*, 236.
19. "We reached Mexico [City] on Sunday, the day before the vespers of St. James." Bandelier and Bandelier, *Journey*, 183. See also Adorno and Pautz, *Álvar Núñez Cabeza de Vaca*, 2:390.
20. Pupo-Walker, *Castaways*, 120.
21. Flint and Flint, "Esteban the Moor." See also Aiton, "Secret Visita against Viceroy Mendoza," 119.
22. Adorno and Pautz, *Álvar Núñez Cabeza de Vaca*, 2:394.
23. Esteban probably was not allowed very often to be in the company of the three Spaniards. His constant presence would have offended Spanish racist and slave-owning prejudices.
24. The story of the Virgin Mary's apparition in 1531 to the Aztec Indian baptized as Juan Diego is believed to have been written first in the Aztec language of Nahuatl about thirty years later by Antonio Valeriano. The original has been lost, but a copy titled *Huei Tlamahuitzoltica* was published 118 years after the event in Nahuatl by Luis Lasso de la Vega. Usually only a much abridged

version is seen in English. The Nahuatl account of Mary's apparitions is best known as *Nican Mopohua*. A record of the apparitions is not in any of Zumárraga's voluminous correspondence or other records. There also is a Virgin of Guadalupe figure in Estremadura, Spain, with a similar story. It says a black Madonna was carved by Saint Luke the Evangelist and buried by priests fleeing Moorish armies in about 711. In the early 1300s a peasant said the Virgin Mary appeared to him and instructed him to tell priests to dig at the site of his reported apparition. A shrine was built where they found the statue, where there now is a large monastery. Downey, *Isabella*, 225.

25. Flint and Flint, "Letter of the Viceroy to the King, 1539," in *Documents of the Coronado Expedition*, 47–48.
26. Goodwin, *Crossing the Continent*, 300–301.
27. Ibid., 301.
28. William K. Hartmann and Richard Flint, "Before the Coronado Expedition: Who Knew What and When Did They Know It?," in Flint and Flint, *Coronado Expedition from the Distance of 460 Years*, 28.
29. Flint and Flint, "The Viceroy's Letter to the King, Jacona, April 17, 1540," in *Documents of the Coronado Expedition*, 240.
30. Terrell, *Estevanico the Black*, 71.
31. Wagner, "'Fray Marcos de Niza' Note," 336. It seems every book, article, and research paper on the Franciscan Marcos de Niza refers to him by the Spanish title of "Fray," which is still a popular reference in Mexico, the American Southwest, and parts of Spain. However, it is a Spanish word. This biography will use its English equivalent of "Friar," except in this quotation.
32. Flint, *No Settlement, No Conquest*, 32.
33. Goodwin, *Crossing the Continent*, 73. Franciscans who knew Marcos de Niza said his nationality was French.
34. Wagner, "Fr. Marcos de Niza," 185.
35. Flint and Flint, "Letter of the Viceroy to the King, 1539," in *Documents of the Coronado Expedition*, 48.
36. Flint and Flint, "Instructions to and Account by Marcos de Niza," in *Documents of the Coronado Expedition*, 65.
37. Ilahiane, "Estevan de Dorantes," 9, 11.
38. "Enslaved Africans in Mexico."
39. Flint and Flint, "Letter of Vázquez de Coronado to the King, December 15, 1538," in *Documents of the Coronado Expedition*, 21. See also Flint and Flint, "Francisco Vázquez de Coronado."
40. Flint and Flint, "Decree of the King Appointing Vázquez de Coronado Governor of Nueva Galicia, April 18, 1539," in *Documents of the Coronado Expedition*, 51.
41. A major African revolt would occur in 1612, resulting in thirty-five blacks being tortured and hanged. The heads of twenty-nine were impaled on poles at the gallows while the bodies of the other six were quartered and hung up to rot

along the main roads leading into the city. Martínez, "Black Blood of New Spain," 479.
42. Terrell, *American Indian Almanac*, 51.
43. This misconception was still true twenty years later when Castañeda wrote his account of the Coronado expedition and decided Asia was not found because Coronado went in the wrong direction.
44. Lowery, *Spanish Settlements*, 263.
45. Wagner, "Fr. Marcos de Niza," 223.
46. Hodge, *History of Hawikuh*, 19.
47. Flint, "Without Them, Nothing Was Possible," 65.
48. For details, see T. Johnson, "Trial and Execution of Don Carlos."
49. Richard E. Greenleaf, "Historiography of the Mexican Inquisition: Evolution of Interpretations and Methodologies," in M. Perry and Cruz, *Cultural Encounters*, 261.
50. Flint, *No Settlement, No Conquest*, 8, and many other sources.
51. Phelan, *Millennial Kingdom*.
52. J. Jorge Klor de Alva, "Colonizing Souls: The Failure of the Indian Inquisition and the Rise of Penitential Discipline," in M. E. Perry and Cruz, *Cultural Encounters*, 12.
53. Flint, *No Settlement, No Conquest*, 223–25.
54. Aiton, "Secret Visita against Viceroy Mendoza," 20. See also Hanke, *Spanish Struggle for Justice*, 89.
55. Flint and Flint, "Narrative Account of Fray Marcos de Niza, August 26, 1539," in *Documents of the Coronado Expedition*, 67. This date is from the Gregorian calendar in use at the time. The departure date in the modern calendar would be March 17. San Miguel was a common way then to refer to Culiacán.
56. Hammond and Rey, "Report of Fray Marcos de Niza," in *Narratives of the Coronado Expedition*, 63.

Chapter 15

1. Flint and Flint, "Letter of the Viceroy to the King, 1539," in *Documents of the Coronado Expedition*, 48.
2. Richard Flint interview, February 11, 2015.
3. Richard Flint, manuscript commentary, October 26, 2016.
4. Flint and Flint, "Letters from Antonio de Mendoza and Rodrigo de Albornoz, October 1539," in *Documents of the Coronado Expedition*, 91.
5. Bakeless, *America*, 71.
6. Allen, "Estevanico the Moor."
7. Marcos said he sent Esteban on ahead on Passion Sunday. Hammond and Rey, "Report of Fray Marcos de Niza," in *Narratives of the Coronado Expedition*, 66.

The date is by the Gregorian calendar. By the modern calendar, Esteban would have left on April 2.
8. Hartmann, *Searching for Golden Empires*, 175.
9. Flint, manuscript commentary, October 26, 2016.
10. Hammond and Rey, "Report of Fray Marcos de Niza," 69.
11. Ibid., 68. Easter Sunday 1539 was on April 17. Hartley, "Easter Date Tables." Whatever date Easter Sunday fell on, Marcos left the next day.
12. Hammond and Rey, "Report of Fray Marcos de Niza," 69.
13. Ibid., 68.
14. Ibid., 66.
15. W. Smith, Woodbury, and Woodbury, *Excavation of Hawikuh*, 128. This was told to Cabeza de Vaca and probably told also to Esteban. The grasslands would come to be known as the Great Plains of the United States.
16. Rogers, *World's Great Men of Color*, 319.
17. Hammond and Rey, "Report of Fray Marcos de Niza," 70.
18. Ibid.
19. Ibid., 74.
20. Flipper, *Memoirs*, 84.
21. Flipper, "Did a Negro Discover," 86–92.
22. Goodwin, *Crossing the Continent*, 337.
23. Houk and Gallagher, *Coronado National Memorial*, 5.
24. Flint and Flint, "Castañeda de Najera's Narrative," in *Documents of the Coronado Expedition*, 388.
25. The reason for the range is that some Spaniards had different distances for a league (see note 29). In addition, a league was an imprecise measurement, depending on the individual counting the paces and considering the roughness of terrain.
26. Hackett, *Historical Documents*, 12.
27. Hammond and Rey, "Report of Fray Marcos de Niza," 74.
28. If the Indians could walk it in thirty days, it's reasonable to think Esteban could, too.
29. Time for some math that would just clog the narrative. When Marcos retreated as fast as he could toward Culiacán, he said he made six to nine leagues in hurried travel per day. So five leagues per day seems a reasonable pace when he was just moving forward and not frightened, and also if he didn't take any more of his regular rest breaks in Indian villages. Giving him the benefit of the doubt, he probably could make five leagues a day. Stepping off a sixteenth-century league over land is imprecise, but this book's conversions range from 2.63 to 3 miles for a league. If Marcos started the route to the final unsettled area at least sixteen days behind Esteban, he had to be from 210 to 240 miles behind Esteban. When he said he was fifteen days from Hawikku at the start of the despoblado, that would put him between 197 and 225 miles away, again

assuming he would travel five leagues a day. If much farther behind, he'd still be in Mexico. As for Castañeda's conservative estimate that Marcos was sixty leagues behind Esteban, that would still put Marcos 158 to 180 miles short of Hawikku before turning back. Even if Marcos is taken at his word that he walked all the way to Hawikku, he couldn't have arrived until weeks after Esteban reached the village.

30. Udall, *To the Inland Empire*, 65.
31. Richard Flint, manuscript commentary, October 26, 2016.
32. The map can be seen at Bandelier and Bandelier, *Journey*, http://www.americanjourneys.org/pdf/AJ-070.pdf.
33. Bandelier, *Gilded Man*, 160. The description of the cross is from Hammond and Rey, "Report of Fray Marcos de Niza," 79. Bandelier was in South America when *Gilded Man* was published, and the late F. W. Hodge believed the book's reference to the cross was inserted without Bandelier's knowledge by an editor. Hodge, "First Discovered City of Cibola," 152.
34. Bolton's book, *Coronado: Knight of Pueblos and Plains*, has been reprinted several times, including in 2015. His map for Coronado's (and presumably also Esteban's) route is on a double-page spread after page 491.
35. Bolton, *Coronado*, 32, 105–17.
36. Richard Flint, manuscript commentary, October 26, 2016.
37. Bolton, *Coronado*, 35.
38. Nugent Brasher, "A Narrative of the Search for the Captain General," in Flint and Flint, *Latest Word from 1540*, 229–55. See also Nugent Brasher, "Francisco Vázquez de Coronado," 325–75.
39. Richard Flint, manuscript commentary, October 26, 2016.
40. Flint and Flint, "Castañeda de Nájera's Narrative," in *Documents of the Coronado Expedition*, 391.
41. Ibid., 393.
42. Wagner, "Fr. Marcos de Niza," 220.
43. Hammond and Rey, "Letter of Coronado to Mendoza, August 3, 1540," in *Narratives of the Coronado Expedition*, 163.
44. Giovanni Battista Ramusio, *Delle navigationi et viaggi* (Venice, Italy: Nella stamperia de Giunti, 1554). English translation by Richard Flint and Shirley Cushing Flint, cited in Flint, *No Settlement, No Conquest*, 228–29.
45. Sauer, *Sixteenth Century North America*, 127.

Chapter 16

1. Estimates vary. Many researchers avoid the issue by never estimating when he arrived. According to Hartmann, *Searching for Golden Empires*, 193, the date of arrival is May 15, but it might have occurred anytime during the month's first two weeks or so.

2. Rentería, "José Cisneros."
3. Hammond and Rey, "Report of Alarcon's Expedition," in *Narratives of the Coronado Expedition*, 141, 145.
4. Hodge, *History of Hawikuh*, 19.
5. Katsinas still can be seen at Zuni and Hopi pueblos in little-publicized public ceremonies. The ancient religion also is still observed among pueblos along the Rio Grande from south of Albuquerque to north of Santa Fe. However, more than three hundred years of Christian missionaries suppressed public appearances of masked katsina figures there.
6. Not surprisingly, there is no record of katsinas or other specific individuals being present at Esteban's appearance. Richard Flint told the author, however, that katsinas probably would appear at such an important event. Flint interview, January 10, 2015.
7. Flint, *No Settlement, No Conquest*, 98–99.
8. Hammond and Rey, "Report of Fray Marcos de Niza," in *Narratives of the Coronado Expedition*, 75.
9. W. Smith, Woodbury, and Woodbury, *Excavation of Hawikuh*, 25.
10. Spaniards would not begin calling these people Zunis until four decades later.
11. Mexican tribes' modern masks are molded and brightly painted with realistic human and animal faces, but protohistoric Mexican masks were more similar to katsina masks except in details.
12. Because priests and Catholics in general considered the Indian masks of Mexico and the pueblos to be satanic, a 1553 Spanish law forbade them. The futility of enforcing the law is clear since the head covers still are used hundreds of years later. Dockstader, *Kachina and the White Man*, 56, with a discussion of the antiquity of katsina masks (55), and the differences between Mexican and Pueblo masks (57).
13. Ibid., 84, 22. When US troops were sent in 1891 to force the Hopis to send their children to government schools, they were confronted by Masaû (also spelled Maasau-u) Katsina, which Puebloans often brought out when they felt threatened because that particular katsina represents death. The Hopis also confronted the troops with the Warrior Twins Katsinas that day. See Trimble, *People*, 69. It's likely Esteban also encountered Masaû at some point.
14. Flint and Flint, "Narrative of Alarcón's Voyage, 1540," in *Documents of the Coronado Expedition*, 197. Zuni women wore "very long garments" and blankets but would not have come out to greet the visitors.
15. This is based on the author's own experiences inside native homes on pueblos between Albuquerque and Santa Fe.
16. Zuni oral history reported by Zuni historian Edmund J. Ladd, "Zuni On the Day," 190.
17. Hammond and Rey, "Report of Alarcon's Expedition," in *Narratives of the Coronado Expedition*, 145. See also Flint and Flint, "Narrative of Alarcón's Voyage, 1540," in *Documents of the Coronado Expedition*, 199.

18. "Aztec" is a word not coined until the 1800s. It is used in this book because it is much better known today. Tenochtitlan was their name for their capital before Mexico City was built on the same site. Nahuatl was the common language on trade routes and in trade centers in the 1500s, much as English is often used in international trade cities today.
19. Ladd, "Zuni on the Day," 189.
20. Guzmán's rampage across Sonora was so rapacious and merciless that he is still referred to as "Bloody Guzmán" in Mexico, where anticonquistador feelings remain strong as is true also in Central and South America.
21. Ladd, "Zuni on the Day," 190.
22. Hammond and Rey, "Report of Alarcon's Expedition," 75–76.
23. Ibid., 76–77.
24. Flint, *No Settlement, No Conquest*, 35. This is Flint's translation from the sixteenth-century Spanish of "Narrative Account by Fray Marcos de Niza," in Flint and Flint, *Documents of the Coronado Expedition*.
25. Hammond and Rey, "Report of Fray Marcos de Niza," 76.
26. Hackett, *Historical Documents*.
27. Indian Pueblo Cultural Center, October 3, 2015.
28. Hammond and Rey, "Castañeda's History of the Expedition," in *Narratives of the Coronado Expedition*, 199.
29. Flint and Flint, "Vázquez de Coronado's Letter to the Viceroy, August 3, 1540," in *Documents of the Coronado Expedition*, 262.

Chapter 17

1. Ladd, "Zuni on the Day," 190. Ladd's explanation is contrary to reasons given by most writers today.
2. Herrick, *Winter of the Metal People*, 31–32. This description was inspired by accounts of kiva meetings by Bandelier in *The Delight Makers* and by Waters in *The Man Who Killed the Deer*.
3. Maura, "Nuevas interpretaciones," 129–54.
4. Ibid., 147–48; my translation. See also Maura, *El Gran Burlador de América*, 290.
5. Maura, *El Gran Burlador de América*, 290; my translation.
6. Simour, "(De)slaving History," 11. See also "Rencontre."
7. Ilahiane, "Estevan de Dorantes," 7.
8. Torture was a routine and accepted interrogation technique that Spaniards often described in the 1500s. While sharp knives, clamps, and fire were the preferred instruments of torture in the field, established European communities also used homemade racks, which would leave their victims crippled for life

afterward. For examples of documented Spanish interrogation by torture, see Morrow, *South American Expeditions*, 176.
9. James E. MacDougald, e-mail to author, April 2, 2017.
10. Although Google Earth or an aerial view shows arroyos that are closer, the nearest dependable water is the Zuni River, two and a half miles west of Hawikku. Flint, "Instructions to and Account by Fray Marcos de Niza, 1538–1539," in *Documents of the Coronado Expedition*, 630n153.
11. Indians told Marcos that the first Zuni village, Hawikku, was fifteen long days of travel from the beginning of the final despoblado. Marcos claimed he began that final leg on May 9. Hammond and Rey, "Report of Fray Marcos de Niza," in *Narratives of the Coronado Expedition*, 74. So, if the friar went at an Indian's pace, he would have arrived at the village on May 24. It's more likely he would have arrived later than that.
12. Flint and Flint, "Vázquez de Coronado's Letter to the Viceroy, August 3, 1540," in *Documents of the Coronado Expedition*, 262.
13. Ibid., 262.
14. Hammond and Rey, "Report of Alarcon's Expedition," in *Narratives of the Coronado Expedition*, 145.
15. Kessell, *Spain in the Southwest*, 27.
16. Ladd, "Zuni on the Day," 190. See also Flint and Flint, "Narrative of Alarcón's Voyage," in *Documents of the Coronado Expedition*, 145.
17. Goodwin, *Crossing the Continent*, 365.
18. Ibid., 369. Many historians, however, would argue that it's a myth that Zunis and other Puebloans were as peaceful in ancient times as they are today, despite Goodwin's lineup of modern Zuni speakers implying or saying otherwise.
19. McDonald, "Intimacy and Empire," 26. This speculative scenario could help resolve the contradiction between the Spanish chronicles saying he was killed immediately and the stories that he was killed because of advances toward women, because Esteban's death might have occurred some time afterward, whether as a result of jealousy or anger.
20. R. Flint, "Eighth De Oficio Witness," 168. See also Hammond and Rey, "Report on Alarcón's Expedition," in *Narratives of the Coronado Expedition*, 178.
21. Flint and Flint, "Coronado's Letter to the Viceroy," 262.
22. Adorno and Pautz, *Álvar Núñez Cabeza de Vaca*, 2:422.
23. Goodwin, *Crossing the Continent*, 372. A unique scenario is that Esteban married an Avavare woman in Texas, took her with him to Hawikku, and then traveled back to Avavare country to live in Texas with her. Lalami, *Moor's Account*, 320. Lalami's book is a fictional novel, and this idea is a product of her imagination.
24. Shepherd, *Discoveries of Esteban the Black*, 40.
25. Jennings, *Aztec Autumn*, 187–95.

26. Maura, "Nuevas interpretaciones," 150. See also Maura, *El Gran Burlador de América*, 281.
27. Flipper, "Did a Negro Discover," 90–91. Flipper, who served in the Southwest as an army officer, might have been the first to record the Zuni oral history that Esteban was held for three days, not one, and that the Zunis did not kill him but instead gave him a "powerful kick" to send him back south.
28. Twitchell, *Leading Facts*, 155. See also Frank H. Cushing in his 1885 talk to the Geographic Society of Boston, recounted in Bandelier, *Discovery of New Mexico*, 94. There's no English translation for the Ka-Ka Clan.
29. Dickens, "Estevan—Early American Negro," 384. See also Shepherd, *Discoveries of Esteban the Black*, 113, and other Spanish and English sources.
30. See "Tesia."

Chapter 18

1. Villagrá, *Historia de la Nueva México*, line 29 of canto 3, 18.
2. Hammond and Rey, "Report of Fray Marcos de Niza," in *Narratives of the Coronado Expedition*, 77.
3. S. Schroeder, *Chimalpahin's Conquest*, 353.
4. Flint and Flint, "Vázquez de Coronado's Letter to the Viceroy, August 3, 1540," in *Documents of the Coronado Expedition*, 262.
5. Ibid., 262.
6. R. Flint, "Definitive Decision of the King and Audiencia," in *Great Cruelties Have Been Reported*, 463.
7. "Santo Domingo and San Felipe," 430.
8. Allen, "Estevanico the Moor." Flint and Flint, "Vázquez de Coronado to Viceroy, August 3, 1540," 262.
9. Lemke, *Cabrillo*, 83.
10. Page, *Uprising*, 14.
11. Simour, "(De)slaving History, 10. Archaeologist Merrill Freeman was more vague in 1917, accusing Esteban of unspecified "indiscretions."
12. Mann, *1493*, 306. See also Rout, *African Experience in Spanish America*, 76; and Rogers, *World's Great Men of Color*, 319.
13. One example is British historian Alan Clark admitting that he "invented" the quotation used as the basis for the title of his World War I study, *The Donkeys*. A. Roberts, "Battle Scars," 59.
14. Twitchell, *Leading Facts*, 156. See also Sanchez, "Historic Trek," A1.
15. Rollins, "Where History Began," 118. His full quote describes "the warranted but untimely death of Estevanico."
16. Reeve, *History of New Mexico*, 86.
17. Kessell, *Kiva, Cross, and Crown*, 6.

18. Lemke, *Cabrillo*, 82.
19. Page, *Uprising*, 14–15.
20. Bandelier, *Gilded Man*, 151–52, 159.
21. One of the most highly fictionalized and idolizing biographers of Cabeza de Vaca—and typical for its time—was Morris Bishop in *The Odyssey of Cabeza de Vaca*. That book also includes one of the more negative portrayals of Esteban due to the author's ethnocentric bias and opinions.
22. Holland, *Hawikuh and the Seven Cities*, 7.
23. Woodbury, "Zuni Prehistory," 469.
24. Chávez, *New Mexico*, 35.
25. Mann, *1493*, 306. Two Moroccan writers came up with the same idea. Simour, "(De)Slaving History," 11, and Ilahaine, "Estevan."
26. Dr. Irving E. Schiek III, a retired surgeon, in e-mail to the author, July 11, 2016.
27. Roberts and Roberts, *New Mexico*, 24–26.
28. Covey, afterword to *Cabeza de Vaca's Adventures*, 141.
29. Koch, *Imaginary Cities of Gold*, 90.
30. W. H. Johnson, *Spanish West*, 28.
31. Hutchins, *Coronado's Well-Equipped Army*, 36.
32. Bishop, *Odyssey of Cabeza de Vaca*, 161.
33. Jaramillo, *History of New Mexico*, 5. An arroyo is a gully cut by erosion.
34. "Esteban," in *Black Heroes in World History*, 34–35.
35. Perry, *Children of the Sun*, 236.
36. Ottmani, *Fils du soleil*, 293.
37. Sando, *Pueblo Nations*, 48–50.
38. Farnum, *Seven Golden Cities*. All of that is in addition to the fact that the term "Seven Cities of Gold" was not known in Esteban's time.
39. Weber, "Fray Marcos de Niza," 140, 27.
40. Loewen, *Lies My Teacher Told Me*, 105–6.
41. Chipman and Weddle, "How Historical Myths Are Born," 258.
42. Sanchez, "Historic Trek," A3.
43. Simour, "(De)slaving History," 11.
44. Ilahiane, "Estevan de Dorantes," 10.
45. Ibid.
46. Bloom, "Who Discovered New Mexico?," 131–32.
47. Weber, "Fray Marcos de Niza," 30.
48. Billard, *World of the American Indian*, 162. This is just one example of giving Marcos the credit.
49. Fritz Thompson, "Black Action Inc.," A1.
50. Holland, *Hawikuh and the Seven Cities*, 1.
51. Katz, *Black West*, 11.
52. Udall, *To the Inland Empire*, 65.
53. MacDougald, "Narvarez Expedition," 27.

54. Ottmani, *Fils du soleil*, 8–9; my translation.
55. Voltaire's phrase of "one of our great minds" is a reference to French philosopher Bernard le Bovier de Fontenelle, who in 1724 wrote *De l'origine des fables*.

Chapter 19

1. D. B. Davis, *Inhuman Bondage*, 32.
2. A translation of the 282 laws of the Hammurabi Code, many dealing with ancient concepts of slavery, can be found in Harper, "Code of Hammurabi."
3. D. B. Davis, *Inhuman Bondage*, 32.
4. Morris, "Breaking the Bonds," 40.
5. Patterson, *Slavery and Social Death*, 13.
6. Ibid., 7.
7. Spicer, *Cycles of Conquest*, 81–82.
8. Gallay, *Indian Slavery*.
9. Schmidt-Nowara, *Slavery, Freedom, and Abolition*, 24.
10. D. B. Davis, *Inhuman Bondage*, 97. The *repartimiento* system was added to the encomienda system in later years, with Indians forced into low-paid or unpaid labor for Spanish-owned businesses and government projects.
11. Downey, *Isabella*, 429.
12. Ibid., 205.
13. "Slavery in French Colonial Louisiana."
14. Mann, *1493*, 67.
15. Simmons, "Slavery Thrived."
16. Rout, *African Experience in Spanish America*, 9.
17. Ibid.
18. Ibid., 22.
19. Price, *Maroon Societies*, 1.
20. Rout, *African Experience in Spanish America*, 23.
21. Ibid., 10–11.
22. One Catholic translation of Genesis 9:25 reads: "Cursed be Chanaan, [Noah] said, he shall be the slave and drudge of his brethren." That same passage in the King James version: "And [Noah] said, cursed be Canaan, a servant of servants shall he be unto his brethren." That passage was interpreted to justify Christians enslaving Africans.
23. Pagden, "Stain," 39.
24. Patterson, *Slavery and Social Death*, 95.
25. "Quotations on the Jefferson Memorial."
26. Finkelman, "Monster of Monticello."

27. Pagden, "Stain," 35.
28. Larson, "African Diasporas," 134.
29. Reséndez, *Other Slavery*, 331n2.
30. Phillips, "India Tops Global Slavery Index."
31. Buckley, "Ava DuVernay," C2.
32. Reséndez, *Other Slavery*, 3.
33. Coe, *Maya*, 25, 141, 146–47.
34. Reséndez, *Other Slavery*, 3.
35. Brett Rushford, "A Little Flesh We Offer You," in Galley, *Indian Slavery in Colonial America*.
36. Brooks, *Captives and Cousins*, 33.
37. Rushford, "A Little Flesh," 361.
38. Brooks, *Captives and Cousins*, 40.
39. Krauthamer, *Black Slaves, Indian Masters*, 17.
40. Yarbrough, *Race and the Cherokee Nation*, 117. For the complete text of Frederick Douglass's lecture, see Douglass, "Inhumanity of Slavery."
41. Yarbrough, *Race and the Cherokee Nation*, 3–4.
42. Brooks, *Captives and Cousins*, 33.

Chapter 20

1. Without saying how he could know, Chouaib Halifi's French article, "Mostapha El Azemmor/Esteban" declares that Esteban's father worked in the Azemmour shipyards, but Halifi says nothing about other family members.
2. Flint and Flint, "Narrative of Alarcón's Voyage, 1540," in *Documents of the Coronado Expedition*, 197.
3. Patterson, *Slavery and Social Death*, 4.
4. Ibid., 5.
5. Ambrose, *Undaunted Courage*, 458. See also Chamberlain, "On the Trail."
6. "York."
7. Theisen, "Expedition of Pánfilo de Narváez," 68.
8. "Searching for York."
9. Quaife, *Narrative*, 84.
10. It's possible that Leonard encountered an African American living with the Crow tribe who pretended to be York.
11. Patterson, *Slavery and Social Death*, 192.
12. Horwitz, *Voyage Long and Strange*, 133.
13. Simour, "(De)slaving History," 15. Throughout his article, Simour refers to Esteban as Mostafa al-Azemmour.

Appendix

1. John Sherrill Houser was born in South Dakota where his father, Ivan Houser, was assistant sculptor to Gutzon Borglum during the carving of Mount Rushmore. He was a sculptor and painter ever since. His world-famous art is in many museums, other public spaces, and many international publications. His best-known sculpture is *The Equestrian*, which is many times larger than life-size of a Spanish conquistador astride a rearing horse. At thirty-six feet high and weighing sixteen tons, the art is the world's largest bronze equestrian statue. Installed in 1999 at the El Paso International Airport, it is one of twelve sculptures planned for the "XII Travelers," which has been proposed to commemorate a dozen notable men and women who traveled at one time through the Southwest close to or through El Paso.
2. John Sherrill Houser, interview on August 15, 2015, Madrid, New Mexico.
3. John Sherrill Houser, telephone interview, April 20, 2017.
4. John Sherill Houser, e-mail to author, July 24, 2015.
5. Houser interview, August 15, 2015.
6. Ibid.
7. G. Smith, "In the Steps of Esteban."
8. These mistakes should be added to any new edition of James W. Loewen's myth-busting book, *Lies Across America: What Our Historic Sites Get Wrong*, as more examples of outdated, Eurocentric, and inaccurate events reported on so many historical markers and exhibits. At least Esteban was remembered.
9. There are several religious Moor statues in the United States, all of Saint Benedict the Moor, the patron saint of African Americans, who is revered throughout Latin America. Saint Benedict was coincidentally a contemporary of Esteban's during his early years, and he lived as a monk in Sicily. There are paintings and stained-glass windows of Saint Benedict the Moor in some of America's multicultural Catholic churches and schools as well as in some homeless shelters.

Bibliography

Abdul-Jabbar, Kareem, and Alan Steinberg. *Black Profiles in Courage: A Legacy of African American Achievement*. New York: William Morrow, 1996.
Abram, Lynwood. "Sculptor Shapes the Faces of El Paso." *Houston Chronicle*, April 22, 2001. http://www.chron.com/news/houston-texas/article/Sculptor-shapes-the-faces-of-El-Paso-2042609.php. Accessed September 23, 2015.
Abu-Talib, Mohammed, ed. *Estevanico el Moro: Requiem huellas comunes y miradas cruzadas*. Rabat, Morocco: de la Universidad Mohamed V, 1995.
Adorno, Rolena, and Patrick Charles Pautz. *Alvar Núñez Cabeza de Vaca: His Account, His Life, and the Expedition of Pánfilo de Narváez*. 3 vols. Lincoln: University of Nebraska Press, 1999.
"African American History Timeline, 1492–1600." African American History Facts, July 4, 2010. http://www.africanamerica.org/topic/african-american-history-facts. Accessed June 2, 2014.
Aguirre, Indalecio Liévano. *Los grandes conflictos sociales y económicos de nuestra historia*. Bogotá: Ediciones Tercer Mundo, 1966.
Aiton, Arthur S. "The Secret Visita against Viceroy Mendoza." In *New Spain and the Anglo-American West, Historical Contributions Presented to Herbert E. Bolton*. Vol. 1. Los Angeles: Privately printed at Lancaster Press, 1932.
Alchin, Linda K. "Estevanico." Elizabethan Era. http://www.elizabethan-era.org.uk/estevanico.htm. Accessed April 15, 2014.
Allen, Anne B. "Estevanico the Moor." *American History* 32, no. 3 (July/August 1999). Also at Weider History Group, http://www.historynet.com/estevanico-the-moor-august-97-american-history-feature.htm, August 19, 1997. Accessed April 15, 2014.
Altman, Ida. "The Revolt of Enriquillo and the Historiography of Early Spanish America." *Americas* 63, no. 4 (April 2007): 587–614.

Ambrose, Stephen. *Undaunted Courage: Meriwether Lewis, Thomas Jefferson, and the Opening of the American West*. New York: Simon and Schuster, 1997. http://louisville.edu/ur/ucomm/mags/summer2003/york.html. Accessed July 5, 2016.

Anghiera, Pietro Martire d'. "The Testimony of Francisco de Chicora," ed. Gary C. Daniels and trans. Francis Augustus MacNutt. The New World, July 6, 2012. http://thenewworld.us/the-testimony-of-francisco-de-chicora. Accessed May 30, 2015.

Arrington, Carolyn. *Estevanico, Black Explorer in Spanish Texas*. Austin: Eakin Press, 1986.

Associated Press. "Large Gold Nugget Sells for about 400K." *Albuquerque Journal*, October 27, 2014, A9.

———. "Pope Celebrates Mass for Mexico's Indigenous People." *Albuquerque Journal*, February 16, 2016, A8.

Ayer, Mrs. Edward E., trans. With annotation by Frederick Webb Hodge and Charles Fletcher Lummis. *The Memorial of Fray Alonso de Benavides, 1630*. 1916. Reprint, Albuquerque: Horn and Wallace, 1965.

"Azemmour." *Lonely Planet: Morocco*. 10th ed. 1989. Reprint, Oakland, CA: lonelyplanet.com, 2011.

Bakeless, John. *America as Seen by Its First Explorers: The Eyes of Discovery*. 1950. Reprint, New York: Dover, 1961.

Bandelier, Adolph. *The Delight Makers*. 1890. Reprint, New York: Harcourt, Brace, Jovanovich, 1971.

———. *The Discovery of New Mexico by the Franciscan Monk, Friar Marcos de Niza in 1539*. Trans. and ed. Madeleine Turrell Rodack. Tucson: University of Arizona Press, 1981.

———. *The Gilded Man (El Dorado) and Other Pictures of the Spanish Occupancy of America*. 1893. Reprint, Chicago: Rio Grande Press, 1962.

Bandelier, Fanny, trans. *The Journey of Alvar Nuñez Cabeza de Vaca*. Adolph Bandelier, ed. New York: A. S. Barnes, 1905. Also available with facsimile edition at Wisconsin Historical Society. http://www.americanjourneys.org/aj-070/index.asp. Accessed September 11, 2014. Also at "The Journey of Alvar Nuñez Cabeza de Vaca." Public Broadcasting System, Archives of the West. http://www.pbs.org/weta/thewest/resources/archives/one/cabeza.htm. Accessed March 20, 2014.

Barrientos, Bartolome. *Pedro Menendez de Aviles: Founder of Florida*. Gainesville: University of Florida Press, 1965.

Bengston, Jonathan. "Images of the New World by Theodore de Bry." Corpus Christi College, University of Oxford. http://www.floridahistory.com/de-bry-plates/de-bry-biography-mirror.htm. Accessed July 19, 2014.

Biedma, Luys Hernández de. "Relation of the Conquest of Florida." In *Narratives of the Career of Hernando de Soto*, ed. Edward Gaylord Bourne, trans. T. Buckingham Smith. New York: Allerton Book, 1904. A facsimile edition can be seen at https://archive.org/details/narrativescaree01smitgoog. Accessed November 22, 2017.

Billard, Jules B., ed. *The World of the American Indian*. Washington, DC: National Geographic Society, 1979.

Bishop, Morris. *The Odyssey of Cabeza de Vaca*. New York: Century, 1933.

Bloom, Lansing B. "Who Discovered New Mexico?" *New Mexico Historical Review* 15, no. 2 (April 1940).

Bolton, Herbert E. *Coronado: Knight of Pueblos and Plains*. 1949. Reprint, Albuquerque: University of New Mexico Press, 1991.

———. *The Spanish Borderlands: A Chronicle of Old Florida and the Southwest*. New Haven, CT: Yale University Press, 1921.

———. *Spanish Exploration in the Southwest, 1542–1706*. New York: Charles Scribner Sons, 1916.

Bonvillian, John D., Vicky L. Ingram, and Brendan M. McCleary. "Observations on the Use of Manual Signs and Gestures in the Communicative Interactions between Native Americans and Spanish Explorers of North America." *Sign Language Studies* 9, no. 2 (Winter 2009).

Bourne, Edward Gaylord, ed. *Narratives of the Career of Hernando de Soto*. Trans. T. Buckingham Smith. New York: Allerton Book, 1904.

Brasher, Nugent. "Francisco Vázquez de Coronado at Doubtful Canyon and the Trail North." *New Mexico Historical Review* 86, no. 3 (Summer 2011).

———. "A Narrative of the Search for the Captain General." In Flint and Flint, *Latest Word from 1540*.

Brooks, James F. *Captives and Cousins: Slavery, Kinship, and Community in the Southwest Borderlands*. Chapel Hill: University of North Carolina Press, 2002.

———. *Confounding the Color Line: The Indian-Black Experience in North America*. Lincoln: University of Nebraska Press, 2002.

Buckley, Cara. "Ava DuVernay on Modern Slavery in America." *New York Times*, October 5, 2016. http://www.nytimes.com/2016/10/06/movies/ava-duvernay-13th-on-modern-slavery-in-america.html. Accessed October 7, 2016.

Cabeza de Vaca, Álvar Núñez. *The Account and Commentaries of Governor Álvar Núñez Cabeza de Vaca, on What Occurred on the Two Journeys that He Made to the Indies*. Southwestern Writers Collection. http://alkek.library.txstate.edu/swwc/cdv/book/1.html. Accessed July 21, 2014.

———. *Naufragios de Alvar Núñez Cabeza de Vaca*. Project Gutenberg e-book, February 16, 2004. www.gutenberg.org/ebooks/11071. Accessed March 24, 2014.

———. *Relacion, Naufragios de Alvar Núñez Cabeza de Vaca*. Early Americas Digital Archives, University of Maryland, 2002. http://eada.lib.umd.edu/text-entries/relacion. Accessed July 22, 2014. Original source: *Naufragios y Comentarios*. Madrid: Calpe, 1922.

Calloway, Colin G. *One Vast Winter Count: The Native American West before Lewis and Clark*. Lincoln: University of Nebraska Press, 2003.

Campbell, T. N., and T. J. Campbell. "Historic Indian Groups of the Choke Canyon Reservoir and Surrounding Area, Southern Texas." Choke Canyon Series 1. San Antonio: University of Texas, Center for Archaeological Research, 1981.

Castanha, Anthony. "Adventures in Caribbean Indigeneity Centering on Resistance, Survival and Presence in Borikén (Puerto Rico)." PhD dissertation, University of Hawai'i, December 2004.

Castillo, Bernal Díaz del, Genaro Garcia, eds. *The Discovery and Conquest of Mexico, 1517–1521*. Trans. A. P. Maudslay. 1584. Reprint, New York: Da Capo Press, 1996.

Chamberlain, John. "On the Trail of Lewis and Clark . . . and York." *Magazine of the University of Louisville* 21, no. 3 (Summer 2003).

Chappell, Bill. "Christopher Columbus Ship the Santa Maria May Have Been Found." *The Two-Way: Breaking News from NPR*, May 13, 2014. http://www.npr.org/blogs/thetwo-way/2014/05/13/312142316/christopher-columbus-ship-the-santa-maria-may-have-been-found. Accessed May 14, 2014.

Chipman, Donald E. "Alonso Alvarez de Pineda and the Río de las Palmas: Scholars and the Mislocation of a River." *Southwestern Historical Quarterly* 98, no. 3 (January 1995).

Chipman, Donald E., and Robert S. Weddle. "How Historical Myths Are Born . . . and Why They Seldom Die." *Southwestern Historical Quarterly* 116, no. 3 (January 2013).

Coe, Michael D. *The Maya*. London: Thames and Hudson, 1966.

Colton, Harold S. *Hopi Kachina Dolls: With a Key to Their Identification*. Albuquerque: University of New Mexico Press, 1959.

Columbus, Christopher. *Journal of Christopher Columbus: During His First Voyage, 1492–93*. Cambridge: Cambridge University Press, 2010.

———. *The Log of Christopher Columbus's First Voyage to America in the Year 1492*. Eastford, CT: Martino Fine Books, 2011.

Covey, Cyclone, ed. *Cabeza de Vaca's Adventures in the Unknown Interior of America*. 1961. Reprint, Albuquerque: University of New Mexico Press, 1983.

Cox, Franklyn. "Estebanico, Black Explorer." In *Rio Grande Stories*, ed. Carolyn Meyer, 138–42. New York: Gulliver Books, 1994.

Coze, Paul. "Kachinas: Masked Dancers of the Southwest." *National Geographic* 112, no. 2 (August 1957).

Cutter, Donald C. Introduction to *The Journey of Coronado, 1540–1542*. Golden, CO: Fulcrum, 1990.

Daniels, Gary C. "Narrative of Le Moyne." The New World, September 24, 2011. http://thenewworld.us/narrative-of-le-moyne. Accessed July 19, 2014.

Dart, John. "Friars Seek Sainthood for Defender of Indian Rights." *Los Angeles Times*, January 26, 1985.

Davis, David Brion. *Inhuman Bondage: The Rise and Fall of Slavery in the New World*. New York: Oxford University Press, 2006.

Davis, Nancy Yaw. *The Zuni Enigma: A Native American People's Possible Japanese Connection*. New York: W. W. Norton, 2001.
Devolder, Eddy. *Incroyables peripeties d'Estebanico El Mauro*. Creil, France: Dumerchez Éditions, 1993.
Diamond, Jared. *Guns, Germs and Steel: The Fates of Human Societies*. New York: W. W. Norton, 1999.
Dickens, Elizabeth. "Estevan—Early American Negro." *Commonweal* 10, no. 15 (August 14, 1929).
Dockstader, Frederick J. *The Kachina and the White Man: The Influences of White Culture on the Hopi Kachina Cult*. Albuquerque: University of New Mexico Press, 1985.
Douglass, Frederick. "Inhumanity of Slavery." University of South Florida, Lit2Go. http://etc.usf.edu/lit2go/45/my-bondage-and-my-freedom/1515. Accessed October 12, 2016.
Downey, Kirsten. *Isabella: The Warrior Queen*. Anchor Books, Penguin Random House, 2015.
Drake, Francis S. *The Indian Tribes of the United States*. Philadelphia: J. B. Lippincott, 1884.
Duncan, David Ewing. *Hernando de Soto: A Savage Quest in the Americas*. New York: Crown, 1996. Norman: University of Oklahoma Press, 1997.
Engelhardt, Zephyrin, OFM. "Full Text of 'Florida's First Bishop.'" JSTOR. http://archive.org/stream/jstor-25011600/25011600_djvu.txt. Accessed June 29, 2015.
"Enslaved Africans in Mexico: The 1537 Rebellion Plot." Sayor.org Academy. https://www.saylor.org/site/wp-content/uploads/2011/08/HIST311-5.3.2-Enslaved-Africans-in-Mexico.pdf. Accessed November 22, 2017.
"The Equestrian Monument." http://johnsherrillhouser.com/Artist.asp?ArtistID=13649&Akey=55ADJN8B. Accessed July 11, 2016.
"Esteban." In *Black Heroes in World History*, 33–42. 1966. Reprint, New York: Bantam Pathfinder Editions, 1969.
"Esteban: Negro or Dark Arab? Historical Issue Turns Political." *Albuquerque Tribune*, October 27, 1972, A11.
"Estevanico." Texas State Historical Society. http://www.tshaonline.org/handbook/online/articles/fes08. Accessed April 15, 2014.
Farnum, Mabel A. *The Seven Cities of Gold: Fray Marcos and the Coronado Adventure*. Milwaukee: Bruce Publishing, 1943.
Favata, Martin A., and José B. Fernández. *The Account: Álvar Núñez Cabeza de Vaca's Relación*. Houston: Arte Público Press, 1993. This translation of the 1555 edition is also available at Southwestern Writers Collection, Texas State University, http://alkek.library.txstate.edu/swwc/cdv/book/1.html. Accessed July 21, 2014.
Fernández, José B. *Alvar Nuñez Cabeza de Vaca: The Forgotten Chronicler*. Miami: Ediciones Universal, 1975.

Finkelman, Paul. "The Monster of Monticello." *New York Times*, November 30, 2012, A25.

Fleming, F. P. "The Story of Juan Ortiz and Uleleh." *Florida Historical Society Quarterly* 1, no. 2 (July 1908).

Flint, Richard. "Eighth De Oficio Witness Juan Troyano." In *Great Cruelties Have Been Reported: The 1544 Investigation of the Coronado Expedition*. 2002. Reprint, Albuquerque: University of New Mexico Press, 2013.

———. *No Settlement, No Conquest: A History of the Coronado Entrada*. Albuquerque: University of New Mexico Press, 2008.

———. "Without Them, Nothing Was Possible." *New Mexico Historical Review* 84, no. 1 (Winter 2009).

Flint, Richard, and Shirley Cushing Flint. "Álvar Núñez Cabeza de Vaca." Office of the New Mexico State Historian. http://newmexicohistory.org/people/alvar-nunez-cabeza-de-vaca.

———. "Esteban the Moor." New Mexico Office of the State Historian. http://newmexicohistory.org/people/esteban-the-moor. Accessed March 23, 2014.

———. "Francisco Vázquez de Coronado." Office of the New Mexico State Historian. http://newmexicohistory.org/people/francisco-vazquez-de-coronado. Accessed February 28, 2017.

Flint, Richard, and Shirley Cushing Flint, eds. *The Coronado Expedition from the Distance of 460 Years*. Albuquerque: University of New Mexico Press, 2003.

———. *The Coronado Expedition to Tierra Nueva: The 1540–1542 Route across the Southwest*. Boulder: University of Colorado Press, 1997.

———. *Documents of the Coronado Expedition, 1539–1542*. 2005. Reprint, Albuquerque: University of New Mexico Press, 2012.

———. *The Latest Word from 1540: People, Places, and Portrayals of the Coronado Expedition*. Albuquerque: University of New Mexico Press, 2011.

Flipper, Henry O. "Did a Negro Discover Arizona and New Mexico?" In *Black Frontiersman: The Memoirs of Henry O. Flipper, First Black Graduate of West Point*, ed. Theodore D. Harris, 86–92. Fort Worth: Texas Christian University Press, 1997.

Friede, Juan, and Benjamin Keen, eds. *Bartolomé de las Casas in History: Toward an Understanding of the Man and His Work*. DeKalb: Northern Illinois University Press, 1971.

Frye, David, trans. *Álvar Núñez Cabeza de Vaca: Chronicle of the Narváez Expedition*. Ed. Ilan Stavans. New York: W. W. Norton, 2013.

Gaffarel, Paul Louis Jacque. *Histoire de la Floride Française*. Firmin-Didot et cie, Paris, 1875. Facsimile at https://books.google.com/books?id=SMvM2dANCcsC&hl=en. Google Books. Accessed December 11, 2017.

Gallay, Alan, ed. *Indian Slavery in Colonial America*. Lincoln: University of Nebraska, 2009.

Galván, Manuel de Jesús. *The Cross and the Sword*. Trans. Robert Graves. London: Victor Gollancz, 1956.

Gardner, Joseph L., ed. *Mysteries of the Ancient Americas: The New World before Columbus*. Pleasantville, NY: Reader's Digest Association, 1986.

Gibson, Daniel. *Pueblos of the Rio Grande: A Visitor's Guide*. Tucson: Rio Nuevo, 2001.

Glasrud, Bruce A., ed. *African American History in New Mexico: Portraits from Five Hundred Years*. Albuquerque: University of New Mexico Press, 2013.

Gómara, Francisco López de. *Historia General de las Indias*. 1552. Reprint, Linkgua: Barcelona, Spain, 2012.

Goodwin, Robert. *Crossing the Continent 1527–1540: The Story of the First African-American Explorer of the South*. New York: HarperCollins, 2008.

Goodwyn, Frank. "Pánfilo de Narváez, a Character Study of the First Spanish Leader to Land an Expedition to Texas." *Hispanic American Historical Review* 29, no. 1 (February 1949).

Green, Jesse, ed. *Zuñi: Selected Writings of Frank Hamilton Cushing*. 1979. Reprint, Lincoln: University of Nebraska Press, 1981. Includes excerpt from "The Discovery of Zuni, in the Ancient Province of Cibola and the Seven Lost Cities," 172–75. Frank Cushing lecture before the Geographic Society of Boston, 1885.

Griffin, Nigel, ed. and trans. *Bartolomé de las Casas: A Short Account of the Destruction of the Indies*. New York: Penguin, 1992.

Guitar, Lynn. "Documenting the Myth of Taíno Extinction." *KACIKE: Journal of Caribbean Amerindian History and Anthropology*, 2002. https://archive.org/stream/KacikeJournal_34/GuitarEnglish#page/no/mode/2up. Accessed January 13, 2015.

Hackett, Charles Wilson, ed. *Historical Documents Relating to New Mexico, Nueva Vizcaya, and Approaches Thereto, to 1773*. Vol 1. Washington, DC: Carnegie Institution, 1923.

Hakluyt, Richard. *Discovery and Conquest of Terra Florida*. 1611. Reprint, London: Printed for the Hakluyt Society, 1851.

Halifi, Chouaib. "Mostapha El Azemmouri/Estebanico: Parcours d'un voyageur du destin: Regard marocain." https://www.researchgate.net/publication/257618636_Mostapha_El_AzemmouriEstebanico_Chouaib_Halifi. Accessed August 29, 2014.

Hallenbeck, Cleve. *Álvar Núñez Cabeza de Vaca: The Journey and Route of the First European to Cross the Continent of America, 1534–1536*. Glendale, CA: Arthur H. Clark, 1940.

———. *The Journey of Fray Marcos de Niza*. Dallas: Southern Methodist University Press, 1949.

Hammond, George P., and Agapito Rey. *Narratives of the Coronado Expedition, 1540–1542*. Albuquerque: University of New Mexico Press, 1940.

———. *The Rediscovery of New Mexico, 1580–1594*. Albuquerque: University of New Mexico Press, 1966.

Hanke, Lewis. "Free Speech in Sixteenth-Century Spanish America." *Hispanic American Historical Review* 26, no. 2 (May 1946).

———. *The Spanish Struggle for Justice in the Conquest of America*. 1949. Reprint, Dallas: Southern Methodist University Press, 2002.

Harper, Robert Francis, trans. "The Code of Hammurabi." Wikisource. https://en.wikisource.org/wiki/The_Code_of_Hammurabi_(Harper_translation). Accessed July 11, 2016.

Hartley, Michael. "Easter Date Tables." Dr. Mike's Math Games for Kids. http://www.dr-mikes-math-games-for-kids.com/easter-date-tables.html?century=16. Accessed October 30, 2016.

Hartmann, William K. *Searching for Golden Empires: Epic Cultural Collisions in Sixteenth-Century America*. Tucson: University of Arizona Press, 2014.

Hartmann, William K., and Richard Flint. "Before the Coronado Expedition: Who Knew What and When Did They Know It?" In Flint and Flint, *Coronado Expedition from the Distance of 460 Years*.

Hazard, Samuel. *Santo Domingo, Past and Present: With a Glance at Hayti*. 1873. Reprint, London: Forgotten Books, 2012.

Hedrick, Basil C., and Carroll L. Riley, eds. *The Journey of the Vaca Party: The Account of the Narváez Expedition, 1528–1536, as Related by Gonzalo Fernández de Oviedo y Valdés*. Carbondale: University Museum, Southern Illinois University, 1974.

Helps, Arthur. *The Spanish Conquest in America*. Vol. 3. New York: Harper and Brothers, 1857.

Herrick, Dennis. "The Tiguex War in Fact, Folklore, and Fiction." In Flint and Flint, *Latest Word from 1540*, 425–38.

———. *Winter of the Metal People: The Untold Story of America's First Indian War*. Mechanicsburg, PA: Sunbury Press, 2013.

Hickerson, Nancy P. "How Cabeza de Vaca Lived with, Worked among, and Finally Left the Indians of Texas." *Journal of Anthropological Research* 54, no. 2 (Summer 1998).

Hnyen, Azzedine. "Remp'Arts Honore Estevanico El Azemmour." Maghress, May 19, 2013. http://www.maghress.com/fr/albayane/117037. Accessed February 12, 2014.

Hodge, Frederick Webb. "The First Discovered City of Cibola." *American Anthropologist* 8, no. 2 (April 1895).

———. *History of Hawikuh: One of the So-Called Cities of Cíbola*. Los Angeles: Museum of the American Indian, Heye Foundation, 1937.

Holland, F. Ross, Jr. *Hawikuh and the Seven Cities of Cibola: Historical Background Study*. Washington, DC: National Park Service, 1969.

Holmes, Richard. *Tommy: The British Soldier on the Western Front*. 2004. Reprint, New York: Harper Press, 2011.

Horwitz, Tony. *A Voyage Long and Strange: Rediscovering the New World*. New York: Henry Holt, 2008.

Houk, Rose, and Derek Gallagher. Coronado National Memorial visitors' guide. Southwest Parks and Monuments Association.

Hudson, Charles. "The Historical Significance of the Soto Route." In *The Hernando de Soto Expedition: History, Historiography and "Discovery" in the Southeast*, ed. Patricia Galloway. 1997. Reprint, Lincoln: University of Nebraska Press, 2006.

———. *Knights of Spain, Warriors of the Sun: Hernando de Soto and the South's Ancient Chiefdoms*. Athens: University of Georgia Press, 1998.

Hutchins, John M. *Coronado's Well-Equipped Army: The Spanish Invasion of the American Southwest*. Yardley, PA: Westholme, 2014.

Ilahiane, Hsain. "Estevan de Dorantes, the Moor or the Slave? The Other Moroccan Explorer of New Spain." *Journal of North Africa Studies* 5, no. 3 (September 2000): 1–14.

———. "Estevan—Moroccan Explorer of the Southwest." *Archaeology Southwest* 19, no. 1 (Winter 2005).

Jameson, J. Franklin, ed. *The Northmen, Columbus and Cabot, 985–1503*. 1906. Reprint, New York: C. Scribner's Sons, 1967.

Jaramillo, Nash. *A History of New Mexico, 1534–1895*. Santa Fe: Distributed by La Villa Real Southwest Books Materials, 1986.

Jennings, Gary. *Aztec Autumn*. 1997. Reprint, New York: Tom Doherty Associates, 2006.

Johnson, Tristan. "The Trial and Execution of Don Carlos: A Political Killing?" Scribd, December 2011. http://www.scribd.com/doc/102495266/The-Trial-and-Execution-of-Don-Carlos#scribd. Accessed January 19, 2015.

Johnson, William H. *The Spanish West*. 1976. Reprint, New York: Time-Life Books, 1979.

"Juan Garrido, African Conquistador." Visit Augustine. https://www.visitstaugustine.com/history/black_history/juan_garrido. Accessed February 23, 2014.

Karunanithy, David. *Dogs of War: Canine Use in Warfare from Ancient Egypt to the 19th Century*. London: Yarak, 2008.

Katz, William Loren. *The Black West*. 1987. Reprint, New York: Touchstone Book, Simon and Schuster, 1996.

Kessell, John L. *Kiva, Cross, and Crown*. Washington, DC: National Park Service, 1979.

———. *Spain in the Southwest: A Narrative History of Colonial New Mexico, Arizona, Texas, and California*. Norman: University of Oklahoma Press, 2002.

Koch, Peter O. *Imaginary Cities of Gold: The Spanish Quest for Treasure in North America*. Jefferson, NC: McFarland, 2009.

Krauthamer, Barbara. *Black Slaves, Indian Masters: Slavery, Emancipation, and Citizenship in the Native American South*. Chapel Hill: University of North Carolina Press, 2013.

Krieger, Alex D., and Margery H. Krieger, eds. *We Came Naked and Barefoot: The Journey of Cabeza de Vaca across North America*. Austin: University of Texas Press, 2002.

Ladd, Edmund J. "Zuni on the Day the Men in Metal Arrived." In Flint and Flint, *Coronado Expedition to Tierra Nueva*, 187–94.

Lalami, Laila. *The Moor's Account: A Novel*. New York: Pantheon, 2014.

Larson, Pier M. "African Diasporas and the Atlantic." In *The Atlantic in Global History, 1500–2000*, ed. Jorge Cañizares-Esguerra and Erik R. Seeman. Upper Saddle River, NJ: Pearson Prentice-Hall, 2007.

Las Casas, Bartolomé de. *Brevíssima relación de la destrucción de las Indias*. Ciudad Seva (in Spanish). http://ciudadseva.com/texto/brevisima-relacion-de-la-destruccion-de-las-indias. Accessed February 5, 2014.

———. *Historia de las Indias*. Book 2. Buenos Aires: Fondo de Cultura Economica, 1951.

Lavender, David S. *DeSoto, Coronado, Cabrillo: Explorers of the Northern Mystery*. Washington, DC: US National Park Service, 1992.

Lemke, Nancy. *Cabrillo: First European Explorer of the California Coast*. Los Osos, CA: EZ Nature Books, 1991.

León-Portilla, Miguel, ed. *The Broken Spears: The Aztec Account of the Conquest of Mexico*. Trans. Angel Maria Garibay K. and Lysander Kemp. 1962. Reprint, Boston: Beacon Press, 1992.

"Life beside the Water." Mesolore.org and Brown University. http://mesolore.org/tutorials/learn/22/Life-Beside-the-Water. Accessed January 22, 2015.

Loewen, James W. *Lies across America: What Our Historic Sites Get Wrong*. New York: Touchstone, 1991.

———. *Lies My Teacher Told Me: Everything Your American History Textbook Got Wrong*. New York: Touchstone, 2007.

Logan, Rayford W. "Estevanico, Negro Discoverer of the Southwest: A Critical Reexamination." *Phylon* 1, no. 4 (1940).

Lowery, Woodbury. *The Spanish Settlements within the Present Limits of the United States*. 2 vols. 1901. Reprint, New York: Russell and Russell, 1959.

MacDougald, James E. "The Navarez Expedition: The Beginning of European Exploration of the American South and Southwest." Limited private publication manuscript, February 2017.

MacNutt, Francis Augustus. *Bartholomew de Las Casas: His Life, Apostate, and Writings*. Cleveland: Arthur H. Clark, 1909.

Major, R. J., trans. and ed. *Christopher Columbus: Four Voyages to the New World in His Own Words*. 1961. Reprint, New York: Carol Publishing Group, 1992.

Mann, Charles C. *1491: New Revelations of the Americas before Columbus*. New York: Vintage Books, 2006.

———. *1493: Uncovering the New World Columbus Created*. New York: Alfred A. Knopf, 2011.

Martínez, María Elena. "The Black Blood of New Spain: Limpieza de Sangre, Racial Violence, and Gendered Power in Early Colonial Mexico." *William and Mary Quarterly* 61, no. 3 (July 2004).

Maura, Juan Francisco. *El Gran Burlador de América: Alvar Núñez Cabeza de Vaca.* 2008. Reprint, Valencia, Spain: Colección Parnaseo-Lemir, Universidad de Valencia, 2011.

———. "La invención de Norteamérica y la muerte de Esteban de Dorantes." In *El Gran Burlador de América: Alvar Núñez Cabeza de Vaca.* 2008. Reprint, Valencia, Spain: Publicaciones de Arnaseo, 2011.

———. "Nuevas interpretaciones sobre las aventuras de Alvar Núñez Cabeza de Vaca, Esteban de Dorantes, y Fray Marcos de Niza." *Revista de Estudios Hispánicos* 29, no. 1–2 (2002).

McDonald, Dedra S. "Intimacy and Empire: Indian-African Interaction in Spanish Colonial New Mexico, 1500–1800." In *African American History in New Mexico: Portraits from Five Hundred Years,* ed. Bruce A. Glasrud, 25–48. Albuquerque: University of New Mexico Press, 2013.

Mell, Michael. Guided History, "Spanish Caballeros—In Context." http://blogs.bu.edu/guidedhistory/historians-craft/michael-mell. Accessed May 26, 2015. Published by Simon Rabinovitch of Boston University.

Melzer, Richard. "Exiled from Isleta: Monsignor Frederick Stadtmuller's [sic] Expulsion from the Pueblo, 1965." *Crónica de Nuevo Mexico,* issue 97 (October 2013).

Miller, Courtney. "First Contact: The Soto Expedition, Part 5: Arrogant and Proud Barbarians." http://courtneymillerauthor.com/2015/01/first-contact-the-soto-expedition-part-5-arrogant-and-proud-barbarians. Accessed February 27, 2017.

Mirsky, Jeannette. *The Gentle Conquistadors: The Ten Year Odyssey across the American Southwest of Three Spanish Captains and Esteban, a Black Slave.* New York: Pantheon, 1969.

———. "Zeroing in on a Fugitive Figure: The First Negro in America." *Midway* 8 (June 1967).

Mitchem, Jeffrey M. "Archaeological and Ethnohistoric Evidence for the Location of Narvaez's Aute." 52nd Florida Academy of Sciences Meeting, Tampa, May 12–14, 1988.

Moriarty, James R. "The Discovery and Early Explorations of Baja California." *San Diego Historical Society Quarterly* 11, no. 1 (January 1965).

Morison, Samuel Eliot, and Mauricio Obregón. *The Caribbean as Columbus Saw It.* Boston: Little, Brown, 1964.

Morris, Marc. "Breaking the Bonds." *History Today* 63, no. 3 (March 2013).

Morrow, Baker H. *The South American Expeditions, 1540–1545.* Albuquerque: University of New Mexico Press, 2011.

Morse, Kitty. "Esteban of Azemmour and His New World Adventures." *Saudi Aramco World* 53, no. 2 (March/April 2002): 2–9. http://www.saudiaramcoworld.com/issue/200202/esteban.of.azemmour.and.his.new.world.adventures.htm. Accessed November 2, 2017.

"Mosquito-Borne and Other Insect-Borne Diseases." Florida Department of Health. http://www.floridahealth.gov/diseases-and-conditions/mosquito-borne-diseases/index.html. Accessed May 29, 2015.

Mundy, Barbara E. *The Death of Aztec Tenochtitlan, the Life of Mexico City*. Austin: University of Texas Press, 2015.

Mursell, Ian. "Moctezuma, Montezuma, Motecuhzoma?" Aztecs at Mexicolore. http://www.mexicolore.co.uk/aztecs/moctezuma/the-name-of-moctezuma. Accessed May 13, 2015.

Mutuku, Tendai. "Estevanico: Africa's Greatest Explorer of the Southwest of the United States and 'Discoverer' of Arizona and New Mexico." *Kenya Historical Review* 3 (1975).

"Naufragios de Alvar Núñez Cabeza de Vaca." Early Americas Digital Archives. http://eada.lib.umd.edu/text-entries/relacion. Accessed November 28, 2017. Original source: *Naufragios y Comentarios*. Madrid, Spain: Calpe, 1922.

Nodal, Roberto. "Estevanico: Pioneer Negro en la conquista de America." *Revista de Historia de America*, no. 89 (January–June 1980).

Olivo, Milton. "La rebelion del Bahoruco—Eco Taino." *Diario Horizonte*, January 12, 2006. Reprint in English at United Confederation of Taino People, http://uctp.blogspot.com/2006_01_01_archive.html. January 29, 2006. Accessed February 5, 2014.

Ottmani, Hamza Ben Driss, *Le Fils du Soleil: L'Odyssée d'Estevanico de Azemor*. Rabat, Morocco: Éditions La Porte, 2006.

Ouarab, Mustapha. مغامرة Estebanico آل Azemmouri، أزموراً في الواية ارزونا، 1500–1530 (Adventure of Estebanico al-Azemmouri in Arizona). Kuwait, 2005. In Arabic.

Oviedo y Valdéz, Fernández Gonzalo. *La historia general y natural de las Indias*. Madrid: Ediciones Atlas, 1959.

———. "A Narrative of De Soto's Expedition Based on the Diary of Rodrigo Ranjel, His Private Secretary." Translated from Oviedo's *Historia general y natural de las Indias*. Vol. 2. New York: A. S. Barnes, 1904. Facsimile at Wisconsin Historical Society, http://www.americanjourneys.org/aj-023/print/index.asp. Accessed September 11, 2014.

Pagden, Anthony. "The Stain." Review of *The Story of the Atlantic Slave Trade, 1440–1870*, by Hugh Thomas. *New Republic*, December 22, 1997.

Page, Jake. *Uprising: The Pueblo Indians and the First American War for Religious Freedom*. Tucson, AZ: Rio Nuevo, 2013.

Paiewonsky, Michael. *Conquest of Eden, 1493–1515*. Rome: MAPes MONDe, 1991.

Parish, Helen Rand. *Estebanico*. New York: Viking Press, 1974.

Parsons, Elsie Clews. "The Humpbacked Flute Player of the Southwest." *American Anthropologist* 39, no. 4 (October–December 1937).

Patterson, Orlando. *Slavery and Social Death: A Comparative Study*. Cambridge, MA: Harvard University Press, 1982.

Patton, Bobby Lee. *A 1,000-Mile Walk*. Pamphlet on Black History Month, 1984.
Perry, I. Mac. *Black Conquistador: The Story of the First Black Man in America*. St. Petersburg, FL: Boca Bay Books, 1998.
———. *Children of the Sun: Cabeza de Vaca's Expedition across America*. St. Petersburg, FL: Boca Bay Books, 1999.
Perry, Mary Elizabeth, and Anne J. Cruz, eds. *Cultural Encounters: The Impact of the Inquisition in Spain and the New World*. 1988. Reprint, Berkeley: University of California Press, 1991.
Phelan, John Leddy. *The Millennial Kingdom of the Franciscans in the New World*. Berkeley: University of California Press, 1970.
Phillips, Catherine. "India Tops Global Slavery Index with over 14 Million People Enslaved." *Newsweek*, November 17, 2014. http://www.newsweek.com/india-tops-global-slavery-index-over-14-million-people-enslaved-284950. Accessed June 15, 2016.
Pike, Ruth. *Aristocrats and Traders: Sevillian Society in the Sixteenth Century*. Ithaca, NY: Cornell University Press, 1972.
Pineda, Alonso Á. "The Pineda Chart." Original map and some of its Spanish labels. http://cartographic-images.net/Cartographic_Images/332_The_Pineda_Chart.html. Accessed July 11, 2016.
Pope Paul III. "Subliminus Dei: On the Enslavement and Evangelization of Indians." May 29, 1537. Papal Encyclicals Online. http://papalencyclicals.net/Pau103/p3subli.htm. Accessed February 5, 2014.
Porter, Kenneth Wiggins. *The Negro on the American Frontier*. New York: Arno Press, 1971.
Price, Richard. *Maroon Societies: Rebel Slave Communities in the Americas*. 1973. Reprint, Baltimore: Johns Hopkins University Press, 1996.
Pullen, Doug. "Travelers Series Continues: Magoffin Sculpture to be Unveiled." *El Paso Times*, July 21, 2009.
Pupo-Walker, Enrique, ed. *Castaways: The Narrative of Alvar Núñez Cabeza de Vaca*. Trans. Frances M. López-Morillas. Berkeley: University of California Press, 1993.
Quaife, Milo Milton, ed. *Narrative of the Adventures of Zenas Leonard*. 1839. Reprint, New York: R. R. Donnelly and Sons, 1934. https://archive.org/details/narrativeofadvenooleon. Accessed October 4, 2014.
"Quotations on the Jefferson Memorial." https://www.monticello.org/site/jefferson/quotations-jefferson-memorial. Accessed July 6, 2016.
Ramdani, Mohamed. "Estebanico al Azemmouri, ce marocain conquistador." *L'economiste* (August 19, 2004). http://www.leconomiste.com/article/estebanico-al-azemmouri-ce-marocain-conquistador. Accessed August 29, 2014.
Ramsey, James G. M. *Annals of Tennessee to the End of the Eighteenth Century*. Charleston, NC: Walker and James, 1853.
Ramusio, Giovanni Battista. *Delle Navigationi et Viaggi*. Venice: Nella Stamperia de Giunti, 1554.

Rangel, Rodrigo. *A Narrative of De Soto's Expedition.* In *Narratives of the Career of Hernando de Soto,* ed. and trans. Edward Gaylord Bourne. New York: Allerton, 1904.
Redfield, Georgia B. Interview with Cleve Hallenbeck. Works Progress Administration, January 9, 1939.
Reeve, Frank D. *History of New Mexico.* Vol. 1. New York: Lewis Historical Publishing, 1961.
Rentería, Ramón. "José Cisneros: Iconic El Paso Artist Dies." *El Paso Times,* November 15, 2009.
"Requerimiento" (in English). Dickinson College. http://users.dickinson.edu/~borges/Resources-Requerimiento.htm. Accessed March 18, 2014.
Reséndez, Andrés. *A Land So Strange: The Epic Journey of Cabeza de Vaca.* New York: Basic Books, 2007.
———. *The Other Slavery: The Uncovered Story of Indian Enslavement in America.* New York: Houghton Mifflin Harcourt, 2016.
"Resolution on Racial Reconciliation on the 150th Anniversary of the Southern Baptist Convention." Atlanta, 1995. http://www.sbc.net/resolutions/899. Accessed May 31, 2015.
Restall, Matthew. "Black Conquistadors: Armed Africans in Early Spanish America." *Americas* 57, no. 2 (October 2000).
Roberts, Andrew. "Battle Scars." *Smithsonian* 47, no. 4 (July–August 2016).
Roberts, Calvin A., and Susan Roberts. *New Mexico: Revised Edition.* 1988. Reprint, Albuquerque: University of New Mexico Press, 2006.
Robertson, James Alexander, ed. and trans. "A Gentleman of Elvas Account," by anonymous Portuguese officer. Florida State Historical Society. http://www.floridahistory.com/elvas-1.html. Accessed June 25, 2014.
Rogers, J. A. *World's Great Men of Color.* Vol. 2. 1947. Rev. ed., New York: Collier Books, 1972.
Rollins, Warren E. "Where History Began in the Southwest." *El Palacio* 6, no. 8 (March 29, 1919).
Rouse, Irving. *The Tainos: Rise and Decline of the People Who Greeted Columbus.* New Haven, CT: Yale University Press, 1992.
Rout, Leslie B., Jr., *The African Experience in Spanish America.* Cambridge: Cambridge University Press, 1976.
Sanchez, Arley. "Historic Trek Lures Modern Wanderer." *Albuquerque Journal,* January 1, 1984, A1.
Sanderlin, George, ed. *Witness: Writings of Bartolomé de Las Casas.* Maryknoll, NY: Orbis, 1971.
Sando, Joe S., and Herman Agoyo. *Popay: Leader of the First American Revolution.* Santa Fe, NM: Clear Light, 2005.
———. *The Pueblo Indians.* San Francisco: Indian Historian Press, 1976.
———. *Pueblo Nations: Eight Centuries of Pueblo Indian History.* Santa Fe, NM: Clear Light, 1992.

"Santo Domingo and San Felipe." *El Palacio* 24, no. 22 (June 2, 1928).
Sauer, Carl O. *Sixteenth Century North America*. 1971. Reprint, Berkeley: University of California Press, 1975.
Schaafsma, Polly, ed. *Kachinas in the Pueblo World*. Albuquerque: University of New Mexico Press, 1994.
Schmidt-Nowara, Christopher. *Slavery, Freedom, and Abolition in Latin America and the Atlantic World*. Albuquerque: University of New Mexico Press, 2011.
Schneider, Paul. *Brutal Journey: Cabeza de Vaca and the Epic First Crossing of America*. New York: Henry Holt, 2006.
Schroeder, Lucinda Delaney. *Plunder of the Ancients*. Guilford, CT: Lyons Press, 2014.
Schroeder, Susan, David Tavárez, Anne J. Cruz, and Cristian De La Carrera, eds. *Chimalpahin's Conquest: A Nahua Historian's Rewriting of Francisco Lopez de Gomara's La Conquista de Mexico*. Stanford, CA: Stanford University Press, 2010.
"Searching for York." Oregon Public Television, October 5, 2010, updated September 4, 2013. http://www.opb.org/television/programs/oregonexperience/segment/searching-for-york-/. Accessed October 4, 2014.
Seymour, Deni J. "Evaluating Eyewitness Accounts of Native Peoples along the Coronado Trail from the International Border to Cíbola." *New Mexico Historical Review* 84, no. 3 (Summer 2009).
Shamsie, Muneeza. "Reconstructing the Story of Mustafa/Estebanico: A Moor in the New World: An Interview with Laila Lamai. *Journal of Postcolonial Writing* 52, no. 2 (March 2016).
Shepherd, Elizabeth. *The Discoveries of Esteban the Black*. New York: Dodd, Mead, 1970.
Simmons, Marc. "Slavery Thrived in Colonial New Mexico." SantaFeAlwaysOnLine.com. http://www.sfaol.com/history/slavery.html. Accessed June 24, 2016.
Simour, Lhoussain. "(De)slaving History: Mostafa al-Azemmouri, the Sixteenth-Century Moroccan Captive in the Tale of Conquest." *European Review of History: Revue européenne d'histoire* 20, no. 3 (May 20, 2013): 1–21.
Simpson, Lesley Byrd. *The Encomienda in New Spain: The Beginning of Spanish Mexico*. 1929. Reprint, Berkeley: University of California Press, 2008.
"Site of First Multi-Year European Settlement in the U.S. Identified by University of West Florida Archaeology Program." University of West Florida. http://uwf.edu/media/university-of-west-florida/about-uwf/images/luna-settlement/LunaMediaKit_2015_Web.pdf. Accessed December 17, 2015.
Smith, Gloria. "In the Steps of Esteban: Tucson's African American Heritage." Arizona Buffalo Soldiers Association. http://parentseyes.arizona.edu/esteban/abriefhistory.html. Accessed November 28, 2017.
Smith, T. Buckingham, trans. "The Falling-Out with Our Countrymen." http://www.explorion.net/adventures-unknown-interior-America/chapter-52-falling-out-our-countrymen. Accessed February 3, 2017.

———. "Full Text of 'The Relation of Alvar Nuñez Cabeça de Vaca.'" The Internet Archive. Online 1542 edition. http://www.archive.org/stream/relationofalvarnoonrich/relationofalvarnoonrich_djvu.txt. Accessed June 21, 2014.

———. "Grammatical Sketch of the Heve [Pima] Language." Project Gutenberg e-book. http://www.gutenberg.org/files/14419/14419-h/14419-h.htm. Accessed February 3, 2017.

———. *The Relation of Alvar Nuñez Cabeça de Vaca*. 1871. Reprint, Cornell University Library, 2009. Also at Lost Trails, http://www.losttrails.com/pages/Tales/devaca.html#38. Accessed February 2, 2016.

Smith, Watson, Richard B. Woodbury, and Nathalie F. S. Woodbury. *The Excavation of Hawikuh by Frederick Webb Hodge: Report of the Hendricks-Hodge Expedition 1917–1923*. New York: Museum of the American Indian, Heye Foundation, 1966. http://ia600706.us.archive.org/17/items/excavationofhawioohodg/excavationofhawioohodg.pdf. Accessed January 14, 2015.

Spicer, Edward H. *Cycles of Conquest: The Impact of Spain, Mexico, and the United States on the Indians of the Southwest, 1533–1960*. 1962. Reprint, Tucson: University of Arizona Press, 1992.

Stewart, Tamara. "The Power of the Kachina Tradition." *American Archaeology* 16, no. 1 (Spring 2012).

Stuller, Jay. "Cleanliness Has Only Recently Become a Virtue." *Smithsonian* 21, no. 11 (February 1991).

Sullivan, Francis Patrick, SJ, trans. *Indian Freedom: The Cause of Bartolomé de las Casas, 1484–1566*. New York: Rowman and Littlefield, 1995.

Swanton, John R. *The Indians of the Southeastern United States*. Washington, DC: US GPO, 1946.

Taylor, Matthew S. "Cabeza de Vaca and the Introduction of Disease to Texas." *Southwestern Historical Quarterly* 111, no. 4 (April 2008).

Tedlock, Dennis. "Stories of Kachinas and the Dance of Life and Death." In Schaafsma, *Kachinas in the Pueblo World*.

Terrell, John Upton. *American Indian Almanac*. New York: Barnes and Noble, 1971.

———. *Estevanico the Black*. Los Angeles: Westernlore Press, 1968.

———. *Journey into Darkness*. New York: William Morrow, 1962.

"Tesia." Nuestra-Mexico.com. http://www.mexico-facts.com/Sonora/Navojoa/Tesia. Accessed August 30, 2014.

Theisen, Gerald, trans. "The Expedition of Pánfilo de Narváez." Booklet. 1853. Reprint, Barre, MA: Imprint Society, 1972. This is a translation of Oviedo's *Historia General*, book 35, chapters 1–6, devoted to the Narváez expedition.

Thompson, Fritz. "Black Action Inc. Is Working to Gain Recognition of Race." *Albuquerque Journal*, September 13, 1970, A1.

Thompson, Ginger. "As a Sculpture Takes Shape in Mexico, Opposition Takes Shape in the U.S." *New York Times*, January 17, 2002. http://www.latinamericanstudies.org/colonial/onate-statue.htm. Accessed September 23, 2015.

Thornton, Richard, "Surprising Late Date on the Map for Word, Timucua." *People of

One Fire, August 13, 2013. https://peopleofonefire.com/surprising-late-date-on-maps-for-word-timucua.html. Accessed May 16, 2017.

Trimble, Stephen. *The People: Indians of the American Southwest*. Santa Fe: School of American Research Press, 1993.

Tunon, Jose T. "An Indian Warrior's Ornament." CZBrats. http://www.czbrats.com/MiNombre/guaymi.htm. Accessed November 28, 2017.

Twitchell, Ralph E. *The Leading Facts of New Mexican History*. Vol. 1. Cedar Rapids, IA: Torch Press, 1911.

Udall, Stewart L. *To the Inland Empire*. New York: Doubleday, 1987.

Vance, Erik. "Mind over Matter." *National Geographic* 230, no. 6 (December 2016).

Varnum, Robin. *Álvar Núñez Cabeza de Vaca: American Trailblazer*. Norman: University of Oklahoma Press, 2014.

Vega, Garcilaso de la. *The Florida of the Inca*. Ed. and trans. John Grier Varner and Jeannette Johnson Varner. 1951. Reprint, Austin: University of Texas Press, 1962.

Vickery, Paul S. *Bartolomé de Las Casas: Great Prophet of the Americas*. Mahwah, NJ: Paulist Press, 2006.

Villagrá, Gaspar Pérez de. *Historia de la Nueva México, 1610*. Ed. and trans. Miguel Encinias, Alfred Rodríguez, and Joseph P. Sánchez. 1610. Reprint, Albuquerque: University of New Mexico Press, 1992.

Wagner, Henry R. "A 'Fray Marcos de Niza' Note." *New Mexico Historical Review* 9, no. 3 (July 1934).

———. "Fr. Marcos de Niza." *New Mexico Historical Review* 9, no. 2 (April 1934).

Wa'rab, Mustapha. *Estevanico el-Azemouri, Mughamir Maghribi fi ardi al Hunudi al humr: Abkar rihla charkiya ila Amerika 1539* ("A Moroccan Adventurer in Red Indians' Lands 1539"). 2009.

———. "Rencontre: 'Estevanico, de l'ombre a la lumiere.'" Morocco: Tifsa Press. Website suspended. Accessed February 3, 2016.

Waters, Frank. *The Man Who Killed the Deer*. 1942. Reprint, Athens: Swallow Press/Ohio University Press, 1989.

Weber, David J. "Esteban." In *African American History in New Mexico: Portraits from Five Hundred Years*, ed. Bruce A. Glasrud, 21–24. Albuquerque: University of New Mexico Press, 2013.

———. "Fray Marcos de Niza and the Historians." In *Myth and the History of the Hispanic Southwest*. Albuquerque: University of New Mexico Press, 1988.

———. *The Spanish Frontier in North America: The Brief Edition*. New Haven, CT: Yale University Press, 2009.

Williams, Eric. *Documents of West Indian History, 1492–1655*. Vol. 1. Port-of-Spain, Trinidad: PNM, 1963.

Wood, Michael. *Conquistadors*. Berkeley: University of California Press, 2000.

Woodbury, Richard B. "Zuni Prehistory and History to 1850." In *Handbook of North American Indians*, vol. 9, ed. Alfonso Ortiz. Washington, DC: Smithsonian Institution, 1979.

Worth, John E., trans. "Biedma's Original DeSoto Writings." University of Alabama's DeSoto Chronicles. http://www.floridahistory.com/biedma.html. Accessed September 11, 2014.

Wright, Barton. *Hopi Kachinas: The Complete Guide to Collecting Kachina Dolls*. Bel Air, CA: Northland, 1977.

———. *Kachinas: A Hopi Artist's Documentary*. Flagstaff, AZ: Northland Publishing with the Heard Museum, 1973.

Wright, R. R. "Negro Companions of the Spanish Explorers." *American Anthropologist* 4, no. 2 (April–June 1902).

Yarbrough, Fay A. *Race and the Cherokee Nation*. Philadelphia: University of Pennsylvania Press, 2008.

Yardley, Jim, and William Neuman. "In Bolivia, Pope Francis Apologizes for Church's 'Grave Sins.'" *New York Times*, July 9, 2015, A4. https://www.nytimes.com/2015/07/10/world/americas/pope-francis-bolivia-catholic-church-apology.html. Acccessed November 29, 2017.

"York." Public Broadcasting System. http://www.pbs.org/lewisandclark/inside/york.html. Accessed July 5, 2016.

Index

Africans on Narváez exp.: other than Esteban, 54, 84; Teodoro's slave at Mobile Bay, 88; African seen in Texas, 88, 94

Alarcón, Hernando de: hears that Zunis killed Esteban, 178; on Colorado River, 178, 185

Alcaraz, Diego de: slave raider, 135; Esteban and three Spaniards turned over to, 135; killed by Indians, 135

ambushes by Apalachees: swamp on retreat to Aute, 78; death of Avellaneda, 80; against Spaniards harvesting fish and oysters, 82

Apalachee Indians: Apalachen, 72; Narváez attack on first village, 73; Narváez takes hostage, 74; fire arrows, 74–75; lake/swamp ambush, 78; arrows pierce expeditionaries' coats of mail, 80; Apalachee fighting tactics, 79–80

Arizona: Tucson's Estevan park, 1, 216–17; Phoenix's Esteban Park, 1, 216–17; Esteban entry near Bisbee, 9, 166; Esteban not on two monuments, 166. *See also* Chichilticale

Aute: Narváez retreat to, 76; St. Marks (FL), 76; Apalachee attack, 81; search for coast, 81–82; cavalry threatened revolt, 82

Ayllón, Lucas Vazquez de: purchases Francisco de Chicora, 44; exp. survivors in Santo Domingo, 44–45; Winyah Bay, 45; Chicora and Africans escape, 45; San Miguel de Gualdape, 45; death, 45

Azemmour, Morocco: birthplace or childhood home of Esteban, 11; Berber city, 13; Esteban's Arab name attached to, 17; drought, 19

Aztec Indians: originally Mexica, xix, 60; Atzlan origin, 219n2

Bandelier, Adolph: editor of wife Fanny Bandelier's translation of *La Relación*, 1; controversy over Bandelier and Bolton routes, 169

Bartolomé from Petatlán: accompanied Esteban, 183; interpreter for Coronado, 186

Berber: Barbary States, 13; Azemmour as Berber city, 13
Bicentennial medal (NM): Esteban and African American placement denied, 7
Biedma, Luys Hernández de: Soto exp. finds Juan Ortiz, 100
bison (buffalo): buffalo hides/robes, 115, 116, 130, 137, 163; hunts, 116; "people of the cows," 117; in Tenochtitlan zoo, 144
Bolton, Herbert E.: Esteban a black African, not an Arab, 14; his proposed route for Esteban and three Spaniards, 98; controversy over his proposed route, 167–71
Brasher, Nugent: background, 169; questions Coronado route, 169–70; his researched route, 171

Cabeza de Vaca, Álvar Núñez: writes of hurricane, 48; treasurer of Narváez exp., 59; tries to dissuade Narváez from abandoning ships, 65; meets Karankawa Indians, 90; self-identified as trader to other tribes, 96–97; escape from slavery, 104; purported healing at Malhado, 108; revives man thought to be dead, 119–20; performs surgery, 121; hears about rich northern Indian cities, 129–59 *passim*; praises Sobaipuri culture, 130; arrives at Village of Hearts, 131; reports eloquent Indian statement, 137–38; changed view of Indians, 137; appointed governor in South America, 151; did not do "healing" in South America, 122
cannibalism: by Carib Indians, 94; by Spaniards, 92, 94
Carib Indians: formidable fighters, 231n14; had bows and arrows, 22

Carlos: as King Carlos I, 26, 36, 40, 58, 149–56 *passim*; Laws of Burgos, 224n2; as Holy Roman Emperor Carlos V, 155, 226n29
Castañeda, Pedro de: Coronado exp. chronicler, 115; starts rumor of Esteban greed, 165; repeats rumor Esteban sought women, 180; reliability as narrator, 194
Castillo Maldonado, Alonso del: one of the healers, xviii; performs reported first healing, 108; goes with Esteban to village near Ojinaga, 117; marries rich widow, 151
Cerda, Álaro de la: Narváez hires, 50; stays behind at Havana, 51; searches for Narváez exp., 52
Chákwaina katsina: represents Esteban, 5; symbolizes social upheaval, 5–6
Chichilticale: Coronado exp. disappointment, 170; natives report Esteban doesn't like Christians, 192; Esteban accused of killing woman, 192
Chicora, Francisco de: captured in slave raid, 44; testifies to royal chronicler, 44; persuades Ayllón to colonize eastern coast, 45; escapes, 45
Chimalpahin: Aztec/Mexica historian, 145; Aztec slaves rebuild Tenochtitlan, 145–46; mentions Virgin Mary statues, 147; writes about Grand Temple, 147
Cíbola (NM): Zuni village of Hawikku, 6; name, 6–7; Seven Cities, 131; Marcos description of, 155, 167; Coronado arrives, 172; Castañeda description of, 172; Esteban's arrival, 175–79
Cities of Gold: not an expression in Esteban's time, 160
Cofitachequi: possibly Chicora, 45; Soto at, 45, 229n11

Colorado River (AZ, CA): Alarcón's trip on, 178; distance from Cíbola, 178

Columbus, Christopher: arrives at San Salvador, 22; virtues of Taínos, 22; Taíno military weakness, 22; captures Taínos to be interpreters, 22; Queen Isabella returns Taínos to Caribbean, 24; Urraca escapes from ship, 38; discovery of Santa Maria ruin, 224n7

Coronado, Francisco Vázquez de: executes Africans suspected of rebellion, 154; escorts Esteban and Marcos exp. to Compostela, 154, 160; appointed governor of Nueva Galicia, 154, 160; leads exp. northward to verify Marcos's account, 155–56; executed women at Chiametla, Mexico, 192

Cortés, Hernán: founded Pánuco/Santisteban del Puerto, 113; *marqués del valle*, 150; conquers Aztecs at Tenochtitlan, xix, 26, 145; opposes Guzmán, 141; palace at Mexico City, 147; greets Esteban at Mexico City, 148; rival of Mendoza, 150; search for Seven Cities, 172

Cuba: hurricane, 35–49 *passim*, 83, 149; Gulf of Guacanayabo, 48; Manzanillo, 48; Trinidad, 49; Cienfuegos, 50; Narváez estate, 50; Havana, 50–52

Culiacán: Esteban and Spaniards arrive, 137–39; Esteban and Marcos depart, 157

Díaz, Bernal (conquistador): smallpox, 35; describes Narváez, 48; describes Tenochtitlan, 145

Díaz, Melchior: greets Esteban and three Spaniards, 139; frees Indians Alcaraz captured, 140; escorts Esteban and Spaniards to Compostela, 140

disease: smallpox, 29–30, 35; malaria, 68; fevers and chills, 68; among Narváez exp. members, 80–81; limited African immunity to fevers, 81; Texas stomach ailment, 93; near-fatal disease for Cabeza de Vaca, 93; death of Ortiz, 101; headaches, 109, 120; dizziness, 120; other pains, 120

dogs: mute Indian dogs, 23–24; Becerrillo, 29; war dogs, 43, 51, 58, 157; in Europe, 58; Indian dog in Texas, 90; Esteban's greyhounds, 162, 175

Dominican friars. Domingo de Betanzos, 26. *See also* Las Casas, Bartolomé de; Montesinos, Antonio de

Dorantes de Carranza, Andrés: purchases Esteban as his slave, xiii; main informant for Joint Report, 46; named trader in Joint Report, 96; turns down Mendoza's request to go north and find Seven Cities, 151; rejects Mendoza's offer to buy Esteban, 151–52; permits Mendoza to possess Esteban, 152

Dulchanchellin: meets Narváez with music, 69; departs from Narváez, 70–71; warriors follow Narváez, 71; defiant guides, 71

Encomienda: motivation of colonists, xvii–xviii, 25; opposition by Las Casas, 25; forced labor like slavery, 25; *encomendero*, 25

Enrique, Enriquillo: Taíno name, 38; leader of Enrique's Rebellion, 38–40; upbringing with Spaniards, 39; tactics of, 39; death, 40

Espejo, Antonio de: 1581 exp. to New Mexico, 115; healers near Ojinaga, Mexico, 115

Esteban, Esteban de Dorantes: other names, ix; assumptions about his death, x, 180, 182–83, 187, 191; pronunciation, 3; speaker of North African and Indian languages, 11–12; Muslim converted to Catholicism, 11, 20, 141; possible sub-Saharan origin, 13–16, 18; Arab name of Mustapha, 16–17; might have volunteered for slavery, 18–19; loyalty to Spaniards, 19; became Dorantes's slave, 20; acculturated as Spanish, 20; arrives at Santo Domingo, 31; hears of Enrique's Rebellion, 38; three Spanish companions, 46, 55; first mention in Joint Report, 47; bodyguard to Dorantes, 50, 74, 78; not first African to Florida, 53; escapes Florida, 86–87; landfall in Texas, 88–89; first mention in *Relación*, 94; enslaved by Indian tribes, 95; theorized as trader, 97; escapes Indian slavery, 104; goes with Dorantes to Anagada village, 104; goes alone to meet Avavare warrior, 104–5; leaves Avavares with three Spaniards, 110; goes with Cabeza de Vaca to find Indians, 111; enters Mexico, 111; alone in Mexican Indian village near Ojinaga, 117; religious influence, 118; becomes a healer, 120–21; depended on to talk with Indians, 122–23; Primahaitu language, 127–28; goes to find slave raiders, 134; return to Spanish slavery, 135, 143; distance Esteban and three Spaniards traveled, 147–48; resides in viceroy's castle, 148; viceroy's personal guard, 152; acquired by Mendoza, 152; viceroy mentions Esteban to king, 152; African revolt in Mexico City, 153–54; Marcos starts with Esteban, 157; influence with viceroy, 159; sent ahead by Marcos, 161; distance ahead of Marcos, 161, 166, 167; sends crosses and glowing reports, 162, 164; enters Arizona, 166; enters New Mexico, 166; reaches Cíbola/Hawikku, 175–79; Ka-Ka Clan kicks him south, 189; viceroy writes to king about him, 191; comparison with York, 210–12

faith healing: with Avavares, 107; claimed at Malhado, 108; with Coahuiltecans, 108; Lévi-Strauss definition, 110; why faith healing can work, 110; placebos, 110; Cerralvo, 114; Ojinaga, 115, 117; not always successful, 117; surgery, 121

Fernandez, Alonso: Portuguese carpenter builds escape boats, 84; death, 92

Flint, Richard: pronunciation of Esteban, 3; "ultimatum" as translation of *requerimiento*, 57, 230n9; Spaniards ban single-ship trips, 227n10

Flint, Shirley Cushing: xi, 148, 246n44

Florida: Ponce de León expeditions, 28–29; all-European conquest attempts, 30; distance to Pánuco, 85, 86; Spanish concept of size of *La Florida*, 85, 151

Florida locations: Tampa Bay, 51, 53; Old Tampa Bay, 60; Tallahassee as Anhaica, 75; St. Marks, 76; Aute, 76–81, 84, 87; St. Petersburg, 99

Forced labor: Spanish *encomiendas*, 25–26, 27, 33; Aztec/Mexica *Tlacotin*, 205; Inca *Mitҫa*, 205; Maya *Pencat'Ob'*, 206

Index

Garrido, Juan: "black conquistador," 53; with Ponce de Léon, 53–54; likely met Esteban, 148
gold: Spain's need for gold and silver, xviii, 21; mining on Hispaniola, 24, 34, 202; taking from the Indians, 28; shipping gold, 33, 150; item in Florida fishing net, 55, 230n6; tale of Apalachee gold, 64; cities of gold, 160; Marcos's sole mention, 173; Zunis didn't know gold, 194
Gulf of Mexico: crossing in caravels, 52; Spanish explorations and maps, 85; crossing in crude boats, 86–88; boats separated at Mississippi River, 88; waves toss boats ashore in Texas, 89
Guzmán, Nuño Beltrán de: hosts Narváez survivors upon their return, 141; arrest and death, 141

Havana, Cuba: Narváez buys replacement ships, 50; Cerda and Miruelo hired, 50; storms drive away Narváez ships, 51; Cerda sails from, 52
Hawikku, Hawikuh: location, xi, ix, 3–5, 128, 163; Marcos description of, 167; architecture, 172; distance Esteban walked to reach it, 174; katsinas and warriors meet Esteban at, 176–77; Esteban's assumed death, 179–80
Hirrihigua: Narváez exp. cuts off nose, 58; war dogs kill mother, 58; sends exp. to Apalachen, 64; captures Juan Ortiz, 99
Hispaniola: now Dominican Republic and Haiti, xiii; name, 22–23; Esteban arrives, 31; first gold mine, 34; population decline, 35; Enrique's Rebellion, 39–40; first black slaves, 202; spelling, 225n15

Houser, John Sherrill: finds model for Esteban bust, 215; XII Travelers monuments, 215, 254n1; creates Esteban bust, 216; Houser bust at El Paso and St. Petersburg, 216; death, 218
hurricane: first description, 49–50; sinks two Narváez ships, 50

illustrations: Chákwaina carving, 5; the New World map, 23; Santo Domingo in 1550, 32; Narváez route to Florida, 51; exp. travel through Florida, 54; Florida Everglades, 61; fire arrows attack, 75; Texas landing sites, 89; boat capsizes, 91; prickly pear, 103; healers' route across continent, 112; Mexico City in 1535, 146; four Coronado routes, 171; Estevan Park, 217
Indios: misnomer for English word for Indians, 21; de guerra Indians captured in war to be slaves, 33; de rescate Indians purchased from other Indians as slaves, 33
Inquisition: fanatical priests, 56, 109; Esteban and three Spaniards are never accused, 109; torture and executions, 121, 156; king removes Mendoza as inquisitor, 156

Joint Report: six chapters in Oviedo's Historia, xviii; believed primarily based on Dorantes testimony, 46; disagrees with Relación about who was trader, 96–97; disagrees with Relación about first healing, 107–8

katsina: sacred beings in Pueblo religion, 4; Neopkwa'i, 6; Masaû confronting Esteban, 177; Masaû at Hopi, 247n13. See also Chákwaina katsina

Krieger, Alex: theories for survivors' route, 111; his theory for route, 113

Ladd, Edmund J.: reason if Zunis did kill Esteban, 2; Esteban "either ignored or avoided by history," 2; discounts Cushing's Black Mexican story, 4; possible kiva scenario about Esteban, 181

Las Casas, Bartolomé de: preaches against "gold fever," 24–25; *encomienda* owner, 25; "Protector of the Indians," 25; critical of Franciscans, 25; repents call to use African slaves, 26; has ear of the king, 26; opposes Narváez, 28; reaction to *requerimiento*, 57

Logan, Rayford W.: evidence that Esteban was a black, 15; notes only other time Cabeza de Vaca referred to someone as *el negro*, 15

MacNutt, Francis A.: peaceable Taínos, 29; warlike nature of mainland Indians, 29

maize: forerunner of modern corn, 33; growing of maize in Florida, 63, 231n5; conquistadors look for, 64, 68; Esteban and three Spaniards seek growers of, 114, 119

Malhado Island: near Galveston, xiv, 90, 148; Esteban arrives, 88; various names for, 90; now a peninsula, 90; Cabeza de Vaca arrives, 90; two boats sink, 90–91; other boats' fates, 92; castaways enslaved on, 95; Cabeza de Vaca and Lope de Oviedo escape, 98; Oviedo returns, 98

Marcos de Niza: leader of exp., 8; Zumárraga friend, 153; leaves Mexico City with Esteban, 157; Vacapa, 161; memorial in Arizona, 166; whether he ever reached Cíbola, 166, 172; claims to have seen Cíbola/Hawikku, 167; issue of lying, 167; report by, 173; theory of collusion with Mendoza, 173; Indian assumptions that Esteban and everyone with him were killed, 180

Maura, Juan Francisco: Esteban's "supposed death," 182; questions assumptions about Esteban's fate, 182, 188

Mayo Indians: accompany Esteban north, 189; report Esteban married and settled with, 189

Mendoza, Viceroy Antonio de (viceroy): Joint Report based on testimonies, 46; rivalry with Cortés and others, 141, 150; attempts to send Dorantes north, 148–49; seeks king's license for exp., 149; acquires Esteban, 151–52; sends Esteban with Marcos, 151, 153; rumored Mexico City slave revolt, 154; led Mixtón war exp., 157; investigated for Mixtón War conduct, 157

Mexican and other Indians of the Americas: Tlaxcalan, xiii, 29, 146; Arawak, 22; Calusa, 29; Inca, 29, 30; Guaymi, 37; Sausolas, 120; Pima/O'Odham, 127; Sobaipuri, 127, 129, 169, 185; Tarascan, 156, 157; Caxcan, 157. *See also* Taíno Indians; Aztec Indians; Yaqui Indians; Carib Indians; Ópata Indians

Mexico City, Mexico: center of Spanish government, 144; built on site of Tenochtitlan, 144; Esteban arrives, 146–48; rumor of slave revolt, 153–54; Indian slaves rebuilding Tenochtitlan into Spanish city, 145–46

Miruelo, Diego: Narváez hires with a brigantine, 50; bad piloting, 51;

returns to Florida with Cerda, 52; location error of Tampa Bay, 62; ordered to sail north, 62; exp. mistakes in believing Miruelo, 85–86
Mixtón War: Mendoza leads exp., 157; execution of war prisoners, 157
Montesinos, Antonio de (Franciscan friar): sermon against cruelty to Indians, 224n2; excerpt of sermon, 225n24
Moors: war between Berbers and Moors, 13; North Africans of the Maghreb, 13–14
myth: history as agreed-upon fables, 9–10, 47, 56, 222n47; groupthink, 11; glamorized versions of events, 47; Eurocentric rationalizations, 56; entertaining fabrications, 99; Spanish fables, 100; rumors, etc., 150; cultural imperialism, 196; fog above a swamp, 196; making of myths, 196; iconic stories, 196; pietistic history, 196; imagined events, 196; histories built on fables, 198; myth-busting book, 254n8

Nahuatl: Aztec historian wrote in, 145; language of Aztecs, 156; used on trade routes, 248n18
nakedness: naked Indians, 22, 80, 130, 239n22; naked Esteban and other exp. survivors, 91, 95, 118, 121; skimpy clothing considered nakedness, 237n37; touch of clothes at the end, 237n37
Narváez, Pánfilo de (conquistador): opposed by Las Casas, 28; might have introduced smallpox, 35; descriptions, 48; invades Florida, 53; meets Tocobagas, 58; war dogs, 58; first exp. death, 70; arrives at Lake Miccosukee, 72; fire arrows attack, 74; don Pedro death, 76;
retreats to Aute, 76, 81; escape boats, 83, 55; launches boats onto Gulf of Mexico, 87; lost at sea, 92
Native Americans: Hopi, 5, 6, 247n13; Calusa, 29; Iroquois, 29, 206; Tocobaga, 55, 58, 64, 83; tattoos, 69; Choctaw, 88, 206; Capoque, 90; Karankawa, 90, 95, 108, 113; Camone, 92; Mareames, 96, 98, 105; Yguaze, 98; Desguanes, 98; Anagado, 103–4; Avavare, 105, 107–8, 110, 113, 119, 211, 249n23; Han, 108; Apache, 115; O'odham (Pima), 127, 239n15; eloquent Indian statement, 137; Creek, Cherokee, and Chickasaw, 206; A:Shiwi (*see* Zuni). *See also* Apalachee Indians; Timucua Indians

Ópata Indians: Esteban and three Spaniards find villages of, 122, 130–31, 135; accompany Esteban northward, 169; naked men, 239n22
Ortiz, Juan (expeditionary): Indians capture, 99; information about, 99–101; Uleleh, 100, 235n33; death, 101
Oviedo, Gonzalo Fernández de Oviedo y Valdéz: author of *La historia general y natural de las Indias*, 46; court chronicler, 46; wrote New World's first novel, 47; Las Casas criticizes, 47; Joint Report, 148
Oviedo, Lope de (expeditionary): arrives in Texas, 90; attempted escape with Cabeza de Vaca, 97–98; "gone native," 101

Pánuco: founded by Cortés as Santisteban del Puerto, 85; inaccurate distance from Florida, 86; failed Malhado attempts to reach, 90–91, 94–95; travelers' goal, 110, 113; distance from Cerralvo, 114

Ponce de León, Juan: expeditions to Florida, 28–29; slaughtered helpless natives, 29; attack in Charlotte Harbor, 29; death, 29; accompanied by Juan Garrido, 53

Pope: Francis, 27; John Paul II, 27; Paul III, 24; *Sublimis Deus*, 225n18

Portugal/Portuguese: custody of Esteban, 11; Gentleman of Elvis, 99; Antilia bishops, 155; Jesuit Antonio Vieira, 201; source of first slaves in US, 202

Primahaitu: Piman language dialects across northern Mexico and into current United States, 127

Pueblo Indians: religion, 3–6; Pueblo influence on Ópata housing and clothes, 122; source of turquoise and gourds, 129–30, 163; influence stopped at Yaqui villages, 132; Indian Pueblo Cultural Center, 180, 186

Requerimiento: opposition as legal basis for attack, 57; first read at Florida, 57; excerpt from, 57–58; read at Apalachee village, 73; text of, 231n11

researchers' comments about Esteban: Kareem Abdul-Jabbar, black explorer of America, 12; Adorno and Pautz, theorized route south along coast, 112–13; John Bakeless, Esteban's importance, 160–61; Robert Goodwin, outstanding achievements, 8; Robert Goodwin, "never far away," 129; Robert Goodwin, Esteban's solution, 165; Chouab Halifi, similarities of Esteban name, 17; Cleve Hallenbeck, starts idea of an Arab, 15; Tony Horwitz, no appreciation of Esteban's service, 212; Hsain Ilahiane, like a viceroy's employee, 153; Hsain Ilahiane, Zunis did not kill Esteban, 182; Hsain Ilahiane, "footnote of history," 197; Laila Lalami, importance as interpreter, 123; Charles C. Mann, group's leader, 125; Hamza Ben Driss Ottmani, Moroccan interest, 16; Hamza Ben Driss Ottmani, "remained obscured," 17–18; Andrés Reséndez, best able to cope, 95; Andrés Reséndez, as a survivor, 140; J. A. Rogers, journey a "veritable triumph," 164; Joe S. Sando, first black man we saw, vi; Paul S. Schneider, least discussed yet most intriguing, 134; Lhoussain Simour, "a real hero," 18; Lhoussain Simour, doubts Zunis killed Esteban, 182; Lhoussain Simour, "excluded actor of history," 196; John Upton Terrell, opened Southwest, vi; John Upton Terrell, personal strengths, 129; Stewart L. Udall, "Expedition of Esteban," 167; Stewart L. Udall, denied recognition, 197; Gaspar Pérez de Villagrá, courageous Esteban, 191; David J. Weber, race, 7, 16; David J. Weber, faith healing, 122; Richard R. Wright Sr., owner's credit for slave's achievements, 126

Rio Grande (TX, Mexico): Esteban and three Spaniards cross into Mexico, 111; confluence with Río Conchos, 115, 116, 119

rivers: Pánuco, xiii, 85, 86, 90–92, 94–95, 113–14; Mississippi, xiv, 88, 101, 207; of Palms, 53; Alabama, 88; Conchos, 115–16, 119, 236n12;

Sinaloa, 135–36, 140; Salt, 170; Mayo, 189. *See also* Colorado River; Rio Grande; San Pedro River

runaway slaves: Enrique's Rebellion, 39; Cabeza de Vaca had opportunities, 97–98, 104; option for Esteban, 165; first in the Americas, 202

San Pedro River (AZ, Mexico): Esteban's entry, 9, 167; source of river, 167; flows northward, 167; Esteban and Coronado both travel, 168; routes split, 169; Brasher conclusion, 170

Santo Domingo: early capital for Hispaniola, xiii; name, 23; description of, 31–32; Esteban arrives at, 31; Ayllón's survivors, 44–45; Narváez route to Florida, 51; surpassed by Mexico City, 144

Seven Cities: Cabeza de Vaca reference, 131; Esteban to find, 134; Spaniards' reference, 150; friar to lead exp., 153–55; Antilia legend, 155; linked with Cíbola, 163; "Seven Cities of Gold" not a term in Esteban's time 160; Spaniards write about, 160–61; distance from Vacapa, 162; Marcos's term, 163

slave raiders: in Florida, 44, 55; in Mexico, 133–34; Esteban and Cabeza de Vaca meet, 135

slave revolt: Hispaniola, 31, 42; Ayllón exp., 45; Florida, 86–87; Mexico City, 153–54; by Wolofs, 227n1

slavery: early Catholic Church support of, xviii, 19, 24; on Hispaniola, 24, 35; encomienda likened to slavery, 25; Indians enslaving Indians, 27, 205–7; Aztec slavery, 26; early denominations condoned, 27; modern denominations denounced, 27; Indian slaves, 33; Esteban and Spaniards enslaved, 95–103; Spanish travelers' change of mind, 133; Tenochtitlan/Mexico city construction, 145–47; slavery through history, 199–207; Bible used to justify slavery, 203; value of women and children, 206

slaves and servants of Narváez exp.: not counted, 86–87; Teodoro's slave, 88; Cuban Indian slave, 88, 89; unnamed African slave in Texas, 94; Avellaneda servant boy, 88

Soto, Hernando de: Acuera defies, 74–75; exp. finds horse skulls from Navárez exp., 84; exp. finds Teodoro's dagger, 88

Suárez, Friar Juan: first Mass on Florida Peninsula, 59; burns boxes with corpses, 79; opposes Cabeza de Vaca plan for ships, 66; whether first Florida bishop, 231n1

Taíno Indians: original Hispaniola inhabitants, 22, 34; no bows and arrows, 22; enslavement of, 22; extinction of full-blooded, 31, 36; mass suicides, 35, 227n12; in Enrique's Rebellion, 39

Tenamaztle: leader of Indians in Mixtón War, 188; in novel advises Esteban, 188

Tenochtitlan: Aztec/Mexica capital, 144; Spanish descriptions, 145; rebuilding into Mexico City, 145–47; Zunis know about Spanish conquest, 178

Timucua Indians: Narváez meets, 69; warning shot fired by, 70; warriors follow Narváez, 71; guides take Narváez exp. to Apalachen, 71–72;

Spanish fort destroyed by, 83; name, 232n21

Urraca: victories against Spaniards, 38; escape from ship, 38
US Highway 191: Coronado Trail National Scenic Byway, 169; internet maps, 169; White Mountains, 170; copper mining, 170

Vacapa, Mexico: Marcos rests at, 161; Marcos sends Esteban ahead, 161; Marcos receives first cross from Esteban, 162
Village of the Hearts (*Los Corazones*) theorized sites: Ures, 131; Mazocahui, 131; Hermosillo, 131; Onavas, 131–32; location lost in modern times, 132
Virgin Mary: Spaniards substitute for Aztec/Mexica female gods, 147, 242n17; figure in Grand Temple plaza, 147; mentioned by Chimalpahin, 147; Guadalupe in Mexico and Spain, 150, 242–43n24

weapons: bows and arrows, 22; atlatl, 22; clubs, 22; poison arrows, 29; cannons, 38, 157; lances, 39, 133; swords, 37, 39, 58, 79; matchlock arquebus, 38, 55, 71, 73, 74, 77, 79; crossbows, 74, 77, 78; horses, 74, 133; firing of arquebus, 77, 78, 79; daggers, 88, 234n12; Manchineel tree, 227n50; Spanish word for arquebus, 228n5

Yaqui Indians: same language as Mayo, 16, 189; repelled Guzmán invasion, 132; Esteban and three Spaniards encounter, 132; with Esteban, 176
York: Clark refuses to give him freedom, 210; Clark sells York's wife, 210; Clark finally frees York, 210; comparison with Esteban, 210–12; report of Zenas Leonard, 212

Zumárraga, Juan de (bishop): support of Mendoza, 150; Lady of Guadalupe, 150, 243n24; recommends Marcos, 153; millenarian, 156; burns Aztec ruler at stake, 156; builds schools and hospitals for converted Indians, 156; persecutes non-Catholics, 156
Zuni Indians: still feature katsinas in public events, 6; A:Shiwi, 177; meet Esteban, 177; stories that Zunis attacked Esteban and his Mexican Indian escort, 179–80; arguments for them having killed Esteban, 183; arguments against them having killed Esteban, 183–86

www.ingramcontent.com/pod-product-compliance
Lightning Source LLC
Chambersburg PA
CBHW022105150426
43195CB00008B/278